Practical Conveyancing: Residential,
Commercial and Agricultural

Practical Conveyancing: Residential, Commercial and Agricultural

Thirteenth Edition

R M Coates, MBE, LLB

Solicitor

LAW & TAX

© Pearson Professional Limited 1995

ISBN 075200 2090

Published by
FT Law & Tax
21–27 Lamb's Conduit Street, London WC1N 3NJ

A Division of Pearson Professional Limited

Associated offices
Australia, Belgium, Canada, Hong Kong, India, Japan, Luxembourg, Singapore,
Spain, USA

First published 1949
Thirteenth edition 1995

A CIP catalogue record for this book is available from the British Library.

Printed in Great Britain by Bell and Bain

Contents

Table of Cases

Table of Statutes

Table of Statutory Instruments

Part 1

Conveyancing procedures

Chapter 1

Running a profitable conveyancing practice

It is commonplace to be asked to provide a quotation before being instructed to carry out a residential conveyance. Competition between conveyancers becomes ever more acute. Much of the competition arises from within the solicitors' profession and not from licensed conveyancers and other institutions that once we feared. Competition has grown at a time when the volume of house transactions has dramatically reduced.

There follows some practical advice on running a successful residential conveyancing department. However, in this edition, we are mindful that many practices have found residential conveyancing uneconomic, and therefore have moved the work of conveyancing executives into the more profitable area of commercial property. Although many of the procedures are the same as between residential and commercial, we try to highlight a number of practical differences and additional considerations for the commercial conveyancer.

Similarly, provincial practices are often involved in work for the farming community; not so much with the sale of farms, but with a number of basic dealings relating to farm land and we have therefore also sought to highlight the considerations to be anticipated in that respect.

Since the 12th edition there have been legislative changes which have had an impact on the work of a conveyancer. These we have incorporated into the text where appropriate and additionally, we have incorporated the up-to-date position concerning land registry practice, the Third Edition of the National Conveyancing Protocol and the latest position concerning Stamp Duty. It is hoped that this revised edition will be a useful practical guide with the latest guidance on the art and practice of conveyancing in all its aspects.

1 Marketing

Principals must recognise the importance of marketing their practice. There are, of course, two ways to market your practice. First, there is the time-honoured method of being involved in the local community, known in the local community, respected by existing clients and the work-referrers and building upon a reputation acquired in a particular locality. Secondly, there is the more recent addition of the preparation of brochures, mailshots using the client database, and of course cross-selling of services with other departments in the film. The following points may be useful:

(1) Know your market. It is important to decide the type of client that you intend to focus upon within your practice. Are you seeking as much residential conveyancing at £200 per transaction as you can obtain? Are you looking for the large commercial client that will provide you with a significant volume of business in their own right? Are you hoping to obtain work from local authorities, charities, or whom?

(2) In every case remember that first impressions count. Marketing literature must present the image of the firm that you wish to portray. For clients visiting the office, their first point of contact is with your reception area and the receptionist. Make sure that your office reception is bright, clean and well organised. Ensure that your receptionist is well trained, cheerful and helpful. Make sure that the telephones are answered promptly and politely and that clients visiting the office are attended to promptly and efficiently.

(3) Using consultants or agencies. Larger firms employ public relations consultants or, in some cases, advertising agencies in order to advise on the promotion of their services. Smaller firms will not be in a position to afford this. In either event, make certain that the service matches the promotion material.

(4) Quotations. People will telephone your office for a quotation, either because your firm has appeared in the Yellow Pages (a very good advertising medium) or because they have been recommended to do so by an estate agent, building society manager, accountant or bank manager. Always be friendly and specific when providing a quotation. Do not hedge your quotations with 'ifs' and 'buts'. You will not get the job. In fact, it is probably better to earmark one member of the conveyancing department/your practice to provide quotations. It may be appropriate to write out a script to use for this purpose. Take names and addresses of the callers, and follow up a verbal quotation in writing *on the same day*. Send it by first class post. This will impress the client and appear to be efficient. Maintain that efficiency throughout the transaction.

(5) Keep existing clients happy. The easier method of marketing your practice is to ensure that your existing clients are satisfied. It is far harder to win a new client than to keep an existing client, and a satisfied existing client will spread the word of his satisfaction to his friends and colleagues, who will then want to use you as well.

(6) Offer no fees for abortive transactions. Most buyers and sellers will re-instruct you if their transaction falls through. It creates much goodwill, and although you will have lost money if a transaction does not materialise, the goodwill is a sound investment for the future.

(7) Most conveyancing clients are looking for a speedy transaction conducted with the minimum of fuss. A transaction conducted in this way is not always possible, but that style of service is appreciated by both estate agents and clients alike. Return all telephone calls (espcially to estate agents) quickly. Advise the estate agents of exchange of contracts immediately. If you are first to ring up the estate agent with this information, it will impress. You will appear to be much more on the ball than your competitors if you note the importance of this tactic.

(8) Create good business relationships. If there are estate agents or building society managers who recommend your firm regularly, it is important to create a good relationship with them. This can be done by being prepared to talk to them, and show an interest in their business, or their own interests. You may have a common hobby or a common interest in sport. Be prepared to do conveyancing work for your referrers on the basis of reduced fees. Be prepared to wine and dine your contacts—sometimes it may be appropriate to take them out to a function. This cements the relationship and provides for a loyal business contact in the medium term.

(9) Good communications with clients, banks, building societies and estate agents are vital at all stages of any business being transacted in the office. So much misunderstanding and anxiety is caused by failure to communicate. Advise those concerned of potential problems as early as possible. Do this without causing undue alarm, but keep everyone informed. It is particularly important with a conveyancing transaction that you are perceived as doing everything you can to keep the transaction alive. Sometimes solicitors are misunderstood to the extent of being perceived as creating as many problems as possible, which eventually lead to the collapse of any given transaction under its own

weight of legal complexities. In this modern day and age, such an approach to the job is not appreciated, and will not create goodwill.

(10) It is also a good selling point to offer evening, weekend and home appointments. Many clients are at work all day and it is not convenient for them to see you during normal working hours. Display a preparedness to visit people outside working hours. Telephone clients outside usual working hours. Either way, they will be impressed and reassured that you are devoting your time to their business and concerns. In practice, out of hours appointments are rare, but it cannot be stressed too highly how much goodwill and what a good impression an offer like this can create.

(11) When you are first instructed by a new client, it is helpful if you can send the introductory letters, including the request for the title deeds; on the same day. Do your best to make sure that any delays are someone else's and not your own.

There is a word of caution concerning a request for title deeds. If you are instructed before the property is sold, there have been many cases where the bank or building society have charged a deeds production fee. In a quiet market, the property may not sell for six or 12 months, by which time the bank or building society will require the deeds to be returned to them. You should, therefore, make it clear to your new client that you would counsel proceeding with caution, prior to ascertaining the marketability of their property, particularly in times such as these, when the market for residential property is so quiet in many parts of the country.

(12) At the end of the transaction, send the estate agents' commission cheque to them on the day of completion. Do not let them wait for a week before you get round to posting it to them. This does not create the right impression, nor is it the way to encourage them to pass future business to you.

(13) Use the telephone. It is important that you are seen as someone prepared to use the telephone, rather than always to rely on letters. Solicitors' work is very much based on letter writing, but in this day and age it is becoming increasingly outmoded. There are, of course, many occasions when letters are quite essential, but for simple questions, try to use the telephone. An increasing number of clients have answer machines on which you can leave a message. In the years to come, homes and businesses are likely to be linked up with 'E-mail' or through the 'Internet' and these new media must be understood and grasped by the conveyancer

if there is any chance that it will speed up the conveyancing process, so that it is as cost-effective and economic as it possibly can be for all concerned.

(14) Corporate marketing of conveyancing. There are some national organisations seeking membership from the more substantial and respected firms who propose to gather a national membership of solicitors' firms and then to market that network to large insurance companies, building societies etc for the purposes of doing their panel conveyancing in their areas. Some of these organisations charge a membership fee and some do not.

The effectiveness of such national marketing exercises remains to be seen. Perhaps they will come into their own if it is finally decided that solicitors acting for borrowers may not at the same time act for lenders too. At the time of writing this book, the debate continues, but if there is a rule requiring separate representation based on the conflict of interest principle, it could have a seriously adverse impact on smaller firms and at the same time a positive impact on larger firms. No doubt in the further deliberations on this issue the profession will have half a mind to claims on the indemnity fund caused by conveyancers.

It may well be that, as with the Legal Aid franchising scheme, an increasing number of the institutional clients—and in the future this may include banks and building societies—will require confirmation that certain practice management standards are in situ, such as the BS5750.

2 How to organise a conveyancing department

There are three possible scenarios:

(1) A small firm of two or three partners, which is not strictly organised in a departmental fashion.
(2) A larger firm with departments, further divided into teams of specialists.
(3) A larger firm with departments, further into teams of fee earners working on different aspects of each transaction.

I will deal with each in turn.

Conveyancing in a small firm

The objective of conveyancing in any solicitors' practice is to make a profit. A profit will not be possible, neither will the service be sustainable, if the task of providing quotes is reduced to an exercise of undercutting one's competitors.

The quality of the service provided is important; proper supervision and observation of the Rules of Professional Conduct are vitally important. A very high percentage of negligence claims against the profession and of calls upon the indemnity fund arise out of conveyancing or conveyancing-related practice.

There will, of course, be different views expressed about the organisation of conveyancing in a small firm but practitioners in this position may find the following suggestions thought-provoking.

(1) Either you as principal or your conveyancer ought to be the person providing quotations in the way suggested under 'Marketing' (above).

(2) The marketing and selling of your service as well respected and one of quality is as important for you as it is for a larger firm.

(3) Ensure that you supervise the work of your conveyancer as may be appropriate and in accordance with the Rules of Professional Conduct. These Rules must be carefully observed if you have a range of small branch offices largely run by unadmitted staff or junior solicitors. Practitioners will note that several costly mistakes can often severely disrupt the cash flow of the firm.

(4) The use of standard precedents stored on a word processor can save time and cost. Develop a range of these. Whilst it may not be good practice to send a pre-printed letter to a client, one will certainly suffice when dealing with other solicitors.

(5) Ensure that the overheads of your office or of your branch office are kept to an absolute minimum. With tight margins on conveyancing, it is important that you are equally careful to ensure that all the overheads (the largest of which is the salary bill!) are tightly controlled and monitored monthly. Many solicitors' practices are failing because of the inability to link overhead costs to fee income. In a properly monitored business with some idea as to the volume of incoming work, one ought to be able to work out what one has to quote in order to maintain a viable practice.

Conveyancing departments divided into specialist teams

Larger firms will often be established firms and the conveyancing department will have as its bedrock a number of substantial clients, both in respect of residential conveyancing and commercial conveyancing.

The firm's managing partner will require the departmental head to prepare an annual budget in terms of gross fee income and the sufficiency of that annual budget will then be compared with the department allocation of its share of the firm's overhead expenses.

As a rule of thumb, many firms (both large and small) will use the one-third rule. This means that the conveyancing executive will be paid one-third of his gross annual fee with the other two-thirds being applied to the firm's overhead expenses. This principle may be used to evaluate the efficiency of the department itself. Such, or similar arithmetical exercises may lead the head of a conveyancing department to decide that the work being done by one or more teams within his department is either not sufficiently profitable to enable that team to continue to exist either at all or in its current format, or that certain types of unprofitable work could be done more efficiently and therefore more profitably. Such pro-active management is not only commonplace, but essential for the continued existence of a healthy firm.

Within a conveyancing department, one might expect one team to deal with residential conveyancing, another team to deal with commercial conveyancing and another team to deal with agricultural conveyancing. It may not arrange itself as neatly as this, and increasingly there may be new teams being set up, for example to deal with a large local authority or housing association contract.

Notwithstanding the fact that large firms are increasingly taking on large institutional contracts, there are certain inherent dangers in this strategy. If a particular company or group of companies go into liquidation or if a contract with the local authority comes to an end, then there are severe problems as to the future employment of the conveyancing executives within that team or within the department. It always remains imporant to have a fair cross-section of clients in all different areas of conveyancing.

A number of larger firms take a different stance to smaller firms on the question of providing quotations, or on the question of providing services for first-time buyers. In developing such strategies, it is important not to forget that a first-time buyer today may be a substantial business client purchasing a £250,000 property in ten years' time. Similarly, a successful business executive today may be bankrupt in five years' time. In other words, individual clients or companies are not static. They may fall into a variety of client categories during their lifetime, and this is a factor that must not be overlooked in developing the firm's marketing strategy.

Computerisation

Larger firms have a greater investment capacity to keep abreast of the latest technology in terms of word processors and linking all fee earners by computer screen. In many large firms, everyone—including partners—now have a screen on their desk. 'E-mail' provides a speedy means of message communication within the office, and as referred to above, it can only be a question of time before this technology links us with many of our clients. In many firms, legal executives are now doing their own word-processing and are operating without secretarial support. Most forms that we use in conveyancing are stored within the word-processing system and can be quickly recalled and filled in and dispatched. Faxes can be sent direct from the word-processing unit, as they are increasingly developed as integral communications systems in their own right. The profession, particularly conveyancers, must continue to grasp all this technology if we are to survive as a sustainable business on current fee rates.

Conveyancing departments divided into cross-disciplined teams

A number of large firms have small teams working on the same case-load. This is not common practice, but does exist. For example, within the residential conveyancing team, one fee earner will take the transaction up to the point of exchange. It will then pass to the next fee earner for exchange of contracts and the post exchange work, and to yet another fee earner for completion and the post completion work. The advantage of this system is that if any one fee earner leaves or goes on holiday, then there are at least two others who know all about the file. It shares the information on the file within the department, and if there are certain procedural nuances overlooked or missed by one person, it is likely they will be picked up by another.

This method of organising work has some advantages, but could confuse clients, many of whom remain keen to deal with one particular person and to know to whom their affairs have been entrusted. Perhaps this style of work would be more appropriate for institutional clients.

Chapter 2

Taking instructions

1 Steps after providing the quotation

Having provided the quotation, a letter should be sent, detailing the fees and disbursements, so as to avoid the possibility of any subsequent misunderstanding. It might also be helpful, particularly with first-time purchasers, to supply a specification of work—such a specification of work would set out step by step what will be done on behalf of the client. You might also enclose an instruction form for completion by the prospective clients, should they wish you to proceed. Such a form would contain all the necessary details required to enable you to have a point of immediate reference on your new file. So often fee earners take instructions without obtaining building society account numbers or telephone numbers etc. This wastes so much time during the currency of the transaction.

The details you need are as follows:

Client name/address and phone numbers

This is self-explanatory, but it is vital to get the spellings correct. There are sometimes curious variations such as 'Freddy', 'Freddie', 'Fredrick', 'Frederick', etc. It is essential to get full names of the client, including any middle names. Such detail will not be volunteered as a general rule.

Identity of estate agent

The estate agent will forward full particulars of the sale that has been negotiated, and in these circumstances, it is important to know his or her identity. It will also put you on notice to expect a commission account after contracts are exchanged.

Agreed price

It is necessary to find out the precise price negotiated between the parties.

11

Sometimes, there will be additional money agreed in respect of fixtures and fittings, or even in respect of items of household and garden furniture. Should this be the case, the price may need to be apportioned. The significance of apportioning the price is particularly acute when it is on the stamp duty threshold, which at the time of writing is at £60,000.

Sometimes, clients make various private agreements between themselves concerning part of the money being paid at a later date, or in cash. A conveyancer cannot afford to become involved in any such scheme and must attempt to dissuade the parties from proceeding in this way. It is your professional duty to ensure that the full price is properly recorded on the conveyancing documentation, and if any part of it is to remain outstanding, it could always be secured by a loan agreement or indeed by a mortgage back to the seller.

Location of deeds

Generally, these will be with a building society or bank or in a solicitor's strongroom. It is important to obtain full particulars from the client as to the whereabouts of the deeds, because until these are located, nothing can happen. If the property is in mortgage, then obtain the account number, as this may be needed when it comes to redemption. The client's written authority will be needed to obtain the deeds from a bank.

The basic rule is that the title deeds—registered or unregistered— together with information from the client equals enough information to prepare a draft contract. However, one without the other is of little assistance in the preparation of this initial document.

Deposit payment

Sometimes, estate agents collect a token deposit from an intending purchaser as a sign of good faith. Estate agents are obliged to inform the conveyancer whether they are holding any money as stakeholder. Make a careful note. It needs to be taken into account when preparing the completion statement.

Otherwise, a deposit needs to be paid when contracts are exchanged. Many clients do not understand the requirement for a deposit, and many do not have the full 10% available.

A draft contract will provide for a 10% deposit, and if it then transpires that the buyer cannot afford to pay this, it is customary to negotiate it down to 5%, but not usually below. It is important to explain to the client the effect of default after exchange of contracts. The deposit will be forfeited, and if less than 10% has been paid, there will usually be a clause in the contract providing for forfeiture of the full 10%.

It is now common practice, and indeed included as part of the conditions of sale (2.2.2) that a deposit may be used by the seller as the deposit on another purchase, although the deposit would need to be held in that transaction as stakeholder until completion. If the passage of the deposit is not prohibited, then it could be lost by being passed to an individual or a company that goes bankrupt or becomes insolvent before completion. The buyer could then be without any deposit money and without any property. It is therefore important for the deposit to be held by a professional conveyancer as a stakeholder at some stage in any given conveyancing chain.

Fixtures and fittings

The Protocol form entitled 'Fixtures Fittings and Contents' should be handed to the seller so that he can tick the relevant boxes as to whether the item concerned is included, excluded or not available at the property. It is now common practice to attach this form to the contract so that there can be no doubt as to what is included in the price on completion.

The seller must be asked whether any of the fixtures and fittings are subject to hire purchase or loan agreements. If fittings are to be removed from the property, the buyer will wish to be assured that no damage will be done to the fabric of the wall, floors and ceilings.

Home improvements

Ask the client whether any additions or alterations have been made requiring planning consent in recent years. If so, ask for the planning permission, building regulations consent and completion certificate. Also ask for any official notices received by that client.

Outstanding borrowing

If there is a mortgage, it is important to write to the mortgagee to give notice of the client's intention to redeem. Certain building societies have minimum periods for notice or a penal charge of interest for a shorter period. There are almost always redemption penalties for fixed rate mortgages and in cash-back schemes part of the cash gift may have to be repaid. Clients who have had a mortgage for only a year or two may find they have to pay three months' penalty interest in any event. Practice varies.

Related purchase

Most transactions proceed side by side, and in such a case it is important to treat them quite separately, using separate instruction sheets and separate file numbers, etc as recorded on your accounts computer. Most clients who require the sale and purchase to run side by side, will be concerned about ending up with no house at all, or two houses. You should explain to them that it is your responsibility to ensure that contracts are exchanged in such a way that this scenario does not arise.

Sometimes, a client does not insist on simultaneity. Here, you should point out the extra costs involved in putting furniture into storage and moving into temporary accommodation, although these may be offset by the interest yielded from the temporary investment of the proceeds of sale. Sometimes, a client will be prepared to proceed with the purchase on the basis of bridging finance. This can prove extremely expensive. The wisdom of not proceeding simultaneously very much depends on the condition of the property market at the time and is inevitably going to be a gamble.

Completion of TransAction forms

The property information form, which is part of the Protocol scheme, should be completed by the seller at the outset. This simply requires the seller to tick the appropriate box, and provides the range of practical information that was previously contained on the preliminary enquiries forms as produced by various law stationers. If the property being sold is the same as that which was purchased, then a suitable plan should be contained with the deeds and documents of title and it should prove no problem. However, in some unregistered titles, there is no suitable plan available and where there is a sale of part only, there will obviously be no plan with the deeds and documents of title. In some of the above circumstances, it may be necessary to ask the seller to provide a plan, either personally or through a surveyor or agent. Nothing is more fundamental than to work on a precisely accurate plan from the outset. It will be needed for search purposes, and it will also be called for by the buyers.

There are some pretty horrendous examples of defective plans dotted amongst the law reports, and they are a major cause of delays in registration of title. It may be that you have an Ordnance Survey plan in your office that you can work on with the seller in order to produce an accurate plan, at least one for identification purposes only. Precise boundary measurements may be the counsel of perfection, and a large-scale Ordnance Survey may well suffice.

On the question of day-to-day outgoings attaching to a property, such as water rates, it is no longer necessary to hand over receipts to the buyers on completion. However, it is necessary to produce receipts for rent and service charges when dealing with leasehold property. In the event of dealing with leasehold property, the seller should be asked to complete an 'additional property information' form, which does in fact contain a series of questions peculiar to leasehold premises such as management accounts, service charges, etc, and you should ask the seller both for evidence that the rent has been paid up to date and for evidence of current insurance cover. An up-to-date schedule should be supplied by the landlord to the tenant each year where it is the landlord's responsibility to insure. Where this is the case, it invariably follows that landlords will recover the cost of doing so from their tenants. Again, details of payment will be called for by the buyer.

The buyer will customarily ask for accounts ranging back for three years in respect of the activities of any management company. A management company is particularly common where there is a large block of flats but it is now increasingly common in smaller developments, such as converted Victorian houses.

The point made above concerning the production of a good plan is crucial for leasehold property. Here, the detail of how the premises is divided is vital. From this you will know what rights are required for services and access.

2 Instructions from the buyer

Client name/address and phone numbers

The points made above concerning the client's personal details apply equally here.

If the buyer is a limited company, it is important to check that you are obtaining instructions from the appropriately authorised personnel. It is also important to check that the limited company has already been incorporated and that it does actually have the power to own the property. This means you should check its Memorandum and Articles of Association.

If you are accepting instructions on behalf of a partnership, it is again a good idea to check that the person who approaches you has authority to act on their behalf.

The question of joint purchase is dealt with below.

It is good practice to make a note of the client's telephone number on the file. You need a daytime and an evening number. Much time is often lost in transactions when looking for telephone numbers. Keep them on the file from the beginning.

Identity of estate agent

It is essential to ask buyers whether they have negotiated transactions through an estate agent and if so, whom. You should telephone the agent and find out who is acting for the seller. You should also ask clients whether they have paid a deposit to the estate agent. If so, make a note on your file accordingly, as it is easily overlooked and your buyer client could end up being asked to pay that particular figure twice unless it is taken into account either at exchange of contracts or on completion.

Use

It is vital to ensure that the use that the buyer intends is authorised for planning purposes. The agents' particulars may give some indication with regard to this. Whether this is the case or not, it is critical to obtain copy planning permissions from the seller's solicitors prior to exchange of contracts. Sometimes the use may be authorised by virtue of the fact that it started before 1948, and it might be prudent to seek a statutory declaration with regard to the long-established use, particularly where that use is of a commercial nature.

If client buyers will require planning permission, it is important to spell out to them that they are running a potential risk by exchanging contracts prior to the grant of that permission. Sometimes, the seller's solicitors will accept a condition being inserted in the contract, which makes the contract conditional upon a successful planning application. Such conditions must be worded extremely carefully in order to ensure that they are effective.

Check the local authority search result carefully with regard to the information it reveals on this issue.

Agreed price

As mentioned previously, it is essential to ensure that this is properly and finally negotiated at the commencement of the transaction. Conveyancers are not normally expected to act as negotiators and, if estate agents are involved, it is important to make certain that they have fully and finally settled the price, both for the legal estate in the property and for any extras, such as fixtures and fittings, or even any chattels that might be left at the property.

It is not uncommon to seek a renegotiation of the price, after a survey report has been received that lists certain works that require attention. The likelihood of the success of this practice depends very much on the current state of the property market, and how badly the seller wishes to move.

Fixtures and fittings

It is very important that the buyer clearly understands what is included and what is excluded. Legal practice in this area has been greatly enhanced by the fixtures, fittings and contents questionnaire. The estate agent's particulars may state what is included and what is not. Since the Property Misdescriptions Act 1991, it has become an offence for an estate agent to attach a misleading description to the property he is selling. This means that estate agent's particulars tend to be more specific and more realistic than they may have been in the past.

The liability incurred by estate agents is similar to that under the Trades Descriptions Act 1968 and applies to all aspects of the description of a property.

Deposit arrangements

If possible, you should work out with your client buyer how much money will be available for the payment of a deposit at the outset of the transaction. It is now common practice for the deposit to be passed along the chain as previously described. If, less than 24 hours before expected exchange of contracts, someone announces they have got only £500 instead of £5,000, this can stall the chain for some while, whilst everyone renegotiates the terms of the contract they each have.

Some clients think of the deposit as the difference between the mortgage advance and the price. The client will not necessarily understand, particularly a first-time buyer, that the deposit has to be paid on exchange of contracts, which is some time before the mortgage advance becomes available. From day one, it is important to explain to the buyer that the usual arrangement is to pay 10% on exchange of contracts and that if this is not available, then a lesser figure will have to be negotiated. There are insurance companies who offer a guarantee scheme that avoids the need to make the payment of any deposit, and instead, upon payment of a premium, provides a guarantee to the seller's conveyancer that should the transaction not proceed, then the appropriate 10% will be made available in the case of forfeiture becoming a legal possibility under the terms of the contract. This arrangement is rarely used and a seller must be aware that they will not have a deposit to use on their related purchase. A seller will also need to know the enforcement provisions.

Survey arrangements

Every buyer should have a survey of the property he or she proposes to buy. It is now possible to rely on the survey that the mortgage company will arrange. Basically, there are three categories that will be offered:

(1) There will be a basic valuation, which is not a survey at all, but merely to assist the mortgage company to ensure it has adequate security for its loan.

(2) There is alternatively a 'House Buyers Report', which is not a comprehensive survey, but is certainly more than a valuation. Generally, this is adequate for most buyers, particularly those purchasing a modern property. The report comes on a pre-printed form, which sets out the various exclusions and caveats in the margin of each page. There will be a note of the work that requires to be done to the property and also a valuation.

(3) Finally, there is a 'full survey', which literally involves the surveyor in scouring the house from top to bottom to include lifting floorboards and examining the timbers in the attic. Not every seller welcomes such a detailed investigation of their home, but it is imperative when you are acting for a client who is proposing to purchase an old farmhouse, for example.

Some clients will not want a survey. It is important to record the fact on your file that you have advised them strongly to have one. Some survey results will point the way to a damp proof report of a structural engineer's report.

Mortgage arrangements

Most estate agents have a financial services manager to organise a mortgage for their buyers. If your client buyers do not fall into this category, for example if they have negotiated direct, then it may well be that your firm has its own financial services department. The provision of financial services can be a lucrative business when one succeeds in organising the pension policies, endowment policies, term policies and so on.

Whether or not your firm has been directly instructed to organise the mortgage, it is important to check the arrangements, and also to scan the mortgage instructions very carefully. Some mortgage companies send pages and pages of instructions to solicitors, and the inclination is to scan them only very briefly. There may be important conditions to be observed (eg to ensure that the road has been adopted by the local authority), and if it is not possible to comply with these, the mortgage may not go through. It is also important to explain the content of the mortgage offer to many clients, as they may not understand the conditions attaching to an offer that they receive directly through the post.

When dealing with bank loans, there may be particular difficulties where the house occupied by husband and wife is used to secure a business loan. There is now, generally, a separate bank mortgage form to deal with a floating overdraft but again, when dealing with a bank, it is vital to check which mortgage form is sent to you.

If the bank mortgage form does not set out the precise amount of the home loan and the terms under which it is to be repaid, then it is important to ensure that the client receives a letter from the bank manager spelling out in precise terms the nature of the loan, the interest rate applicable to it and the regularity of the instalment payments.

The final point of caution is that as the conveyancer for the buyer, you should check that any endowment mortgage arrangements are suitable. Endowment policies are not always appropriately matched to the client and sometimes a low-cost endowment would suffice instead of a full endowment policy, or a term insurance policy would be more appropriate than an endowment.

It is very necessary to ensure that you do not give financial advice unless your firm is appropriately registered under the Financial Services Act 1986. This is more fully dealt with in Chapter 18.

Joint purchase?

At the outset, it is important for the buyer's conveyancer to explain the difference between the significance of joint tenants holding in trust for themselves either as tenants in common or as joint tenants. *Walker v Hall* (1984) 5 FLR 126 established that failure to give such guidance can amount to negligence and is a clear breach of professional duty. Therefore you may care to produce a handout to be given to joint purchasers at the beginning of each transaction.

Basically, the way you should explain it to your buyer client is that the share of a joint tenant passes automatically to the survivor on death, whereas the share of a tenant in common passes under the terms of their will to whomsoever their beneficiaries may be. They will exclude the other tenant in common.

You may well be asked for your advice. Point out that in the case of a married couple or a permanent relationship, the joint tenancy is the surest guarantee that on the death of either there will at least be a roof over the heads of the surviving family, particularly if there is to be a mortgage supported by a life endowment policy. Explain too, how easily a joint tenancy can be converted to a tenancy in common by, for example, simple notice in writing by one party of his or her intention given to the other.

A tenancy in common is usual in a business situation such as a solicitors' partnership.

Insurance arrangements

Condition 5.13 of the Second Edition of the standard conditions of sale states that the seller is not under a duty to maintain an insurance policy but that the risk in the property does stay with the seller until completion. Despite this condition, some buyers may wish to insure after contracts are exchanged in order to be doubly certain about their investment, but this is a practice that should now no longer be strictly necessary.

Related sale

As noted above most clients will be very worried about whether they will end up with two properties or none. It is of course your duty as a conveyancer to ensure that this does not happen.

Clearly, it is a matter of skill to ensure the two transactions are exchanged simultaneously. However, it is good practice to make sure that both your sale and your purchase file are kept at roughly the same level. Some firms will need chasing, and others will push you.

It is worth reiterating that throughout every conveyancing transaction the conveyancer should keep in touch with the client. In some ways it is better to communicate with the client and say that nothing has happened, than not to communicate with the client because nothing has happened. Set up a system within your office whereby you monitor every file, so that your daily work is not simply a question of responding to incoming post and phone calls, but also a task of initiating approaches to clients and to other firms and to estate agents. A pro-active approach to the job is essential to build up your client base. Why not devise a weekly or fortnightly report sheet to be sent to the estate agent?

The National Conveyancing Protocol — Third Edition

The Third Edition of the National Protocol came into force on 1 May 1994. The Protocol applies to domestic conveyances.

At the beginning of every transaction, every solicitor acting in a domestic conveyance must notify the solicitor acting for the other party whether or not the Protocol will be used in that transaction. Once such notice has been given, and it has been agreed that the Protocol will be adopted, the procedures laid out must be followed, subject to the right at any time by either solicitor to give notice to the other that he intends to vary those procedures.

The aim of the Protocol has always been to provide as much information about the property being sold as possible at the outset. This should help to shorten the time the transaction takes. Sometimes there will be difficulties which require either solicitor to adopt different or additional procedures. The solicitor's overriding duty is to act in the best interests of his client, and in complex cases, he must not hesitate to go outside the provisions of the Protocol.

The word 'TransAction' is the marketing or brand name for the

Protocol procedures. The word and the logo is exclusive to solicitors and is not available for use by licensed conveyancers. This applies equally to the range of forms prescribed by the Protocol. Such forms can be purchased only from the Law Society. However, a general licence has been granted to the legal profession to reproduce these forms by word processor only. Photocopying is not permitted, except for taking a file copy of the already completed form.

Chapter 3

Steps up to exchange of contracts

1 TransAction—the seller's package

Assemble the appropriate range of documentation at the outset. If the seller's answers to the question on the property information form refer to copy documents, obtain these from the seller and place them on file.

Once the seller's property information form is duly received, the answers given should be compared with the information available on the title deeds. This will enable the conveyancer to complete the seller's property information form Part 2. The Part 2 form must be signed personally by the solicitor and basically verifies or otherwise the answers given personally by the client seller.

Upon receipt of the title deeds, you will be able to ascertain whether the land is already registered or not. In the former case, you will need to apply for office copy entries (cost £5 without the filed plan and £10 with a filed plan) and in the latter instance, you should prepare an epitome of title in readiness.

When a sale is negotiated, dispatch the following:

(1) A draft contract in duplicate, incorporating the Second Edition of the standard conditions of sale. Use standard form unless you have it on word processor.
(2) Office copy entries or an epitome of title as appropriate.
(3) The fixtures, fittings and contents questionnaire duly answered, signed and dated.
(4) The property information forms Part I and II duly completed and signed and dated.
(5) Any enclosures referred to in the above documents, such as NHBC documentation, planning papers and guarantee certificates.

The buyer's response

Upon receipt of the Protocol documentation, the buyer's conveyancer will closely examine all the papers submitted. The raising of additional enquiries is not encouraged, but may be necessary in order to fulfil the conveyancer's professional duty to his or her buyer client.

If there are problems with the answers given to the questions on the property information form or if the contract or the title appears to be unacceptable, then these questions should be raised.

The old rule was that requisitions on title were dealt with after contracts had been exchanged, and that prior to that time the questions were to be of a practical nature, as per the form of preliminary enquiries. The standard condition (Condition 4) deals with time limits for the raising of requisitions and it is now becoming increasingly common practice to mix in requisitions with any additional enquiries under the vague heading of 'Observations'. Most conveyancers do not now object to dealing with requisitions on the title before exchange of contracts, although time limits are imposed for raising of requisitions after contracts have been exchanged (six working days after the date of the contract).

Contracts should be able to be approved by the buyer's conveyancer as soon as a satisfactory survey has been concluded, a satisfactory set of responses received from the seller's conveyancer concerning the Protocol documentation, and a loan has been agreed where applicable. Make sure any conditions attaching to the loan offer are capable of being observed.

Searches

The buyer will undertake a local authority search, and where the land is not registered, a public index map search from the Land Registry appropriate to the location of the property.

For rural property, it may be appropriate to address a commons registration search to the appropriate county council and also, particulary but not exclusively in the case of rural property, certain additional Part II loal authority search questions may be applicable. Check the position carefully (eg footpaths).

Local authority search fees vary widely and for the current cost you should check the local authority in question.

With regard to local authority searches, there is no 'priority period' applicable. Most solicitors regard a search as valid for three months after its date, but this is by no means a fixed rule. In these circumstances, The Law Society has set up a local search validation scheme. A master policy has been arranged with Lombard Continental Insurance Plc and underwriters and with Legal & Professional Indemnity Ltd as the administrators. To operate the validation insurance, solicitors are issued with certificates which they may then use in an appropriate case, thereby providing cover under the master policy for the benefit of their client buyer. The solicitor must send the premium to Legal & Professional Indemnity when the certificate is issued. The certificate should be placed with the title deeds at the end of the transaction.

Qualifying properties under this scheme must be residential with a purchase price of less than £500,000. The maximum time span covered is six months from the date of the result of the search. The premium payable depends upon the value of the property and ranges from £15 to £40. The cover provided is the difference between the market value of the property at the date of exchange of contracts caused by an adverse entry registered against the property in the period between the date of the earlier search and the date of exchange.

Three is no time limit for the notification of a claim. However, the loss is not index-linked, so that if the claim is not discovered for many years, inflation rate rises in the value of the property will not be taken into account.

2 The traditional style—the seller's package

The seller's conveyancer will send a draft contract in duplicate, probably referring to the old National conditions of sale or Law Society's conditions of sale. The contract will accompany a suitable letter of introduction.

The contract should contain a plan to enable the buyer's conveyancer to undertake a local authority search. Upon receipt of preliminary enquiries and any additional enquiries, the seller's conveyancers should answer those that they can from the deeds and documents of title and the balance from information given to them by their client.

When the buyer's conveyancer receives a local authority search result and a loan offer, and a satisfactory survey report, he or she will proceed to approve the contract, and subject to any related transaction, move towards exchange of contracts.

Under the traditional style, it was common practice for the seller's conveyancer to supply office copy entries on the title with the contract, but not to supply an epitome of title for unregistered property until after contracts had been exchanged. This practice was varied only if there was some known defect in the title, and if that was so, one could expect to find a special condition on the contract, indicating that the buyer would take the title as it stood, and would not raise requisitions after contracts were exchanged.

The buyer's response

Apart from noting omissions in the documents provided, it may be that the buyer requires the draft contract to be amended. There may be certain special conditions that are unacceptable. For example, the stipulated interest rate that applies, should there be delay in completion, may be too high. The property may not be very precisely described, or the description of the property may omit to refer to necessary rights of way and easements for the enjoyment of services. It is important to consider the content of the contract very carefully, and it is particularly important to examine the special conditions. If there are a lot of special conditions, they are generally there for a reason, and one has to try to work out why.

Under both the TransAction scheme and the traditional style, the preparation of a transfer is usually undertaken by the buyer's conveyancer. This does not apply where a pro forma is supplied by the seller's solicitors as in a new housing estate or where there is a sale such as by a mortgagee in possession. Since December 1990 all areas of England and Wales are compulsorily registrable. The need to prepare a conveyance deed is rare, because Rule 72 transfers are used instead. This is dealt with later in the text (see head 9 of Chapter 5).

3 Initial letters

For economy of every kind—time, energy, money—the 'one bite at the cherry' principle can't be over-emphasised. On this principle write all initial letters together on the day you receive instructions, or at the latest the following day. You'll find specimens of most of the kind of letters you will need to write at every stage of a simple conveyancing matter in Appendix II. These will normally be as follows:

(1) *To your client*, to acknowledge his instructions. You should confirm your costs quotation and draw attention to your client care arrangements. Record the salient terms of the sale (eg the purchase price, whether the property is freehold or leasehold, desired date of completion, etc; in the case of a buyer, that the purchase is subject to selling the buyer's own house or seeking a mortgage and to keep you informed as to his or her success). At the same time remind a seller or buyer of anything you still need (eg last receipts, or particulars of a seller's building society whose loan is to be repaid and who can give you particulars of your client's title).

(2) If you know who they are, write *to the conveyancers for the seller or buyer*, as the case may be, confirming that you are acting for

your client, and if your client is the buyer asking for the draft contract documentation, or if you act for the seller, either sending or promising to send the draft agreement for sale.

(3) Telephone the *seller's conveyancer* and ask if he or she intends to adopt the National Protocol.

(4) If you haven't already heard, telephone the *selling agent* for full particulars of the sale and parties etc.

(5) If you act for a seller whose unregistered title deeds are with a bank, building society, etc, write *for the deeds*, or (if they are not clients of yours) for the name and address of the conveyancers to whom they will be sent, and from whom an abstract can be obtained. A bank will usually be willing to send deeds to you upon your giving an undertaking in its standard form, although they will require their customer's written authority.

If the title is registered, telephone or write to the mortgagee for the title number and obtain office copy entries and filed plan.

The Law Society insists that a solicitor's undertaking is near absolute, and must be honoured. If need be, don't hesitate to amend any undertaking put before you by a bank etc, to terms you are confident you can fulfil. For example, ensure that the undertaking provides for payment to the bank *out of money coming to your hands*; then if, for some reason beyond your control, you don't receive the purchase money this condition won't have been fulfilled, and you will be exempt from the obligation to pay.

When writing to a building society, never omit the mortgage reference number, or there may be some delay in receiving a reply, and if you act for your client's bank, building society etc, you will of course normally ask them to send the deeds direct to you; in such a case include in your letter, if there is an existing mortgage to be discharged on completion (as there will be in the case of a building society and may be in the case of a bank), an undertaking to hold the deeds on behalf of the bank or society, to return them on demand, not to part with the same except on completion of the sale, and to discharge the society's mortgage.

(6) This is the time, if you have not before acted for your client, to send a polite note of thanks *to the person who introduced your client to you*.

4 Preparing a draft contract—seller

Before you do this you'll need to peruse the title (see Chapter 6) to ensure that all easements, rights and liabilities on the title are disclosed to the buyer, and that any defects or difficulties are disclosed and the buyer shut off from objecting to them after exchange.

Be brief. With an unregistered title don't stick slavishly to the description in old deeds. A typical clause on the sale of a registered title is as follows:

All that property known as   the title to which is registered as Absolute at HM Land Registry under Title No   *Together* with the rights and *Except and Reserved* and *Subject* as mentioned in the Entries on the Property and Charges Register of the said Title.

A typical clause on the sale of an unregistered title is as follows:

All that property known as   *Together* with the rights and *Except and Reserved* and *Subject* as mentioned in a Conveyance (hereinafter called 'the Conveyance') dated   and made between   of the one part and   of the other part.

It's common practice to supply, in addition to the top copy, an extra copy of the draft contract and of the transfer.

Send the epitome or abstract of an unregistered title, or Office Copy Entries and filed plan with the draft contract. This gives notice to the other side of all they should know.

A seller's conveyancer must be alert not only to supply copies of all known restrictions, but to guard against the absence of copies of old restrictions, as sometimes occurs. In *Faruqi v English Real Estates Ltd* [1979] 1 WLR 963, a property was registered with absolute title. An entry in the charges register disclosed that it was subject to restrictive covenants imposed by a deed of 1883 but did not reveal what those covenants were, because on first registration neither the deed nor a copy or abstract of it had been produced. Although the contract for sale was 'subject to the entries on the register of title', it did not disclose that there was a defect in the title. The buyer asked for a copy of the restrictions; they were not forthcoming, the seller having no copy. On a seller and buyer summons the court declared that the seller had not made a good title, and ordered the return to the buyer of the buyer's deposit on the equitable principle that it is a seller's duty to disclose fully and frankly in the contract any title defect.

Talking of restrictions, it often happens that your client wants to develop a property that is subject to old restrictive covenants in a manner that would be a breach of covenant. The Law of Property Act 1925 s 84 makes provision for application to the court in such a case to modify or discharge the restrictions, and now, under the Law of Property Act 1969, similar powers are given to the Lands Tribunal on grounds that the restriction impedes a use of the land that would be reasonable.

For a discussion of such applications see [1985] *Gazette* 6 March, 658.

A more common method today, however (because it is much quicker, often cheaper and one which can give certain security even before contracts to sell are exchanged), is the *insurance indemnity policy* issued on payment of a single premium. To obtain a quotation for such a policy you need to give the insurers full particulars of the restrictions, the proposed development (often after outline planning permission has been obtained) and the amount of indemnity required. Reference to such a policy when this is appropriate—that the buyer is to have the benefit of a policy the seller has obtained, for example, or that the sale is conditional on such a policy being issued to one of the parties—should be made in an appropriate case.

If, on a sale of *unregistered* land, there is any personal obligation on the part of a seller client to observe restrictions (as, for example, where the seller is the original covenantor or has given a personal covenant to observe these), it is desirable to provide in the contract for a similar covenant indemnifying the seller against any future breach. But to avoid loading a title with a chain of such covenants, it is perhaps better draftsmanship, when first imposing restrictions, to provide that the owner for the time being shall be responsible *only* for breaches committed whilst he or she is such owner. In cases where a covenant must be imposed to observe existing restrictions, on behalf of a buyer always insert in the covenant such words as 'so far as the same affect the property hereby conveyed and are subsisting and capable of being enforced', because for one reason or another the odds are ten to one that nobody *can* legally enforce them; but the case might be otherwise if you impose the restrictions afresh.

In the case of *registered leasehold* land the position is taken care of by s 24(1)(*b*) of the Land Registration Act 1925, which implies a covenant by the transferee to perform and observe the covenants and conditions in the lease and to indemnify the transferor. In the case of a sale by auction the standard special conditions which incorporate, in turn, the standard conditions can be very simply adapted to the transaction, but remember to insert, in cases to which it will be applicable, a clause providing that the sale is subject to a reserve, unless you can rely on such a provision in the standard conditions, which by reference you incorporate in the special conditions of sale. Without such a condition the auctioneer is under an obligation to knock down the property to the highest bidder, which could be a financial tragedy for the seller (and for you, in the shape of an action for negligence) if the highest bid was below its fair market value. Standard condition 2.3 deals with auctions.

Remember, too, when acting for a seller on a sale by auction to attend the sale itself to answer any questions that a prospective buyer may raise on the title or the special conditions — and be wary of the questioner who seeks to suggest that the title is faulty or that restrictions prohibit development, etc, in the hope of abating the bids offered. It is sometimes useful to consider quietly, in advance of the auction, possible objections and their answers.

If you act for the seller of a building estate, even though it comprises no more than a dozen houses or flats, it will repay you to print as many documents as possible (drafts and engrossments of conveyance or lease, contract etc) and to anticipate as far as you can a buyer's preliminary requirements. In many cases it will also repay you, in subsequent work saved, to register the title to the property. The preparatory work is considerable and demands the attention of an experienced conveyancer; but this preparation makes possible the delegation of much subsequent work, the smooth running of every sale, and an enormous overall saving of time.

When the purchase price includes fixtures or furniture, these should be specified in detail in the draft, and if their value is substantial it is sometimes useful to agree and state the value at which they should be taken in order to reduce the consideration, and the stamp duty payable thereon, in the ultimate conveyance or transfer of the property. In such a case a seller will give a separate receipt, on completion of the sale, in such words as these:

re . . . . . .

I   hereby acknowledge that I have received from   the sum of £   in payment for the fixtures, fittings and chattels now in or about the above premises listed in the Schedule below AND I confirm that I am absolutely entitled to the same free of any charge, hire-purchase agreement or other incumbrance affecting the same or any of them.

Properties around the stamp duty threshold of £60,000 may benefit significantly from an apportionment of the price between the legal estate and the contents of the property.

Assembly of information to prepare a draft contract

Most draft contracts now incorporate the standard conditions of sale (third Edition). This represents a merger of the previous Law Society and National conditions of sale, use of which is being discontinued. The new conditions are considerably simplified and written in plain English. The terms 'buyer' and 'seller' are used rather than 'purchaser' and 'vendor'. Solicitors may produce their own contract on word processors and are permitted to reproduce the standard contract incorporating the standard conditions of sale by reference.

The conditions are available in a printed booklet, which solicitors are advised to provide to their client in instances where the conditions are incorporated by reference. The new conditions of sale have been drafted for both domestic and commercial transactions and are not restricted to transactions where the National Protocol is followed.

Drafting the contract

The standard conditions do not need to be expressly referred to unless an alteration is sought.

The following information needs to be put on the front page:

(1) The agreement date and the name and address of the seller and the buyer. The date is left blank until contracts are actually exchanged.

(2) The description of the property together with the interest being sold by the seller. In the case of unregistered land this description should be by reference to an attached plan. The description of the property will generally be similar to that contained in the conveyance to the seller but sometimes such descriptions need to be improved by updating. The description of the property should include easements, such as rights of way that the property enjoys, rights of light across neighbouring property or support from neighbouring property. The description will also include all exceptions and reservations in favour of the seller, the benefit of which is to be sold to the buyer.

(3) If the property is sold subject to restrictive covenants contained in the title deeds, these should be noted as burdens on the property. Sometimes the root deed itself will refer to the restrictive covenants and sometimes new restrictive covenants will be imposed in this transaction, for example, if it is a sale of part only of the seller's property. In any of these events, a special condition needs to be inserted in order to make it clear which restrictions the property is being sold subject to, and copies of any restrictive covenants should be supplied. As an alternative to restrictive covenants (eg the buyer may build only one single-storey dwelling on the land hereby agreed to be sold), there may be positive covenants that the buyer is to be required to observe (eg the buyer must erect a larchlap fence on the length of the left-hand boundary of the property). If there is a positive covenant, not only should this be referred to but also the buyer should be required to enter into an indemnity covenant in the conveyance to him or her in respect of the future observance of it. The reason for an indemnity is that such a covenant does not automatically pass on each

transaction; the burden of it needs to be handed down expressly to each subsequent buyer.

(4) It is necessary to disclose the capacity in which the seller sells. There are a number of alternatives:

(i) *With full or limited title guarantee*. With effect from 1 July 1995, the Law of Property (Miscellaneous Provisions) Act 1994 comes into force. This will replace the words 'as beneficial owner', 'as trustee' etc. They will be replaced by two possibilities, namely, 'with full title guarantee' and 'with limited title guarantee'.

As has been the case until now, covenants are implied by statute only if the key words are used, and that is a matter to be agreed between the parties' solicitors.

From 1 July 1995, the transferor's capacity is irrelevant. For example, it may well be agreed that trustees can transfer 'with full title guarantee'. This is the equivalent of being a beneficial owner. Conversely, it may be agreed that a beneficial owner may transfer with 'limited title guarantee'.

If the key words are used, the covenants will be implied, even if there is no consideration (eg a deed of gift). This reverses the position in s 76(1)(a) and (b) of the Law of Property Act 1925.

(ii) *Mortgagee*. Sometimes it may be necessary for a mortgagee to exercise its powers under the Law of Property Act 1925 as enhanced by the provisions of the relevant mortgage deed in order to take possession of a property from a defaulting borrower. The ultimate sanction—and one which is most commonly applied—is for the mortgagee to sell. Under the new arrangements, the mortgagee will decide in which of the above two capacities it will opt to sell.

(iii) *Personal Representatives*. Where the proprietor of the legal estate has died, the sellers will be the personal representatives of the estate. When title is deduced, the sellers will be obliged to produce a grant of probate or a grant of letters of administration to show they are entitled to sell. A certified copy or office copy of this must be handed over on completion. Again, the personal representatives will have to opt in which capacity they sell.

(iv) *Trustees*. Trustees for sale may include owners of business property or trustees under a will trust. Again, they have to opt in which capacity they sell under the terms of the new Act.

(5) The completion date should be inserted when contracts are exchanged. If this is not done, standard Condition 6 will prevail. This provides for completion 20 working days after the date of the contract, but further provides that time is not of the essence unless a notice to complete has been served.

If the money due on completion is received after 2 pm, completion is treated as taking place on the next working day.

(6) Interest payable if completion is delayed. This provision may cause confusion to clients as they will not understand that it relates only to a late completion date. The provision normally provides for the buyer to pay interest on the balance purchase money and this should now be fixed at the Law Society's Interest Rate. The rate is published regularly in the *Law Society's Gazette*.

(7) The root of title or title number. For unregistered conveyancing, the provisions of the Law of Property Act 1969 provide that a good root of title is a conveyance on sale or legal mortgage which is at least 15 years old. If there is no such deed of that age, then one has to trace the title back further until a deed is found. Bad roots of title include leases (when one is conveying the freehold), wills and equitable mortgages. In certain transactions one might be requested to accept a root of title that is less than 15 years old or a document other than a mortgage, or a conveyance on sale as the root deed. On these occasions further enquiries should be made in order to ascertain why the request is being put. It may mean that the legal title to the property is defective, and if this is so, certain remedial steps may be necessary, such as obtaining a defective title indemnity policy from an insurance company and a statutory declaration from the seller or the seller's neighbours. Such additional requirements may give rise to a special condition being attached to the back of the contract.

(8) The price of the property being sold and provision for a deposit. Sometimes these are left blank until exchange of contracts is imminent. It saves having to re-print the contract if the transaction does not proceed and the contract is required for an alternative proposed buyer. Where a deposit is inserted the standard conditions provide for this to be 10% of the price. However, a deposit of less than 10% may sometimes be agreed by negotiation between the parties' legal representatives, and this negotiation usually takes place immediately before contracts are exchanged. It may necessitate a further special condition on the back of the contract.

The deposit does constitute clients' money and the seller is entitled to interest earned on the deposit money in accordance with the provisions of the Solicitors Accounts Rules 1991. The rate is the rate currently payable on small deposits by the bank or building society where the money is held. A table of minimum balances applies.

Standard condition 2.2.2 provide that if the seller is buying another property in a related transaction, he or she may use all or part of the deposit as a deposit in that transaction, to be held in that transaction as stakeholder. This means it may not be further used. Any part of a deposit that is not required as described above must be held as stakeholder by the seller's solicitor until completion. If this arrangement is to be varied a special condition is required.

(9) The amount payable for chattels at the property is separately set out on the standard conditions contract form.

5 Plans

As noted above a plan is essential to the proper description of a property, and this is especially so in the case of leases the title to which is to be registered, and indeed of leases of flats in general. A plan is commonly essential, too, on the sale of a part of a property, registered or unregistered.

While it is the responsibility of your seller-client to prepare the plan where necessary (and don't be persuaded to take on this heavy responsibility in your client's stead) you should, as the conveyancer, scrutinise what is handed to you with a critical eye coupled with your knowledge of the title and the property. Bring to your client's attention any errors, uncertainties or omissions which you may discover, with any suggested amendments. Check that all necessary rights of way are shown. Check that the whole of the property to be sold is included in the plan, no more, no less, and that the boundaries shown leave no room for doubt. And ensure that your client prepares the plans to a reasonable scale, not too small or too large—if on a size A4 page, that will not only annex conveniently to a lease or transfer of part but will also facilitate the taking of photocopies. No architect's working drawings of wallpaper size. Be firm.

Conveyancers are not trained or expected to prepare original plans: it is the duty of the client to supply these. But it's the clear duty of a seller's conveyancer to recognise the nature of any plan required, and to obtain this from the seller, or, with authority, to instruct a professional draughtsman to prepare one. And it is the equally clear duty of a buyer's conveyancer, with the buyer, to consider whether a plan correctly and adequately describes the property.

When acting for a buyer note that standard condition 4.3 exempts a seller from the obligation to prove the exact boundaries of a property or to prove who owns the hedges, ditches, fences etc.

The UK is virtually completely moving over to the metric system by 1 October 1995. The Law Society recommends that henceforth conveyancers should use only metric units of measurement, for the avoidance of doubt.

6 Special conditions of sale

These are included for the purpose of supplementing and altering the standard conditions of sale. It is not possible to provide the reader with a comprehensive list of these, because they vary from one transaction to another. They do appear on many of the precedents commonly used by practitioners. The following are examples of special conditions:

Whether the sale is with vacant possession on completion, or subject to an existing tenancy. In the latter case, details should be inserted and in the former the alternative deleted.

The authorised use of the property for the purposes of current planning legislation.

The chattels included in the sale are as set out on the fixtures, fittings and contents form attached.

Here are some further special conditions, some of which in a suitable case may be useful. Others will be suggested by the circumstances and terms of a particular transaction.

For all freeholds
   A   The property is sold subject to the [burdens and other provisions] contained in [the said conveyance] [entries on the Register other than financial charges] and a copy thereof having been supplied to the buyer's conveyancers the buyer shall be deemed to purchase with full knowledge of the same and shall not raise any requisition or objection relating thereto.

For all leaseholds
   B   The title shall commence with the lease and the property is sold subject to the [entries on the Register other than financial charges and to the] covenants, terms and conditions contained in the lease. [A copy] [copies] thereof having been supplied to the buyer's conveyancers the buyer shall be deemed to purchase with

full knowledge of the same and shall not raise any requisition or objection relating thereto.

For registered leasehold titles

C   The lease and counterpart shall be prepared by the Lessor's solicitor and the Lessee shall contribute the sum of £   plus VAT towards the engrossing costs.

or

D   This Contract shall represent all the terms agreed between the parties hereto and the buyer hereby admits that no statement made by the seller or his agent has induced him to enter into this Contract except written statements, if any, made by the seller's conveyancers.

E   The seller shall prior to completion of the purchase carry out and complete in a good and workmanlike manner and with good quality materials the following works to the property, namely:

F   AB the [wife] of the seller hereby acknowledges that she has no claim to or interest in the property hereby agreed to be sold adverse to the interest of the buyer and in consideration of the buyer entering into this agreement she hereby agrees that if so required she will join in the [conveyance] [transfer] [assignment] [lease] for the purpose of vesting the said property in the buyer free from incumbrances.

G   The buyer shall in the transfer of the property covenant with the seller by way of indemnity against any breach of the covenants contained in [the said conveyance dated   ] [the said Lease] [referred to in Entry No 1 on the Charges Register].

H   The seller undertakes to make an irrevocable offer to enter into the form of agreement HB 5 prescribed by the National House-Building Council.

I   All provisions of this agreement which are not expressly or by necessary implication to merge and be extinguished in the transfer hereunder shall continue in full force and effect after completion.

Where less than 10% deposit paid

J   If the buyer pays by way of deposit a sum less than 10% of the purchase price then in the event of the seller becoming entitled to forfeit the deposit under the terms hereof the buyer shall forthwith pay to the seller or the seller's conveyancer a sum equal to the difference between the deposit already paid and 10% of the total purchase price.

On sales of short leases and some others

K   The seller shall use his or her best endeavours to procure the lessor's licence to assign and the buyer shall use his or her best endeavours to supply all references and information reasonably required by the lessor.

7 The property information forms

The property information questionnaire is specially prefaced for the client and is directly intended for the client's use. It has some important advice on the front page, and explains the effect of the answers given. It underlines the importance of accuracy. Most clients are able to cope with answering the questions since the answers will be a matter of their personal knowledge as a result of residing in or using the property they are selling.

It is then your task as the seller's conveyancer to compare the answers on the information form with the deeds or land certificate and then complete Part II of the information form.

The additional property information form deals with the more complex questions that relate to leasehold property. They are concerned with a management company and the details relating thereto. There are questions concerning insurance, maintenance costs and any problems with the landlord/tenant relationship.

All these forms, including the fixtures, fittings and contents form, need a signature. This is particularly important if any query arises upon any of the answers given at a later date.

It is sometimes important for the buyer's conveyancer to raise observations on the content of these information forms. However, the practice of raising pages and pages of additional enquiries is now strongly discouraged, and the enquiries necessary are simply those to fulfil one's professional obligations to one's client.

8 Preliminary enquiries and additional enquiries

Under the old system of conveyancing and for commercial conveyancing, the preliminary enquiry form remains in use. Readers will recall that upon receipt of the draft contract in duplicate together with the accompanying plan and any copy covenants, the buyer's conveyancer will make an index map search and a local search, and also raise enquiries before contract. Enquiries before contract are a method of ascertaining as much practical information as possible from the seller about the property to be bought. The buyer's conveyancer will generally send a standard form to the seller's conveyancer, accompanied by a copy and also further questions, which ideally should be tailor-made for the particular transaction.

Standard enquiries include the following:

(1) *The ownership and maintenance responsibilities of the boundaries of the property.* Ownership of boundaries is commonly marked on deed plans with an inwardly facing 'T'. There will be occasions where there is no indication with the title deeds as to who owns the boundaries and in that case custom and practice will prevail. On modern housing developments boundaries are commonly 'party' structures (ie 50:50).

(2) *Disputes.* The seller will be required to supply information about any disputes with the neighbours in the recent past and to supply copy correspondence etc.

(3) *Notices.* The seller will be expected to supply details of any correspondence with the local authority in respect of planning matters either relating to the property to be sold or to neighbouring property. Sometimes an older property will have been listed as a building of special architectural or historical interest and again details should be supplied. A notice may have been served with regard to an intention by a local authority compulsorily to purchase the property or part of it and again notices may have been received by the seller where the property is subject to occupation by a tenant.

(4) *Guarantees.* The property may be sold with the benefit of certain guarantees as to its condition. The most common of these is the 'Buildmark' guarantee supplied by the National House-Building Council. Details of this appear below in Chapter 8.

Other guarantees may be supplied by a double glazing, damp-proofing or woodworm treatment company. Details of all these should be supplied to the buyer's conveyancer on request.

(5) *Services.* The buyer will wish to know which services he or she has the benefit of, and here we refer to gas and mains water. It may well be that the property does not have the benefit of mains drainage and this will lead to the further enquiry as to arrangements for septic tank drainage, whether or not that septic tank drains onto neighbouring property and, if so, what rights are in existence for such an arrangement. Similarly, the buyer will wish to know whether there are rights for services to pass over neighbouring land.

(6) *Exclusive facilities.* This deals with those facilities enjoyed exclusively by the property to be sold over neighbouring property. Most commonly, this might relate to a right of way across

the neighbouring property, and details as to whether or not that right has been interrupted or whether charges have been made for its use will be required.

(7) *Shared facilities*. This enquiry is similar to the one above, but refers to those facilities that are jointly used by neighbours over a third person's property. Again, details of maintenance responsibilities will be required and the proportion in which the costs of upkeep have been shared by those entitled.

(8) *Rights of occupiers*. This enquiry refers to the rights of those who do not actually own the property but who may, for example, occupy it. Adult occupiers should be required to sign the contract on completion in order to signify their consent to granting vacant possession in accordance with the obligations of the owners on exchange of contracts. Details of occupiers, including their names and ages, will be required in answer to preliminary enquiries.

(9) *Restrictions*. It will be necessary to confirm that all restrictions have been observed and if they have not been observed, to confirm that consent to vary or discharge them has been forthcoming. A restrictive covenant imposed after 1925 binds future owners if registered as a land charge Class D(ii) or on the Land Register. Earlier covenants affect buyers for value if they buy with notice although this must depend on whether anyone is available legally entitled to enforce them.

(10) *Use of the property*. It is necessary to state current use of the property and whether that has been continuous. Where a property is being used in breach of planning permission, an enforcement notice may be served by the local planning authority on the owner/occupier requiring the use to cease. Failure to observe that enforcement notice can result in a prosecution in the local magistrates' court. The existence or otherwise of an enforcement notice will be revealed by the local search result. Once an enforcement notice has been entered against a property as a local land charge it will not be removed. This will not materially affect the buyer unless he or she is seeking to continue with the unauthorised use.

(11) *Environmental enquiries*. Consider raising environmental enquiries far more widely than at present. Under new legislation it is proposed the buyer will take the risk—*caveat emptor* applies. A tenant can be liable for pollution from land as 'occupier' of that land, even if only on a short term lease. Liability to repair premises may include clean up costs.

The Environmental Information Regulations 1992 establish

the positive right for any person seeking information on the environment to obtain it from any public body which holds it.

Note the Environment Act which received Royal Assent on 19 July 1995. It contains important powers and responsibilities for local authorities and harsh penalties on those who pollute land.

Preliminary enquiries should be treated seriously and the seller's legal representatives should do their best to supply full answers.

When you act for a buyer, always go through the answers you receive to your preliminary enquiries, search and additional enquiries made of the local authority, marking each of these with a tick if it is satisfactory, or with a cross if it is not, or if it requires further elucidation. Then go through the replies again if any are marked with a cross, taking whatever action may be appropriate on each (asking the seller's conveyancers to provide a copy of a planning consent that your search has revealed, and telling your client that the drainage is combined with that of adjoining properties, or — this merely to pass on interesting information — that the house is in an area designated as one of special natural beauty or historical interest). *As you deal with each point* then tick the cross, but not before.

This practice of *marking* searches, requisitions etc, should be an invariable one for three reasons:

(1) it compels you to consider each question and reply before marking it;
(2) it will save you time in selecting answers that require further action, and will avoid you reading through the enquiries again later on to make sure that the replies to them are in order; and
(3) it is a permanent record that at the time of the transaction you not only made your search etc, but duly considered and dealt with the replies.

You can never entirely eliminate human error and oversight, but this procedure of marking replies to searches, etc, minimises the possibility of your forgetting to pass on to your client vital information that might give time to consider whether or not to proceed with the purchase, such as the fact that redevelopment of the area within the next ten years is contemplated. You will commonly, of course, advise your client of any facts of interest, which you have discovered by your enquiries; for example, that the road has not yet been taken over by the local authority, that plans for building on the property were submitted to and rejected by the local authority, etc. Write the word 'client' in the margin against any information that it is necessary to impart (and your client should be kept fully informed on every matter that might be of material interest), ticking this, as already mentioned, when you have done so.

There is one enquiry you should always make when buying a flat: otherwise the buyer may, in the next year, be confronted with a quite unacceptable bill for major repairs—repainting the block, a new roof etc. A similar enquiry should also be made in the case of 'right to buy' purchases (see Chapter 9).

Is the seller [or lessor, on the grant of a new lease] aware of any major work of repair or otherwise, anticipated in the foreseeable future towards which a purchaser [lessee] might be required to contribute?

When acting for a buyer of *vacant land* who intends to build on it, or for a buyer of a *recently erected house*, a hidden danger has recently been highlighted—the possibility that the foundations may be at risk of subsidence or of sliding either through infilling of the site, or a dangerous geological stratum. In the case of a building, the seller may be ignorant: if the seller knew of a risk and sold without disclosure, he or she is probably liable at law, but builders come and builders go, and those who deliberately mislead mostly go.

The local authority will have all the information that would reveal the danger, but, surprisingly, it is under no obligation to volunteer this information, either in a development permit or otherwise—it is the absence of such an obligation that has been the source of hardship and complaint.

So, when acting in such a case, add to your additional enquiries made of the local authority, or better in a letter, some such enquiry as this:

Is the Authority aware of any infilling or any geological stratum which might result in the instability of the foundations of any building erected on the site for which planning consent has been granted?

If they say the enquiry is too wide to answer, that's nonsense—they know wherever infilling has occurred, and they have their geological maps of the area. Press them.

Examples of additional enquiries

(1) Is the seller aware of any development or proposals for the development or use of property in the neighbourhood which might adversely affect the property or the amenities of persons living in it?

(2) Has the property to the seller's knowledge been affected at any time by structural, building or drainage defects, flooding, dry rot, timber infestation or rising damp?

(3) Please confirm that any damage caused to decorations by the removal of fixtures and fittings will be made good by the seller before completion.

(4) Are there to the seller's knowledge any adverse rights or informal arrangements or licences affecting the property not disclosed in the draft contract?

(5) If the property has central heating:
  (i)   approximately when was it installed?
  (ii) when was it last serviced?
  (iii) is it working satisfactorily?

(6) Have there been any disputes between the seller and the lessor and/or the owners or occupiers of adjoining or neighbouring properties? If so, please supply particulars.

(7) Has any work to the seller's knowledge been done at the property requiring planning permission or Building Regulations 1991 (SI No 2768) consent? If so, please supply copies.

(8) (i) When was the property last rewired and when last tested by the electricity authority?
    (ii) Is a current test certificate available? If so, please supply a copy.

(9) If the property is *leasehold*:
    (i) please confirm that the seller has complied with all the covenants in the lease;
    (ii) does the seller know whether any items of substantial expenditure for decoration, maintenance or repair have been carried out by the lessors recently but not yet charged to tenants, or are any such contemplated in the near future?

(10) Is the seller aware of any overriding interest under the Land Registration Act 1925, s 70(1)?

(11) Please confirm:
    (i)   that all gas and electrical installations are the seller's absolute property and are included in the purchase price;
    (ii) that the electric light installations down to the bulb holders will be left intact;
    (iii) that all furniture, furnishings and fittings not included in the sale and all rubbish will be removed before completion.

(12) Please notify us before exchange of contracts if you become aware of any change of circumstances which make inaccurate your replies to the foregoing enquiries.

9 Rights of spouses and third parties

Most husbands and wives are joint owners of their matrimonial home. A non-owner spouse does, however, have rights under the Matrimonial

Homes Act 1983 and may acquire an equitable interest in the property through contributions to the purchase price of the property. Contributions may be calculated in various ways.

The presumption of joint ownership between husbands and wives may be varied, either as part of a tax planning scheme, or where one partner is particularly vulnerable in court proceedings, or faces the threat of bankruptcy. As suggested before, a condition should be added to the contract so that the non-owning spouse signs prior to exchange of contracts, in order to signify his/her consent to the transaction and further to confirm that he will grant vacant possession on the appointed completion date. The form of wording may look like this:

I hereby undertake that in consideration of your entering into an agreement to purchase the above property, any interest which I may have or acquire therein shall be deferred to any interest of you, or any mortgage or chargee and that I will not apply for the registration of any Land Charge, Caution, Notice or Restriction in respect thereof.

The 1983 Act does not protect unmarried, non-owning partners, although their position may be secured by being able to establish an equitable or overriding interest.

10 Approval of draft contract

We have already noted the stage at which it will become possible for the buyer's conveyancer to approve the contract. It is important that when contracts are approved, both parts are identical. If any alterations are made to the contract, or conditions added to it, then such must be initialled by the parties to the contract. Sometimes, this may be delegated to the conveyancer acting, but this delegation must clearly be with the client's authority.

After contracts are approved and signed, and the deposit money is ready at the appropriate place in the chain, the exchange process may begin.

11 Contract races

A solicitor is sometimes instructed by a seller to deal with more than one prospective buyer at a time, sending a draft contract to each. If the client can't be dissuaded, the Law Society has directed that the following steps by a solicitor are obligatory:

(1) A solicitor must, with his clients' authority, at once disclose in writing his clients' decisions to the solicitor for each prospective buyer (or to the prospective buyer if he or she is unrepresented).

If the seller refuses to authorise disclosure, the solicitor must forthwith cease to act for him or her.

(2) Notwithstanding exceptions to the rule that a solicitor may not act for both seller and buyer, in any such case a solicitor cannot act as there is a conflict of interest between the parties. A contract race increases the risk of such a conflict, and if, in an exceptional case, the solicitor decides to act for both seller and one of the prospective buyers, this decision must be disclosed, in writing, to both the two clients and the other prospective buyers or their solicitors.

(3) Where draft contracts are submitted to more than one prospective buyer, a solicitor must not accept instructions to act for more than one of them. (See Council Direction published in [1977] *Gazette* 6 October, 834 repeated 28 November 1979, 1177.)

New Rule 6(a) of the Solicitors Practice Rules 1990

The revised Rule 6(a) came into force on 1 March 1995 and applies to all conveyancing transactions, whether commercial or domestic, freehold or leasehold.

(i)   It applies when you know that the seller/client is dealing with another prospective buyer without your being directly involved.

(ii) There is an absolute prohibition on acting for both buyer and seller if a further prospective buyer is introduced during the course of the transaction. This is even if one of the standard exceptions (within Rule 6) applies.

(iii) If you use the fax to tell the other side that they are now in a contract race, it is no longer necessary to confirm that fax by letter. See note in [1994] 47 LSG 36.

12 The alternative methods of exchanging contracts

Exchange is more commonly effected either by post or by telephone.

If by post, the buyer's conveyancer posts or delivers to the seller's conveyancer the part of the contract signed by the buyer, together with a cheque for the deposit. Exchange occurs when the seller's conveyancer posts their part to the buyer's conveyancer. From that moment, there is a binding exchange of contracts. If exchanging contracts through the post and dealing with a sale and purchase, the steps must be carefully synchronised. On the sale, the buyers post their part to you first. On the purchase, you then post your client's part to the other side. You wait for the other side to post their part back to you on your client's purchase, thereby leaving you with the initiative to complete the exchange procedure on your client's sale, and this you should do immediately.

However, it is much more satisfactory to exchange by telephone, using one of The Law Society's formulae.

The Law Society has published a statement recommending the procedure to be followed in a case of exchange by telephone or telex ([1980] *Gazette*, 13 February, 144). This was slightly amended in 1984 to include the DX delivery system. Two formulae are suggested: one (Formula A) where one solicitor holds both parts of the contract; the other (Formula B) where conveyancers hold their own client's signed part of the contract. In practice, most firms use a standard form of memorandum to record the salient detail of what is agreed.

Under Formula A
   (1) A completion date is agreed. Holding solicitors confirm to the others that their client's part is signed and is identical to the part signed by the other party; they agree they will forthwith insert in both parts the agreed completion date.
   (2) The solicitors agree that exchange shall take place from that moment and holding solicitors confirm that as from that moment:
      (i) they hold the part signed by their client to the order of the other; and
      (ii) undertake that day to post by first-class post or to deliver their signed part of the contract to the other solicitors, together, in the case of the buyer's solicitor holding both parts, with a bank draft or a solicitor's clients' account cheque for the deposit.

Under Formula B
   (1) A completion date is agreed. Each solicitor confirms that they hold their own client's part of the contract in the agreed form; agree forthwith to insert the agreed completion date.
   (2) Each undertakes to the other thenceforth to hold the part in their hands to the other's order, and that day by first-class post or hand delivery to send their part to the other, together, in the case of the buyer, with bank draft or a solicitor's clients' account cheque for the deposit.

Under Formula C
Since 1986 under the Law Society Formula 'C', a chain of transactions may be exchanged over the telephone more satisfactorily. The solicitors at the end of the chain are asked to release their contract for a

specified period of time to the solicitors acting for the buyer next in line. Precise details of times etc should be carefully recorded and each solicitor should be available to speak to the other throughout the agreed duration of the release. Memoranda should be prepared accordingly. The solicitors in whose favour the contract has been released, are then free to undertake a telephone exchange of contracts in accordance with Law Society Formula 'A' or 'B', as appropriate, and can then return to the original solicitors at the end of the chain in order to complete the exchange of the released contract in the same way as they would if dealing with Law Society Formula 'A' or 'B'. Law Society Formula 'C' therefore involves two phone calls. However, the contractual commitment stems from the first of those calls on the basis that it is followed up by the time agreed.

The above formulae are also used by licensed conveyancers.

13 The deposit paid on exchange

This has been referred to previously in the text, but there are two additional points to note.

Under the Solicitors Accounts Rules 1991, solicitors have a duty to account to their clients for the interest earned by the placing of deposit money in a solicitors' client account as stakeholder.

Standard condition 2.2 now deals with the payment of deposits and provides for a 10% deposit to be taken. Standard condition 6.8.4 provides that where a deposit of less than 10% is taken on exchange, the balance of the 10% becomes payable immediately on service of a notice to complete. Indeed if the contract is not fulfilled the 10% deposit is forfeited.

The condition requires the deposit to be paid only by a banker's draft or solicitors' cheque. In an auction contract, this will need to be amended. A special condition will be required if the deposit is being funded by a guarantee scheme. This scheme may be used only with the seller's agreement.

The condition also allows sellers to use part of the deposit to fund their own deposit in a related transaction, and such part of the deposit as is used in this way will be held by the seller's conveyancer as agent, and the balance as stakeholder. Finally, the condition provides that interest shall be paid on stakeholder deposits to the seller on completion.

14 Pre-exchange checklist—seller

(1) Take full instructions on instructions sheet.
(2) Peruse and check title.

(3) Have seller supply replies to property information form and fixtures, fittings and contents questionnaire.

(4) Interest rate.

(5) Deposit?

(6) Restrictions, covenants in leaseholds etc.

(7) Plans? adequate, correct. Have client supply plan.

(8) Misrepresentation: safeguard against buyer relying on any representations except those made by you in writing (eg in replies on property information form etc).

(9) ? Provide for indemnity by buyer against breach of restrictions, covenants in lease etc.

(10) Vacant possession. Check adults in occupation.

(11) Completion date—synchronise in linked sale and purchase.

(12) Completion date—new building.

(13) ? Vary standard conditions.

(14) ? Provide for NHBC agreement.

(15) Obtain client's approval of contract before exchange.

(16) Hold exchange until completion dates and readiness to exchange on sale and concurrent purchase established.

(17) Then exchange by telephone.

(18) On sale of a flat:
   (i) Check outgoings (rent, maintenance charge etc).
   (ii) When a management company, check share position; if lessees are members, get share certificate.
   (iii) Check insurance position.
   (iv) When lessor's licence required, insert appropriate special condition.

15 Pre-exchange checklist—buyer

(1) Take full instructions on instructions sheet.

(2) In sale of leaseholds, go through lease and draft contract with client, make notes on information supplied on the Protocol forms.

(3) Peruse contract; dispatch additional observations.

(4) Insurance? If leasehold, consider position.

(5) Peruse title.

(6) Check provisions in draft contract for interest; deposit; restrictions; plan; indemnity to seller; misrepresentation.

(7) Check contract plan with buyer.

(8) Undertake local search, water authority search and other searches relevant to the transaction.

(9) Check financial arrangements with client.

(10) ? Provide for seller's spouse to renounce interest in property.
(11) Provide for vacant possession.
(12) In linked transactions synchronise completion dates.
(13) Check and provide for NHBC cover on new or recent building.
(14) Provide for completion guarantee of new building.
(15) Check agreement for fixtures and fittings etc.
(16) Check position with regard to restrictive covenants etc. ?Consult or advise client.
(17) Obtain client's approval of contract before exchange.
(18) Leaseholds; if licence required, obtain, take up buyer's references.
(19) Leaseholds; check outgoings and past and present maintenance charge with client.
(20) Hold exchange until completion dates and readiness to exchange on concurrent sale and purchase established.
(21) Then exchange by telephone.

Chapter 4

Searches and registrations

Searches, and the registrations that occasion them, are pivotal to modern conveyancing. They are the shield against fraud and deception. The only serious chink in the armour of the buyer is the 'overriding interest' of registered land, which is described in Chapter 5.

The subject is one of such importance to the conveyancer that readers are advised to acquire one of the books and booklets devoted to the subject, of which the following are three examples: *Guide to Enquiries of Local Authorities* by Trevor Aldridge (Longman Professional); *Handbook of Conveyancing Searches* by E O Bourne (Sweet & Maxwell); and *Searches and Enquiries—A Conveyancer's Guide* by Frances Silverman (Butterworths).

Who cause the entries in the various registers to be made? Broadly, those who have an interest in a parcel of land that is not otherwise apparent in the title to that land. And who is concerned to discover what may be those interests, which, by registration, are deemed to be notified to the world? Broadly, those who seek to acquire that piece of land, or an interest therein: prospective buyers, lessees, mortgagees.

Particulars of the principal Registers and the persons and bodies who should register and search are given below. Some references to the details of search procedure, where material to action at various stages of a conveyancing transaction, are also given in succeeding chapters.

1 The Local Land Charges Register

Contents of the Register

Established under the Land Charges Act 1925, this is of importance to every buyer, lessee and mortgagee of any property in England and Wales, because the matters registered are not referred to in either the Registers of registered land nor in the Central Land Charges Register.

As well as the contents of the official register (use official form of request for certificate of search), search is invariably made at the same time for other information noted on the records of the local authority of which a buyer needs to be informed (two forms here; one for London boroughs and one for all other district councils).

The Register proper consists of 12 parts, as follows:

Part 1   General financial charges
Part 2   Specific financial charges
Part 3   Planning charges
Part 4   Miscellaneous charges
Part 5   Fenland ways maintenance
Part 6   Land compensation charges
Part 7   New towns charges
Part 8   Civil aviation charges
Part 9   Opencast coal charges
Part 10   Listed buildings charges
Part 11   Light obstruction charges
Part 12   Drainage scheme charges

The form (Con 29) containing additional enquiries is in two parts: Part I contains questions of universal application, and replies are sought and paid for by one comprehensive fee; Part II enquiries are relevant only to particular properties and will not be answered unless indicated by the searcher, a separate fee being paid for each entry searched. No more than headings are given below—for details, readers are referred to the forms themselves.

Who registers?

The local authority is responsible for making all the entries on its Register.

Who searches? When and how?

Every prospective buyer or owner dealing with someone interested in acquiring an interest over land, such as a right of way or other easements.

Complete the application for an official search using a carbon for the duplicate copy comprised in the one form. Complete the request for further information on form Con 29 in duplicate, using two forms for the purpose. Send the forms, together with the appropriate fee to the Registrar of local land charges at the municipal offices for the authority concerned. Longman's *Directory of Local Authorities* provides a list of the appropriate addresses. Note that there is no longer a fixed national scale figure. The amount charged varies from one authority to another, and independent enquiries should generally be made when dealing with authorities outside one's own area.

In most authorities there is some delay. The validity of a local search result lasts for only three months, and if there is delay in finding a buyer, the search may be extended under the local search validation insurance scheme. The idea is that the master policy indemnifies the buyer and the buyer's mortgagee for any diminution in the market value of the property arising from adverse entries between the date of the search and the date of exchange. This insurance cover deals with replies to both form LLC1 and Con29. The indemnity only covers market value claims as at the date of exchange. There is no time limit for claims, and accordingly, the certificate of insurance should be kept with the title deeds.

The cost of cover is £10 for properties up to £250,000 and £20 for properties up to £500,000. To take out the insurance, a solicitor simply completes a form from the pad supplied and sends a cheque for the premium to London & Professional Indemnity. The detachable remittance slip is the proof of the cover and goes with the deeds.

To speed the local search result it is possible, though expensive, to arrange a personal search in some local authorities by a local search agency or indeed by doing it yourself.

Action on receipt of replies

First peruse each reply carefully, consider its significance; and if the reply is benign, pass on to the next, but before you do, tick the answer in the margin, or if it calls for clarification or action, put a cross in the margin, so that when you have considered every reply, you can go over them all comprehensively, and take whatever action is called for. This procedure avoids possible oversight, and is a record that the answers have been considered, thus avoiding possible duplication of work if for any reason the matter is handed to another to deal with. The same procedure should be followed in the case of other searches, the Schedules that may be attached to the official certificate of search, and also answers to your preliminary enquiries and requisitions on title made of the seller.

Not all positive replies are sinister: on the contrary, some are desirable or necessary. If the certificate of search discloses that a resolution has been made adopting the provisions of the Clean Air Act, that's an advantage to a buyer as a measure of protection against pollution. Question 1 of the additional questions will reveal whether or not the road has been adopted and all charges paid. If not, the buyer should be alerted and his other instructions taken. When a road is taken over by the local authority there are usually substantial charges to be paid, but often, in the case of estate roads, the developers have accepted responsibility and entered into a bond with the local authority to secure their liability. Your enquiries should, again, yield positive information about the existence or otherwise of mains drains.

When you've gone through all the answers, take up with the seller any that call for clarification, for example the absence of a planning consent (suggested by your preliminary enquiries) revealed by your search. Don't exchange contracts until you and your client are satisfied on every point and in particular about adoption of roads and drains. A retention from the price should be negotiated if you are not satisfied on these points.

Lastly, report to the buyer every matter of significance or interest— eg that the property is in an area of outstanding natural beauty. Remember the golden rule of legal PR—keep the client in the picture— and keep the picture moving quickly.

2 The Central Land Charges Register

Contents of the Register

The Central Land Charges Register, like the Local Land Charges Register, was established under the Land Charges Act 1925 for the purpose of protecting various interests of a less parochial nature than the Local Land Charges Registers.

Section 10 establishes the Register of Land Charges consisting of five classes to which has been added a sixth, Class F. They are described below and apart from the bankruptcy entries, relate to unregistered land.
Class C
(i)   Any legal mortgage *not* protected by the deposit of documents (a *puisne mortgage*).
(*Note*: usually this means a second or subsequent mortgage, the first mortgagee holding the title deeds as his security.)
(ii) Any equitable charge acquired by a tenant for life or statutory owner under any Finance or other Act by reason of the discharge by him of any inheritance tax or other liabilities to which special priority is given by the statute (a 'limited owner's charge').
(iii) Any other equitable charge not secured by a deposit of documents not arising under a trust for sale or a settlement and not included in any other land charge ('a general equitable charge').
(iv) Any contract by an estate owner or by a person at the date of the contract entitled to have a legal estate conveyed to him or her, including a valid option of purchase, a right of pre-emption or any other like right (an 'estate contract').

(*Note*: this is the means whereby the contractual purchaser of an unregistered property can protect his or her priority.)

Class D

   (i)   Any charge acquired by the Commissioners of Inland Revenue for death duties.

   (ii) A covenant or agreement (other than in a lease) restricting the use of land (a *'restrictive covenant'*).

  (iii) An easement, right or privilege affecting land and being merely an equitable interest (an *'equitable easement'*).

Class A (rare)

A rent, annuity or principal sum being a charge (otherwise than by deed) created pursuant to the application of an individual under the provision of certain Acts of Parliament specified in heads (i) to (vi).

Class B (rare)

A charge on land (other than a local land charge) of any of the kinds described in Class A created otherwise than pursuant to the application of any person.

Class E (rare)

Certain annuities created before 1920.

Class F

The right of a spouse (commonly the wife) to occupy the matrimonial home though having no legal estate therein under the Matrimonial Homes Act 1983.

There is also a Register of Pending Actions affecting land or any interest in land kept by the Land Charges Registrar, but a buyer (the term includes a lessee and mortgagee) for value who does not have express notice of such an action will not be bound by it unless it is registered as a land charge.

Who registers? How and where?

In general, the persons or bodies with an interest to protect in unregistered land will effect registration. The Receiver in Bankruptcy applies for registration of a receiving order. The mortgagee registers a puisne mortgage. Buyers are usually the people fearful of their contract being overreached who register an estate contract, but sometimes lessors will register, or require a lessee to register an option for renewal or for the purchase of the reversion contained in the lease, lest they be pursued under their covenant if, in the meantime, the reversion has been sold before an estate contract has been registered.

Complete Form 15 (from your law stationer) and send it with the appropriate fee, to The Registrar, Central Land Charges Registry, Burrington Way, Plymouth. Fees are payable by cheque, postal order or through a Land Registry credit account. Searches can also be made by telephone or fax transmission. The latter applies only to credit account holders. The service is available from 9.30 am to 5 pm from Monday to Friday on fax no 01752 766666. Only the front page of the printed forms should be transmitted. The result will be posted to the applicant in the normal way.

Registration is appropriate only for unregistered land. New registrations are therefore of decreasing importance.

Who searches? How and where?

Every buyer, prospective lessee and mortgagee of *unregistered* land should *search before completion*—no search is necessary in the case of registered land, the Registers of which contain all the protective entries a purchaser needs (except overriding interests—see head 10 of Chapter 5 below). Apply on Form K 15 to the Registrar.

There is one exception to this rule of not searching the unregistered Land Charges Register in the case of registered land: prospective mortgagors who are buying a registered property have, as yet (until they complete their purchase), no title to the registered land; and therefore a bankruptcy or a receiving order made against them would not be disclosed by a title search. Therefore, when acting for a mortgagee such as a building society or bank as well as for the buyer-borrower, *always* make a bankruptcy search against your client on Form K16.

There are two search forms: one for the whole Register (K15) or for bankruptcy only (K16). The fee is currently £1 per name.

If only a bankruptcy search is required in the case of registered land use Form K16. If on the other hand your client is buying an unregistered property, make the full search of the Register, which will include bankruptcy, and you can therefore add your client's name to the list of names searched. Form K15 requires a period of years to be stated. This will be the period during which the estate owners have owned the property. The search cannot pre-date 1925. Form K15 also requires the county to be stipulated. It is not necessary to state the full address of the property being purchased.

On investigation of an unregistered title (Chapter 6) you'll have noted the names of owners, against whom the results of land charge searches are noted, and you'll search against any in respect of whom the seller can't give evidence of prior search.

Action on receipt of replies

Replies to a land charges search give the number of any land charge (eg C iv), which may relate to your land. Replies tend to play safe, and often give names which clearly don't refer to the land you're interested in. Then you can disregard the reply. But often the information will be ambiguous and may refer to the land or individual in respect of which you are searching. Then pass the matter to the seller's conveyancer and send the certificate of search, for verification on the form that the entry does not relate to the property offered to your client.

If a reply clearly refers to the land you are interested in, consider whether you have already had particulars of this on the title you have investigated. If not, obtain an *office copy* of the application that gave rise to the entry, which will supply not only information as to what is the protected interest but also as to who is the individual claiming protection and his or her conveyancer. Apply to the Registry on Form K19 and send the copy, when received, to the seller's conveyancer to give full particulars. If you are still in any doubt, take your client's instructions. The fee for an office copy including any plan is £1.

3 Public index map

Contents of map

The map is kept at Local Land Registries of the area covered by the Registry, which is responsible for its maintenance.

A search will reveal:

(i) whether the freehold or leasehold title is registered;
(ii) if the title is unregistered, whether any caution against first registration or priority notice is registered.

Who registers?

Any person who has an interest in the unregistered property can apply to register a caution against first registration (LR form 13) with a supporting statutory declaration (LR form 14).

Who searches? How and when?

Under the Protocol it is the duty of the buyer to search. A plan may be needed to accompany the application for a certificate of search. Application is made on Form 96 and costs £5.

Action on receipt of reply

Consider whether any unregistered disposition of the property for value has been made since registration of title became compulsory or consider whether property has been registered and you have not been shown the registered title.

Satisfy yourself and dispose of any entry before proceeding to exchange contracts.

4 Registered land—application for official searches

What the Registers contain

The three Registers that make up the entries on the Register—the Property Register, the Proprietorship Register and the Charges Register—contain the whole title of the registered proprietor including entries protective of the rights and interests of third parties by registration of notices, cautions, inhibitions and restrictions. (One exception: sometimes a document, like a complicated estate transfer, is bound up in the certificate.) They are the counterpart in registered land conveyancing of the protection afforded third parties in unregistered conveyancing by the Central Land Charges Register.

Notices show on the Register many matters that in unregistered conveyancing would appear in the Land Charges Register or on the title, such as restrictive covenants, a spouse's interest under the Matrimonial Homes legislation, and a special form of registering a charge over a land certificate (an equitable charge) known as a deposit of land certificate.

Caution against dealings provides that a third party claiming an interest such as the courts would enforce, must be notified of any proposed dealing with the land so that he or she might challenge it.

Restrictions are a warning that there is some restriction on the powers of dealing with a registered property by the registered proprietor; eg by a tenant for life.

Inhibitions are rare except for a bankruptcy inhibition, which serves the same purpose as a land charge in unregistered conveyancing. Entry of a notice or a restriction can (and more commonly does) procure a restraint on the uninhibited exercise of the powers of a registered proprietor.

As well as the warnings and restraints of notices etc, registered land is always subject to the interests known collectively as '*overriding interests*'—see head 10 of Chapter 5 below. Such interests are not apparent from the Registers.

Who registers? When and how?

The person or body having an interest to protect is the one to register as soon as possible after the interest is vested in them.

To register a caution, complete and file an application (LR form 13) with supporting statutory declaration (LR form 14) in accordance with instructions on the forms. Lodge in District Land Registry under Land Registry Cover A4 with the prescribed fee.

To register a notice of a lease (LR form 84); notice of deposit of land or charge certificate (LR form 85S); notice of intended deposit on first registration of title (LR form 85B); notice of intended deposit to accompany a dealing (LR form 85C), lodge under Land Registry Cover A4 or A5. There is no prescribed form of application for any other form of notice, but lodge a letter of application under A4 or A5 cover.

A restriction such as restrictive covenants is commonly contained in a transfer or (before first registration of title) a 'Rule 72 transfer' is noted on the Charges Register on the transaction being registered.

An inhibition as mentioned above, is rarely used. No prescribed form of application. Apply to the Chief Land Registrar or to the court (on counsel's advice). Avoid if possible.

Who searches? How and when?

Every buyer, lessee, mortgagee of registered land should search shortly before completion. The cost is £5.

Any entries will be disclosed by office copy entries supplied by the seller to the buyer. Pre-completion search made by every buyer etc, will reveal any entry made since office copy was issued. Office copies cost £5 without the filed plan and £10 with.

Action on receipt of replies

If any adverse entry, don't complete until, as buyer's or mortgagee's conveyancer, you are satisfied as to the position. In appropriate case take up with the seller's conveyancer for clarification or action, and if necessary advise client and take instructions before completing. Do not forget your 'client' may also be the mortgage lender.

5 The Registers of common land

Who registers?

The Commons Registration Act 1965, established the Registers. No further registrations can be made under the Common Land (Rectification of Registers) Act 1989. There is a procedure by which certain land may be removed from the Registers of Common Land and Town and Village Greens. These are kept by county councils. Certain areas, however, are exempt from registration under the Act, including Epping Forest, the New Forest and the Forest of Dean. For a full list of exempted areas see the Act.

Who searches? How and when?

Under the Protocol, it is the duty of the buyer to search.

Search on Form CR 21; complete it and plan (the plan is a 'must' in all cases) in duplicate, send with fee of £6 to Registrar of Local Land Charges in the London boroughs, or to the county council.

Action on receipt of reply

If the search reveals any adverse entry, advise the client accordingly and ask the seller for further details.

6 The Companies' Registry

Contains the registers of every company, public and private, which comprise their vital statistics and information.

Who registers?

Each company is responsible for its annual return. It's the obligation of the company to register with the Registrar of Companies particulars of all mortgages and charges (including debentures) and the duty of every mortgagee to ensure compliance with that obligation. Registration must take place within 21 days of completion.

Who searches? How and when?

Every buyer, lessee and mortgagee of unregistered land from a company before exchange of contracts. If, in an unregistered title, a company is one of the parties to a title deed, search after exchange, on investigating title; but when buying *direct* from a company, better to search before exchange to confirm that the company has power to sell under its articles etc. Mortgagees of a company should check power to borrow, possible limit on authorised amount of borrowing etc.

All mortgages by companies of registered land must be registered both at the Companies' Registry and the Land Registry. Search can be made by post (see explanatory leaflet published by the Registrar of Companies), by personal attendance or (the preferable and more common method) through your law agent. Larger firms may have direct computer links enabling an instant registered office search.

Action on receipt of reply

The circumstances in which searches are made and the variety of information elicited are too wide for a short answer. Confer with clients on any material information received but not in a way that confuses them. The most crucial thing for you to know is that the company is still trading and is not subject to any winding up proceedings.

7 British Coal

What the records contain

British Coal's records show land where underground or opencast workings are (or are contemplated) except for the anomalous Forest of Dean Coalfield, Gloucestershire and area, where ancient private rights of mining are not recorded by British Coal.

Who registers?

British Coal is responsible for maintaining its records. In the Forest of Dean field local operators register with the Deputy Gaveller and Crown Receiver, Forestry Commission, Crown Offices, Coleford, Gloucestershire.

Who searches? How and when?

Every buyer, lessee and mortgagee of property in or in the vicinity of a coalmining area should search before exchanging contracts. Although British Coal pays compensation for damage resulting from mining subsidence there can be no adequate compensation for the emotional loss of one's home or for some material loss. British Coal can publish notices withdrawing support from specified areas.

Search by letter, or use the form CON 29 M and enclose a clear and exact plan, to the Survey Department, British Coal relevant area office. The relevant address can be supplied by British Coal's London Survey Department (Mining Branch: 0171-235 2020) or a list of area offices and their addresses and phone numbers is given in Bourne's *Handbook of Conveyancing Searches* (Sweet & Maxwell) and Silverman's *Searches and Enquiries* (Butterworths).

Action on receipt of reply

Always inform clients of result of search; if any material entry, confer with them and take their instructions before exchanging contracts.

8 Water Authorities

What information the Authority has

Details of all rivers, streams or brooks.

Who registers?

Water Authorities are responsible for maintaining records.

Who searches? How and when?

Every buyer, lessee and mortgagee of land bounded by, adjacent to or crossed by a river, stream or brook should search before exchange of contracts, to ascertain any rights exercised over the property, liability for repair and maintenance of banks, and liability to flooding.

Apply by letter, with plan, to the regional office—a list of addresses and telephone numbers and a suggested pro forma letter are given in Bourne's *Handbook of Conveyancing Searches* mentioned under British Coal searches above, and a list of authorities in Silverman, *Searches and Enquiries*.

Action on receipt of reply

Advise client in all cases of contents of reply, and if any material information is given, take instructions.

9 The British Waterways Board

What information the Board has

Details of all canals.

Who registers?

The Board and its local offices are responsible for maintaining the records.

Who searches? How and when?

Every buyer, lessee and mortgagee of property bounded by or adjacent to a canal should search before exchange of contracts by letter, with a plan, for information similar to that sought in the case of rivers. A list of addresses and a suggested pro forma letter are given in Bourne's *Handbook of Conveyancing Searches* and in Silverman's *Searches and Enquiries* referred to under British Coal searches, above.

Action on receipt of reply

Advise client in all cases of the contents of the reply, and if any material information is given, take instructions.

10 British Rail/Railtrack

What information the Authority has

All rights and obligations attaching to land adjoining a railway.

Who registers?

The Board.

Who searches? How and when?

Every buyer, lessee and mortgagee of land adjoining a railway should by letter, with a plan, search before exchange of contracts for details of any rights of the Authority over the land or any liability for maintenance of boundaries attaching to it. A list of addresses of rail offices and telephone numbers of British Rail offices and a suggested pro forma letter are given in Bourne's *Handbook of Conveyancing Searches* and Silverman's *Searches and Enquiries* referred to under British Coal searches, above.

Action on receipt of reply

Advise client in all cases of the contents of the reply and if any material information is given, take instructions.

11 Other searches

The following is a list of other searches of more limited application.
(1) *Rent officers.* For particulars of a 'fair rent' registered when a property is subject to a regulated tenancy.
(2) *Rent assessment panels.* For particulars of rents registered in respect of a restricted tenancy.
(3) *The Cheshire Brine Subsidence Compensation Board.* For information as to possible risk of subsidence.
(4) *The English China Clay Company, Cornwall.*
(5) *Chancel repairs and corn rents.* No register to search, and in this ancient and complex field there can be quite substantial financial liability. If your client's property is near an ancient (medieval or earlier) Church of England parish church, advise him or her to

enquire of the vicar. Public Record Office leaflet No 61 provides a useful guide. In any case of possible liability, confer with client. The Law Commission has recommended that these be abolished after a run-out period of ten years (Law Commission Report No 152, published November 1985). The Law Society is firmly of the view that this antique and uncertain liability should be abolished forthwith, without any run-out period. For a reasoned appeal for its recommendation, see letter from the Society to the Permanent Secretary to the Lord Chancellor [1986] *Gazette* 2 July, 2076.

(6) *Cornish Chamber of Mines*. For possible old or new mine workings.

Chapter 5

Registered title

1 Registrable land

With effect from 1 December 1990, the entirety of England and Wales became an area of compulsory registration. This means that on every conveyance on sale of the freehold, previously unregistered property must be presented for first registration to the appropriate District Land Registry. Compulsory first registration also applies to a lease for a term of more than 21 years and to the assignment of a lease which has more than 21 years left to run. All other transactions of freehold and leasehold land which do not fall into the above categories, (eg a deed of gift or leases for less than 21 years) do not require registration upon the conclusion of the dealing.

2 The Land Registries

On 2 July 1990 the Land Registry became an executive agency.

In 1990 the Government also removed the statutory requirement that the Chief Land Registrar, who will be the agency's Chief Executive, must be a barrister or solicitor of at least ten years' standing.

An executive agency is a non-statutory management device aiming to ensure that the executive functions of the government are run efficiently and effectively and within available resources.

The work of the Land Registry is carried out by a number of District Land Registries located throughout the country. These District Land Registries accept responsibility for the registration of dealings and for first registrations of land within their allotted geographical areas.

The areas that are the responsibility of each District Land Registry vary from time to time, although now that compulsory land registration is completed throughout the country, it may not be necessary to seek further variations in the future.

See the current Longman *Directory of Local Authorities* in order to know which Land Registry you should approach for the area that is the subject of your conveyancing transaction.

3 Forms

Every office should keep a portfolio of official forms, obtainable from any law stationer, including all the basic applications for registration, transfers, charge, notice of deposit and intended deposit, applications for search and office copies, etc. If you practise in an area where rentcharges are common you'll also need a few more forms (see your law stationer's catalogue or the Land Registry list of official forms) dealing with these.

4 The format of a certificate

Land and charge certificates are now smaller than their predecessors and are generally bound in a buff or blue cover.

Even though the certificates have taken on a different appearance, their structure remains the same. There are three registers.

The first is the Property Register. This describes the property, usually by reference to an address, and goes on to include any easements or other matters that the property has the benefit of and will also mention any declaration, exception or reservation.

The second register is the Proprietorship Register. Here, the owner for the time being is recorded. If there are two owners, there may also be a restriction recorded with regard to the ability of one of them to dispose of the property. It will depend on the wording of the transfer deed that induces the registration.

The third and final register is the Charges Register. This will record any restrictive covenants that may be set out in full in the body of the certificate or may more commonly be referred to in a transfer deed, which may be sewn into the back of the certificate. Also recorded in the Charges Register are any outstanding mortgages, and these will be listed in order of priority. Again, the appropriate mortgage deed will be sewn into the back of the certificate.

Neither the certificate, nor any of the enclosures sewn into it, may be altered, other than by the Land Registry, and indeed it is an offence to attempt to do so.

Additional details of other entries that may be found in the certificate (eg notices) are set out later in this chapter.

5 Types of title and their effect

Acting for the buyer of a leasehold interest, remember that nowadays one seeks to register with an *absolute* title, instead of the *good leasehold* title that some time ago was much more common and acceptable. To obtain this the lessor's title must be strictly investigated and proved. If the lessor's title is already registered as absolute, this is a simple matter—but remember to have in the contract for sale or your requisitions on title, a special condition that before or immediately after completion the lessor will lodge or cause to be lodged in the Registry the land or charge certificate of his title, and will furnish the buyer with the deposit reference.

If, however, the lessor's title is itself registered only as good leasehold (if, for example, the lessor is granting an underlease out of an older leasehold title) you may not be able to obtain a better title than good leasehold for the underlease; a position that a mortgagee will normally accept if there's no alternative. Now that many good leasehold titles are quite a few years old, however, this might well be the time to apply to the Registry to convert a good leasehold to an absolute title. See also 'First Registration with Absolute Leasehold Title', *Registered Land Practice Notes*, p 1.

Sometimes a freehold title may be registered as 'qualified' or possessory (eg a record of squatters rights only). Whilst this occurrence is rare, it is important to keep a look-out. You may need a defective title indemnity policy.

6 Office copies

Application for office copies of register and title plan are lodged on Form 109 by post or fax pursuant to the Land Registration (Open Register) Rules 1993.

The form should be addressed to the appropriate District Land Registry and should contain the title number and a full description of the property by reference to the necessary elements of its address. Persons making the application should complete their name and address and should indicate what they are applying for. The appropriate fee should either accompany the application form, or will be debited to your firm's credit account where appropriate.

There is no longer any need to have the authority of the registered proprietor to inspect the register or indeed to obtain office copy entries, and fees are now levied pursuant to the Land Registration Fees Order 1994 (with effect from 30 October 1994).

7 Searches

The key to security: a search made by a buyer or mortgagee with priority receives 30 working days' priority against any subsequent application—that's around six weeks' priority. But so many applications for an official search are rejected that the Registries have a printed list of four frequent reasons for rejection, as follows:

(1) no plan on search of part;
(2) plan lodged does not enable the property searched to be identified on the filed plan;
(3) the estate plan referred to has not been approved by the Registry for use with Form 94B;
(4) approval of the estate plan has been withdrawn, therefore any application for a search must be accompanied by a plan.

The Land Registration (Official Searches) Rules 1993 provide for a search against a pending first registration, which gives priority to prospective buyers and chargees, and enables them to ascertain what other applications may be pending. They also provide for searches by telephone and fax.

In the matter of searches the only search necessary before completion is against the title, on the appropriate Form 94A (search relating to whole of land in a title) or 94B (search relating to part). In a search of *part*, the land searched against *must* in general be defined by a plan *unless* the seller has lodged an officially approved plan of his or her development in the Registry: see official form of search (Form 94B). The form is simple and foolproof if you follow its wording and directions carefully. The form should name the registered proprietor in full. As mentioned above, the authority is now commonly given in a special condition in the contract itself. No fee is payable if request for search is made by post. Searches can be made by telephone or by post. Searches by telephone in respect of the whole of the land in a registered title now carry priority. They cost £8 payable upon quoting your firm's key number.

If you've had office copy entries, the date from which to search is that given at the top of each page, when the office copy entries were issued; your search will then reveal any entries that may have been made since that date. If only an ordinary copy (not an office copy) has been delivered to you, then the date to search from is that on which the land certificate was last checked with the entries on the Register, this being the date given in the land certificate which will be supplied by the seller on appropriate requisition—'What is the date on which the land certificate was last compared with the entries on the register?' Or if in doubt, you can search from the last date of any registration disclosed (of registration of the seller or of a mortgage, etc).

It is better to insist that your seller obtains and lets you have office copies, which will almost certainly be an obligation under the contract.

Make your title search four or five days or a week before completion (five days if you think there may be a *pending* registration), to enable you to complete well within the period of priority that your search gives you—but remember that to gain full protection you must not only *complete* the purchase within that period, as with unregistered title, but must also *within the same period* lodge your application to register the transfer or mortgage. Every District Land Registry sends its replies by first-class mail, often by return of post, to all searches received by *first-class post*; therefore it should be your invariable practice to send your requisition by first-class mail, too; otherwise, being delivered by second delivery (and sometimes later than that), it will be dealt with only the following day. Use of the DX system is the most common practice, now.

In response to your application you'll receive, on the top of the form you have sent to the Registry, an official *certificate of search* that will reveal whether any entry or pending entry has been made *since* the date from which you searched. This official search serves two vital purposes for a buyer:

(1) it gives an assurance that no adverse entry has been made since the date searched from; and

(2) it gives the buyer priority for the registration of transfer (or mortgage, when a prospective mortgagee is searching) *provided* the buyer's own transfer or mortgage is lodged in the Registry before 11 am on the thirtieth *working* day from the date of the certificate.

This gives the buyer a period of at least six weeks' priority ('working days' don't include Saturdays, Sundays or public holidays). The priority is available only for a *buyer* defined as a buyer for valuable consideration, or a mortgagee. If the latter makes a search, the priority extends to cover the transfer, too, or the lease where there is a lease instead of a transfer; but note that the converse isn't true, so the mortgagee must *always* search, and shouldn't rely on any search made by the borrower, who *can* properly rely on the search made by his or her mortgagee. So if you act for both, search in the name of the mortgagee; if the mortgagee is separately represented, and you are satisfied that a search has been made, you may think it unnecessary to search too, if you are confident that the mortgagee will lodge the application to register transfer and mortgage promptly.

It may be that there is some delay *after* completion, which makes it impossible for the buyer's conveyancers to lodge their transfer within the period of priority. In that case make a second search before the first has expired.

When delay may result from the need to adjudicate stamp duty on a transfer, the procedure first mentioned should be followed.

The certificate of search conveniently gives both the date at which the search was made, and the date on which the period of priority will expire—and note, again, that to have the protection of that priority you must not only complete your purchase or mortgage, but *also* lodge the application to register the transaction (LR form A4 or A5) within the priority period—hence the virtue of the procedure for effecting registration when there is unavoidable delay mentioned above.

When buying a property on a *registered building estate* or other development in respect of which the layout plan has been lodged and officially approved, make your search on Form 94B, when (unlike other searches against part only of a title) reference to the approved plan avoids the need to enclose a plan with your search.

Remember, if the buyer is borrowing on the security of a mortgage of the registered property, that the *buyer* is not yet the registered proprietor, and accordingly a *land charges search* in bankruptcy on the appropriate land charges form should be made against the buyer on behalf of his or her mortgagee in the unregistered Land Charges Register at Plymouth.

8 Deducing and investigating title

If the title is still unregistered, deducing and investigation of the unregistered title proceeds as subsequently described. When buying property with an *unregistered* title make an index map search. This is maintained by the Registry, based on the Ordnance Survey map, which shows every registered property and all land subject to cautions against first registration. It is open to public inspection; as described above an official certificate may be obtained by application on Form 96 to confirm the land you are buying is not already registered; and to confirm there is no caution or priority notice against first registration registered against it. In urban areas, a plan will seldom be necessary because there the local authorities are obliged to notify the Registry of all changes of streets and house numbers; in country districts the property should be described by reference to a plan.

When lodging the papers with your application for first registration of title on behalf of a buyer remember that the abstract *must* be marked as examined, even though it consists of an epitome of title and photocopies of documents.

When acting for a *buyer* remember to make spare copies of the transfer and any mortgage for use as certified copies on registration, as mentioned above.

Early on in the transaction, check the filed plan with the contract plan, if any. Normally, except on the sale or lease of a part only of a property, the supply of a copy of the filed plan by the seller avoids the need for a contract plan. Then work steadily through all the entries, noting and raising requisitions on any matters that call for this.

The Protocol package now includes 'Completion Information and Registration on Title' in standard format. This format includes question 6 which ask the seller's solicitor to confirm that all outstanding mortgages will be discharged on completion and to list those mortgages which will be discharged. This will include the repayment of any discount under the Housing Act 1985. The question further goes on to provide for an undertaking so to discharge those outstanding mortgages.

The form is clearly labelled 'warning' with regard to the proposed giving of undertakings, both in terms of The Law Society's code of completion by post at question 4 and in terms of the undertaking to discharge the subsisting borrowing at question 6.

The provision of a prescribed form does not mean that additional requisitions are precluded. It is indeed your obligation to your client to raise any questions you find necessary.

A notice of deposit or notice of intended deposit is not dealt with by a discharge of mortgage (normally LR form 53), but by a 'withdrawal' thereof. When the whole of the charge secured by that entry is to be repaid the form of withdrawal endorsed on the back of the lender's official notice of deposit is completed and handed over; when the notice of deposit relates to other property as well as that being sold, and so will continue in respect of that other property after completion, the notice of deposit must of course be retained by the lender. Form 86 or a quite informal letter is then sufficient—such as:

We hereby consent to the property known as   [shown edged red on the accompanying plan] being part of the land comprised in the above title being transferred free from the [Intended] Notice of Deposit registered on the

But some banks (which favour this type of security in appropriate cases) have their own favoured form of withdrawal; acting for a seller you will satisfy yourself on this point and obtain the necessary withdrawal in time to hand over on completion. And there's also an official (though not compulsory) form of application to withdraw notice of deposit of which a supply could be kept in your office—Form 86.

Acting for a buyer in such a case the appropriate requisition is:

Withdrawal of Notice of Deposit (entry no   on the charges register) relating to the property must be handed over on completion.

Acting for a *seller* on the development of an estate, large or small, registered title has great advantages, particularly in respect of plans. When the lay-out of the estate is settled send two prints to the appropriate Land

Registry (no form necessary, only a covering letter). The plan should show plot numbers, but a warning is necessary here: builders have a way of changing boundaries, plot numbers and details of plans without informing their solicitors. Warn them that you *must* be notified of any changes at all, so that in such an event a revised estate plan can be lodged at the Registry in substitution for the previous one. Not a bad idea to remind them of this more than once during the development of an estate; and remember, acting for either seller or buyer, that on the granting of a long lease of a *flat* a plan is essential. Here again, builders sometimes have a way of varying the internal party walls without telling anybody, sometimes plaintively observing (as the troubles that ensue from this fall about their lawyer's ears), 'But the contract said the plan was only for identification'.

When such a plan has been lodged it will only be necessary for a buyer to search against the plot he is buying on the appropriate form for a search of part (Form 94B), indicating thereon the plot or flat number 'as shown on the estate development plan lodged in the Registry on the   '—no plan being then necessary as would be the case if no estate plan had been lodged.

Lastly, when acting for a buyer prepare your land registry cover or application form (which you will require when lodging your application to register the transfer or for first registration of title, as the case may be) at the same time as you make your requisitions and prepare the draft transfer and other documents preferably in the buyer's response described in head 2 of Chapter 3).

9 The transfer deed

In a simple sale of the whole of a seller's property, the title to which is registered, the form of *transfer of whole* will apply; it's so simple that commonly one proceeds straight to an engrossment (Form 19 or 19 JP).

Remember to complete or delete, as appropriate, the certificate of value incorporated in all printed forms. It is not invariable practice amongst conveyancers even to keep a third copy of a simple transfer for themselves (but always keep one if it contains restrictions, or the grant or reservation of rights, etc, or if you will require one for your mortgagee's solicitors); normally one prepares top and carbon, both of which are sent to the seller's conveyancers with a suggestion that the top copy, too, should be retained and used as the engrossment if its terms are approved. In the case of a joint purchase it will save time if, as buyers' conveyancer, you have them execute the engrossment print before you send it to the other side.

A *transfer of part* of land in a registered title is a simple matter, too, but requires a plan to define the land (and see remarks already made as to the need for accuracy) and the document may also, of course, contain mutual rights and obligations such as rights of way, of support, of liability for maintenance of common parts, covenants to observe restrictions etc.

A transfer normally requires signing only by the seller. When should it be signed by the buyer? Like a conveyance, in three cases:

(1) When the purchase is by two or more persons, when they must sign in order to commit themselves to the terms on which they hold. For joint buyers there's an official form of transfer (Form 19(JP)), having attestation clauses for sellers and buyers. The form includes a declaration to be completed according to whether a survivor of the buyers can or cannot give a valid receipt for purchase money.

This provision in joint purchases—can the survivor give a valid receipt on a subsequent sale?—is also included in land registry covers for dealings with whole or part of a registered property. Before Form 19(JP) was introduced this was often—still is, sometimes—relied on to establish the position. But preferable to have it stated under the buyers' own signatures, and by you on taking instructions.

(2) If the transfer contains covenants to be observed by the buyer, he or she must execute the document in order to be bound, and seen to be bound, by its terms.

(3) If the buyer is to give the seller an indemnity against breach of covenants under which the seller might have continuing liability (eg the original lessee under a lease or a seller who has previously given a personal covenant not limited to his or her period of ownership), then again, to bind the buyer to the covenant, the buyer must execute the document. But avoid unnecessary covenants of indemnity; they should be given only if someone is truly under a continuing liability. Acting for a buyer, look closely—don't accept a seller's facile inclusion of such a covenant, perhaps taken from an unsuitable precedent. Clarify the point *before* exchange of contracts and avoid your clients becoming liable even after they've parted with the property on a subsequent sale.

When, acting for a buyer, you come to draft the document that will vest the unregistered property in your client, this can be either a conveyance or a form of transfer adapted to the particular property and title. Do not use an old style 'Rule 72' transfer because of the new covenants for title introduced by the Law of Property (Miscellaneous Provisions)

Act 1994 (see head 4 of Chapter 3). Until new forms are available use an old style conveyance.

If a 'Rule 72' transfer of unregistered land is used, the Registry requires only the original document to be lodged (except when fresh restrictive covenants are imposed) without a copy; but it's still the preferred method to lodge with the original transfer a certified copy, when the copy will be returned with the new land certificate.

If you act for a mortgagee on such a purchase of unregistered land, you will again need a certified copy of the mortgage document; so be wise in time and have a spare carbon or print (if you are using a building society or other printed form) prepared when engrossing.

Remember that whenever either a conveyance, lease or transfer defines the land by reference to a plan attached to the document, the plan *must* be signed (sealed and attested by director and secretary in the case of a company) by all parties—except that the conveyancer for *buyers* can sign on their behalf if they state the capacity in which they sign it: 'Solicitor for the transferee.' When, as conveyancer for a buyer, you send the engrossment of the conveyance, lease or transfer to the other side for execution, it is wise to remind them to have the plan signed (or sealed, as the case may be) by the seller—and even then it's remarkable how often the requirement can be overlooked. But it is vital, because, as mentioned above, a seller's conveyancer (unlike a buyer's) can't sign on behalf of his or her client; and if on completion, checking the execution of a transfer on behalf of the buyer, you find this requirement has not been observed, you should refuse to complete until it has.

10 Overriding interests

Overriding interests are the Achilles' heel of registered land conveyancing, whose 'principal object . . . is to confer certainty' (Ruoff & Roper, *The Law and Practice of Registered Conveyancing*, (4th ed) Sweet & Maxwell, p 43). But not all the skills and ingenuity of law draftsmen could wholly circumvent the deviousness of ancient land law. By the Land Registration Act 1925, s 70(1):

All registered land shall . . . be deemed to be subject to such of the following overriding interests as may be for the time being subsisting in reference thereto.

There follows a list of these interests, some of which are not of frequent significance for the conveyancer, or will be covered by the searches discussed in Chapter 4. The complete list is printed inside the cover of every certificate, and the following are samples only: rights of common, customary rights, public rights, right of sheepwalk, rights of way, rights of water, liability to repair highways by reason of tenure, liability to repair the chancel of any church, liability to repair embankments and sea or river walls, rights under local land charges, rights of fishing and sporting, manorial and seignorial rights of all descriptions (until extinguished), leases for any term not exceeding 21 years granted at a rent without taking a fine, etc (s 70(1)(a)–(k)).

But it is s 70(1)(g) that is the nightmare of conveyancers:

The rights of every person in actual occupation of the land or in receipt of the rents and profits thereof save where enquiry is made of such person and the rights are not disclosed.

So how do buyers ensure that they will not, as they walk into their new home, be saddled with an unwanted bedfellow (to mix a couple of metaphors)? There's no other register they can search as in the case, for example, of local land charges. Little consolation for the frustrated buyer that the seller has contracted to give vacant possession of the whole property: a successful claim to damages might not be your client's idea of a happy home. So enquiry and inspection of a property must always be made.

There's really no absolute guarantee of security. The preliminary enquiry of a seller as to what other persons occupy the property is one precaution. It is wise, when the seller has a spouse, to have him or (more commonly) her execute the contract and this even where the other spouse is absent from the property. And land charge Class F (unregistered title) or a notice (registered title) give notice of a prior claim under the Matrimonial Homes Act. With all this, and with conveyancers, if not always their clients, being professionally responsible, the chance of disaster is really extremely rare.

11 Notices, cautions, restrictions

Notices may be entered on the Register of Title to protect 'minor' interests—for example, an estate contract, a grant of easements over registered land, a lease or agreement for a lease which is not an overriding interest, and many other matters that it is desired shall come to the notice of all persons dealing with the land.

The application to register is on Form A4 and must be accompanied by the document creating the interest and a certified copy or examined abstract thereof. The land certificate should also be produced; if there is a registered charge the charge certificate is needed if the chargee is to be bound. The consent of any cautioner must be lodged and the prescribed fee paid.

Bankruptcy of a registered proprietor, and the interests of creditors, are protected by a *bankruptcy inhibition* and a *creditors' notice* respectively. The liquidator of a company can have notice of his appointment entered on the Register.

The registration of a notice is a friendly proceeding carried out, in general, with the co-operation of the registered proprietor. When that person is unwilling to be a party to the application, however, there is a hostile procedure available by the *caution against dealings*. This is made on LR form 63, signed by the cautioner or his or her solicitor and accompanied by a statutory declaration (printed on the same form). The interest protected must be such as *the court would enforce against the land or charge*, and the cautioner must be a person interested in any land or charge registered in the name of another person.

Examples of interests that can be so protected are the following:

(1) Beneficial owner in fee simple.
(2) Person beneficially entitled to the lease referred to.
(3) Tenant for life within the meaning of the Settled Land Act 1925.
(4) Purchaser under a contract for sale.
(5) Plaintiff in an action in the Chancery Division of the High Court of Justice.
(6) Equitable mortgagee under a memorandum of charge.

A further example is the registration of either a notice or a caution to give priority to a charge and bridge the gap between its creation and registration.

The effect of registering a caution against dealings is that no dealing will be registered without the cautioner's consent until the expiration of a 'warning off' notice (14 working days) served on the cautioner by the Chief Land Registrar. Within the period of the notice the cautioner must withdraw or justify the claim.

Last amongst these devices for the protection of interests in registered land, is the *restriction* on the powers of registered proprietors to deal with their land; for example, that partnership property shall not be disposed of after the death of one of the partners without the consent of his or her personal representatives; or that no disposition is to be registered without the consent of the proprietor of a registered charge (this last one a not uncommon precaution of building societies).

Application to register a restriction must be made on LR form 75 signed by the applicant or the applicant's solicitor; the land or charge certificate must (in all but exceptional circumstances) accompany the application.

As to interests *not* requiring protection by noting on the Register ('overriding interests'), see head 10 above.

12 Minor interests

Protection is afforded by registration of a notice (see above); minor interests are in fact mainly what would be described as *equitable interests* in unregistered conveyancing. They include in the case of land held by trustees for sale, all interests and powers capable of being overridden by the trustees for sale; in the case of settled land, all interests and powers capable of being overridden by the tenant for life or the statutory owner. They also include the rights of beneficiaries when any fiduciary owner is the registered proprietor; the rights and interest of a buyer who has asked for registration of title in the name of a nominee; and the right of a buyer whose contract has not been registered on the seller's title.

So acting for a buyer, if no protective entries appear on the Register you need have no qualms; if they do, you will of course question them by requisition or otherwise.

Acting for the owner of a minor interest, if protection is required this will be by registration of a notice, caution, restriction or (rarely) inhibition. One of the commonest and most important is a contract for the buyer of a property, protected by a notice (the equivalent, in unregistered conveyancing, of the registration on the Central Land Charges Register of an estate contract). It's not common practice to register notice of a contract, but when there's an unusually long deferred completion date, or when your buyer-client suspects the good faith of the seller, or if there is a contract by correspondence, or for any other special reason peculiar to the particular transaction, a notice should be seriously considered and the client consulted and advised.

13 Positive covenants

Positive covenants don't run with the land; therefore they are not registrable. Original covenantors (the first buyers) who continue liable under their covenants should therefore be protected by a covenant of indemnity against breach from subsequent buyers. But it's easy for a seller's conveyancer to overlook positive covenants.

If such covenants are mixed with negative covenants, which appear on the Register, or if they are contained in a document that is bound up in the certificate, they will be apparent, and a conveyancer acting for an original covenantor who is selling should peruse these covenants, providing in the contract for a covenant of indemnity against breach of any positive covenants by the buyer (see below). Acting for a buyer, see warning above as to liability after a re-sale.

Another case where a covenant of indemnity by a third or subsequent buyer is appropriate arises when the first buyer (A) has entered into positive covenants, and as the original covenantor will continue liable after selling; A therefore takes a covenant of indemnity from A's buyer (B), *not* limited to A's period of ownership; B therefore takes from B's buyer (C) a covenant against liability under B's covenant with A. Very complicated, but logical.

If a seller's unregistered title on a purchase is subsequently registered, the seller's conveyancer, on a sale, should peruse the original conveyance to the seller (returned with the land or charge certificate) for positive covenants.

In the case of positive covenants *contained in transfers* of registered property, it's the practice of the Registry to bind up in the land or charge certificate a copy of the transfer containing such covenants, because the transfer containing them is retained in the Registry, and so the registered proprietor's conveyancer could otherwise easily overlook them.

Specimen covenant:

The Transferee hereby covenants with the Transferor by way of indemnity only that [so long as he the Transferee is the registered proprietor of the property hereby transferred] he will observe and perform the [positive] covenants contained or referred to in Entry No 1 of the charges register of the said Title.

14 Fees and arrangements for their payment

Fees change from time to time: an account of fees at the time of going to press might be misleading. Keep the latest Land Registration Fee Order in the office. If in doubt as to a fee, telephone Land Registry Enquiries.

Notwithstanding this the fee scales were significantly simplified by the three scales introduced by the 1994 Fee Order: Scale 1 applies to first registrations and dealings for value. Scale 2 applies, *inter alia*, to voluntary transfers. Scale 3 applies to mortgages.

Credit account facilities offered to solicitors for the payment of Land Registry fees are a convenience in more than one way. A credit account avoids errors and saves time.

Apply for facilities to the Accounts Section, HM Land Registry, Burrington Way, Plymouth, PL5 3LP.

15 Avoiding errors

Treat the application forms, whether for a dealing or application for first registration, with the care they demand: in the end you'll thereby save yourself and Land Registry officials much time and trouble.

Year after year the annual report of the Chief Land Registrar refers to errors by solicitors in their applications, a source of delay, expense and frustration for all concerned.

The most common error by solicitors concerns the incorrect calculation of fees, and the following also appear frequently:

(1) Failure to lodge form 53.
(2) Failure to sign application forms.
(3) Form L(A) 451 not enclosed when required.
(4) Leaving uncompleted spaces in building society and other mortgages.
(5) Failure to include, on application for first registration, a land charges search against the seller or a certified copy of the transfer.
(6) Failure to lodge a probate or letters of administration, or to mark the abstract thereof as examined.

This conclusion of a conveyancing transaction demands careful and unhurried attention, free from distraction, if the matter is to be satisfactorily disposed of without unhappy aftermath.

16 Merger of freehold and leasehold titles

Merger can be applied for when the freehold and leasehold estates become vested in the same person, whether or not both titles are registered. Application can also be made when the freehold title is registered but not the leasehold, when the leasehold is registered but not the freehold, and when the leasehold is either registered or unregistered and application is being made for first registration of the freehold title. A fee is payable for each title closed unless an *ad valorem* fee is payable on a linked transaction (such as the purchase of the freehold or leasehold title) when no fee is payable.

When you act for buyers who intend that a leasehold interest shall merge in the freehold (leaseholders buying the freehold reversion on their lease, or freeholders buying the lease to which their title is subject) it is convenient to express the *intention to merge* in the transfer or other instrument vesting the second estate in the owner of the first if this is intended, but beware of such an application in the case of a flat—if, for example, your client owns a leasehold flat and buys the freehold of the whole building in which it is situate. In such a case, don't merge: a merger would create a 'flying freehold', which is anathema to a mortgagee and would prejudice your client and probably any future sale when no building society, bank or other mortgagee is likely to advance on such security.

17 Estate conveyances

Registration of title has great advantages in simplifying conveyancing when an estate is to be developed by the sale or lease of individual plots or flats. It is desirable to lodge at the District Registry an *approved estate plan* (two copies); searches by individual buyers can then be made by reference to the plot number alone.

18 Devolution on death

Since registration is compulsory only on a *purchase for value* it isn't necessary to register the devolution of unregistered property on a death. If the title is registered it still isn't essential to register the devolution, because personal representatives can deal with a registered title without themselves being first registered as proprietors; but if the property is not to be disposed of forthwith, either on sale or by a vesting assent, it's desirable to register the devolution to the personal representatives as soon as practicable. When personal representatives sell *without* first effecting registration of their title, proof thereof and of the death of the registered proprietor must of course be lodged: a copy of the grant of probate or letters of administration *certified as a true copy* by the seller's conveyancers (when acting for a buyer you should make this requirement the subject of one of your requisitions on title) is sufficient evidence. Death of one or more joint owners or of a sole proprietor is proved by lodging a certificate of death, or a copy of such a certificate certified as a true copy by the seller's conveyancer, with the appropriate application.

19 Expediting registration

By paying a fee of £40 it is possible to expedite a registration; in such a case, if a survey isn't required and no Land Registry requisitions are necessary, registration normally takes place within 14 to 21 days.

Expedition is useful in the case of property being resold very shortly after the unregistered title has been purchased, when it is desired to give the new purchaser a registered title and completion is to take place before the title would normally be registered. Include the item 'Expedition fee—£40' in the fees panel; and it may facilitate the matter, as well as showing courtesy towards the Land Registrar and his staff, if a covering letter with the application cover tells briefly why expedition is required. Don't forget to charge the fee in your bill of costs!

The procedure is often of great value, but it is suggested that for two reasons it should be used *only* in urgent cases—both out of consideration for Land Registry staff, and to avoid the possibility of their being swamped by too many such applications, resulting in delay, which would defeat the whole purpose of the operation. Over-use is counter-productive and prejudices the whole profession.

20 Old title deeds

Some of these should often be preserved; use intelligent discretion, remembering that they belong to the client. Registration of title is no guarantee of boundaries, showing general boundaries only, although the clarity and accuracy of the filed plan (based as it is on the Ordnance Survey) is commonly superior to most of the plans you'll find on the unregistered title. Old deeds can be very useful for such a purpose, and certainly any containing plans should in general be retained. Further, the plans may indicate the ownership of fences and so may help in solving problems in that connection. It is also important to preserve original documents imposing restrictive covenants, granting or reserving easements etc, since the terms of these are often not set out fully on the Register, and reference to them, and to the exact terms of a covenant, may be necessary at a later date.

You may not need to keep very old deeds, engrossed in manuscript on real parchment, often with impressive seals: but your client will often much appreciate them, so remember to send him any such documents. The county archivist may be interested in them, too, subject to the client's rights.

But don't retain unnecessary papers such as old local searches—the only one worth having is your own recent search; or, without consideration of their contents, old drafts.

The Law Society's non-contentious business committee has given guidance on this subject, referring to its careful consideration in *Cordery on Solicitors* (8th ed, Butterworths 1988 p 99). The effect of the committee's pronouncement is that documents prepared for the client and paid for by him (drafts, deeds and documents etc) belong to the client. So do documents prepared by a third party and sent to the solicitor in the course of his retainer.

Documents prepared by the solicitor for his or her own benefit or protection belong to that solicitor; so do documents sent by the client, which are intended to pass to him or her.

Lastly, under the Value Added Tax Act 1983, Sched 7, para 7(2), as amended, records and papers relevant to VAT liability must be kept for six years.

Chapter 6

Investigating the legal title

1 The 'traditional' system

Under the traditional system of conveyancing, it was common not to deal with matters that were germane to the legal title until after contracts had been exchanged. This particularly related to unregistered land.

In the above circumstances, there would simply be a special condition attaching to the draft contract, which would recite the deed that was to be the root of title, and the matter would be left at that until after contracts were exchanged. When contracts were exchanged, the conditions of sale would stipulate the time for the delivery of an abstract and thereafter the time for the raising of requisitions upon it.

Even before the introduction of The Law Society's Protocol, it was becoming common practice for evidence of title to be supplied before contracts were exchanged. Indeed, it was usual practice where the land was already registered, and buyers' conveyancers would call for proof of title at the outset of a new conveyancing transaction.

Whether title is dealt with before or after exchange of contracts, the procedure for investigating title is exactly the same.

If land is already registered, and the seller's conveyancers have supplied office copy entries on the Register, the details of the title can be rapidly assimilated by the experienced conveyancer, and if there are any errors or omissions, these can be quickly spotted. This may not be so where the title is unregistered. Sometimes, the legal title can be lengthy, and where land has remained in one family for many years, as is often the case with agricultural land, the chain of title can be complex.

When dealing with unregistered agricultural land, it will take time to examine the title carefully. This time must be set aside before proceeding to raise requisitions. The need to deal with complicated unregistered titles will slowly disappear, but at the time of writing, it is very important to be able to read through an unregistered title and spot any errors that should form the subject-matter of requisitions on title.

2 The TransAction system

Under the new system, delivery of the evidence of title is always necessary as part of the original package supplied by the seller's conveyancer at the commencement of the transaction. The preparation of the title is one of those tasks that can be undertaken in advance of a transaction being negotiated, and should form part of the early work of a seller's conveyancer.

If there is a defect in the title, it is as well that it be dealt with and agreed from early on in the transaction, and if the defect cannot be put right, it may be necessary to make arrangements for a defective title indemnity policy. Again, this would now be dealt with before contracts are exchanged.

One of the main practical impacts of the TransAction system is that almost all the conveyancing is now dealt with before exchange of contracts, and this means that the tasks that have to be undertaken in between exchange and completion are relatively minor, thereby reducing the average time between exchange and completion to two weeks or even less. The precise timing will depend on the convenience of one's clients and the need to obtain a mortgage advance cheque. Institutions vary in the speed with which they are able to dispatch the necessary money.

3 An abstract of title

Now that the entirety of England and Wales forms an area of compulsory registration, the preparation of an abstract of title is becoming less and less common.

To deduce title to unregistered land, you need to locate a good root of title that is at least 15 years old. If you cannot find such a deed, you have to keep going back in time until one is located. A good root would preferably comprise a conveyance on sale, or if not, a legal mortgage. Wills, leases and assents are among those documents that do not form a good root of title. Sometimes, a conveyancer may be asked to accept a vesting assent as a root of title, but this is not very satisfactory.

Having located a good root of title, you then need to form a chain of title from the date of that document right up to the present time. Having selected the deeds and documents from the deeds packet, you then need to photocopy them, and pin them together with a front sheet, which is entitled 'Epitome of Title'. An epitome of title is basically a list of the copy documents behind it, and the columns on the epitome should be appropriately completed, with each document being numbered consecutively.

Prior to photocopiers, the preparation of an epitome of title in the way described above was not possible, and this meant that abstracts of title had to be created by our predecessors, who were in fact charged with the duty of tracing back title over 30 or 40 years or more. The creation of an abstract of title is an art-form in itself, and one that has now largely died out. What happened was that each of the documents comprising the abstract were listed on large abstract sheets, and a special form of short-hand was devised in order to prevent the need for each of the deeds and documents to be set out in full.

As an aside, readers should note that if these abstracts or epitomes are marked by the seller's conveyancer as being true copies of the originals, and that marking is then signed and dated, the abstract or epitome will form an original title, and this is common practice when dealing with a sale of part. In the case of selling part, the seller does, of course, retain the original deeds packet.

In creating the epitome of title, it is important to include land charge searches, as well as the old conveyances and mortgage deeds, and, where appropriate, it would also be necessary to include: marriage certificates to deal with apparent changes of name; death certificates to deal with the death of one of two joint tenants; a grant of probate to deal with the death of the owner and the appointment of executors; and any other document that is necessary to prove a coherent line from the root deed. Clearly, it is not conveyancing practice to include local searches and planning permissions within an abstract of title.

4 Office copy entries

It is important to apply for these when acting for a seller, as soon as you know your client's title number. The fee will be £5 (£10 if filed plan included) and the application should be made to the appropriate District Land Registry for the area in which the property is situated. It is best to obtain a complete set of office copies, to include any transfer deed that may be filed at the Land Registry and a copy of the filed plan.

The office copy entries replace entirely the deeds and documents of title described above. However, the old deeds and documents of title may be helpful in resolving any detailed matters that do not appear as part of the land registration process.

5 Investigation of title

In a busy office, time is the main difficulty in perusing a possibly lengthy abstract, although the length of most has been greatly reduced since the statutory minimum length of title was reduced to 15 years. The chief dangers are that some flaw in the title will be overlooked, or that requisitions on title will not be delivered within the stipulated time (now six working days after delivery of abstract), so that a seller's conveyancer might plead this breach of the conditions of sale as an excuse for not clearing up a genuine difficulty.

In examining an unregistered title it's a help to make 'Notes on Title', which are really an abstract of the abstract. The virtues of this procedure, which doesn't lengthen but in fact shortens your investigation, are as follows:

(a) The actual investigation is simplified, as you don't have to keep turning back an unwieldy abstract to see which documents contained restrictions, whether the seller named in one conveyance was the buyer named in the previous deed, etc. The method is of special advantage in cases when a seller delivers an epitome of title accompanied by photographic copies of the title documents, some perhaps complicated and lengthy; in such a case it may be expedient to make your own 'notes on title' on the epitome itself to save duplication of documents.

(b) It prevents the overlooking of such standard matters of enquiry as the existence of undischarged mortgages, covenants for production covering all the title deeds which will not be handed over, the proper stamping of documents etc.

(c) It makes the dictation of requisitions on title hours or days after your examination a simple matter (although preferably this should be done at once — one bite at the cherry), and obviates the chance of missing any points you observed on investigation. The common practice of putting pencil notes on the abstract itself is to be deprecated as defacing an important document, and it is also easy to miss these notes on an old and tattered abstract that has already been marked by previous investigators.

(d) You'll have on your file a permanent record of the title and all its principal features in a much more manageable form than that of an abstract; your notes will remain with your papers for future reference; and from them at a later date you should be able, if necessary, to answer any questions or difficulties that may arise.

(e) This record also saves time when you come to deal with the replies to your requisitions, and to decide whether or not they're satisfactory. It's a frustrating exercise to wander backwards and forwards through a full-sized abstract, its plans and pages held together by a thread or a rusty pin, pursuing some trivial and tedious point. Your notes on title will save you some, at least, of this sort of irritation.

(f) If, perhaps years later, your client sells the property now being bought, you'll still find your notes on title helpful in deciding on the root of title, in preparing the draft contract, and in dealing with your buyer's requisitions on title. To this end it's sometimes useful, when an abstract is unduly long, to mark on your notes on title the document that might become a future root.

(g) The notes are also useful for the preparation of any report on title that may be required for your client's bank, building society or other mortgagee, the form of which sometimes requires you to state the last purchase price etc.

(h) Your notes on title will help you deal with any possible requisitions by the Land Registry and will also indicate at a glance deeds containing restrictive covenants, easements or plans, which should be retained after registration as giving fuller information and exact wording on matters of possible dispute.

In preparing notes on title, points to observe are as follows:

(1) Year, date and stamp duty go in the left-hand margin.

(2) Give a simple description of the document: eg conveyance instead of indenture for old deeds etc.

(3) Give the names of the parties in the first abstracted deed, but where these recur (as, for example, where a buyer becomes a seller, or where personal representatives become sellers) give *initials* only, so that after the first deed the seller, etc, of an abstracted document will commonly be shown by initials and so indicate that there is an unbroken chain of title.

(4) Make a note of the purchase price, and then, if it is correct, tick the stamp duty to show you have checked this. If there is any discrepancy between the two, mark it (see (6) below) for a requisition.

(5) Make a note of any major point in the parcels: eg the name of a house, or that the land is coloured pink on a plan. By doing this you simplify your final consideration of whether or not the identity of the property with that described in the abstracted documents is satisfactory.

(6) Mark *any* point that at the time of perusing the abstracted deed does not appear clear to you by scoring the margin heavily against your note, or in any other manner that will catch your attention. If, later in the abstract, you find that the point is cleared up, you can then put a tick through your marking with or without a note of how it's disposed of. For example, if a deed includes restrictive covenants, enter 'restrictions' on your notes, but then check with the contract whether or not these are disclosed, and if they are, tick it and mark 'disclosed by contract'. You may find an

apparent discrepancy in the parcels, and mark this in the same way, although later deeds may clear it up. If they don't, your own conveyance may do so. In general, your attitude whilst investigating a title should be thoroughly suspicious.

(7) Whenever you come across a mortgage or a charge put 'M' prominently in the margin; tick this as you come to any subsequent statutory receipt or other discharge.

(8) When an abstracted deed includes a covenant for production of documents, put a 'P' in your margin against *each* of the abstracted documents included in the covenant and the date of the deed containing the covenant. When, at the end of your investigation, you run through your notes to see that there are covenants for the production of all documents not likely to be handed over, you can pick out at once those already covered by some existing covenant for production. Remember that if on completion you obtain either a document or a covenant for the production of a document, which itself contains a covenant for the production and an undertaking for the safe custody of *earlier* documents, the benefit of that covenant and undertaking will enure for the benefit of your client, the buyer.

This procedure is also a help when you come to check the reply to your standard requisition: 'Which of the abstracted documents will be handed over on completion?' Remember that when a probate or letters of administration constitute one of the title documents it's unlikely in any event to be handed over, so look for a covenant for its production and if one isn't abstracted, make a requisition on the point, although you should note covenants for production are not necessary in deeds giving rise to first registration. Look, too, for a memorandum of a subsequent conveyance etc, endorsed on a probate or letters of administration; if there's none, but there ought to be one, make a requisition on the point, such as:

The abstract does not reveal a memorandum of the conveyance of   endorsed on the probate dated   . Please confirm the position, and if not endorsed that a suitable memorandum will be endorsed on or before completion.

If it transpires from the answer to this requisition that such a memorandum should and will be endorsed, make a note there and then on your completion agenda to obtain a copy of it. And when your client is buying from executors or administrators, remember, as you make your notes on title, to include a reminder to make a requisition asking for a memorandum of the conveyance to your client to be endorsed on the probate or letters of administration on completion, and to be furnished with a copy.

(9) If there are two or more abstracts, mark where each supplemental abstract commences. It will save time in finding the abstract of a particular deed should you later need to refer to this.

(10) Entries in the Land Charges Register (not local land charges) being matters of title (although certificates of search are not 'documents of title') that should be abstracted, note these, too, on your notes; when considering these comprehensively (see (11) below), note for requisitions (see (6) above) any which may be missing: if necessary make a search yourself before completion when searching against your seller. You may find it convenient, as enabling you to decide quickly when the time comes to make your searches shortly before completion, to write 'LC' against the name of every party to a document against whom a prior land charges search has been made, using your own search to supply any missing searches.

(11) When you've finished your investigation and your notes on title are complete, it's useful at the foot of your notes to make a table of the major matters you must commonly consider, and mark them as satisfactory or otherwise. The virtue of this procedure is that you will then consider and decide finally whether you should make any requisitions upon, for example, the absence of a covenant for production of one of the title documents, an outstanding mortgage that should be discharged, restrictions that were not disclosed by the contract, etc. The headings that I tabulate in this way (but you may like to include others) are as follows: *identity*; *outstanding mortgages*; *restrictive covenants*; *covenants for production*; *land charge searches*; *registrations with freeholders* (for sales of leaseholds); *endorse memorandum* (when there's been a probate or letters of administration, or a sale of a part only of the land comprised in a prior conveyance); and *stamping of documents*. A rubber stamp of these headings, which you can impress on the last sheet of your notes on title and each of which you then tick or mark appropriately, saves undue strain on your memory.

6 Completion information and requisitions on title

As soon as you've concluded your investigation of title, and whilst, with the help of your notes on title, it's still fresh in your mind, prepare your requisitions on title (with, of course, an additional print or carbon copy for the use of the seller's conveyancer). For the standard enquiries use the Protocol form of requisitions. Add your own special requisitions arising on the particular title. The Protocol form of requisitions starts with the property information question. The usual reply to this requisition is:

> Confirmed, except as they may have been varied or added to by subsequent correspondence between us.

7 Replies to requisitions

When, as a buyer's conveyancer, you receive the seller's replies to your requisitions, you should go through these carefully, as in the case of your property information forms and local search, ticking each one the reply to which is satisfactory. Where any action needs to be taken, make a note in the margin; eg when the replies contain information that should be passed on to your client, put a marginal note 'Buyer'; when the reply indicates that there is an error in the abstract supplied to you, mark it 'Abstract'; and tick these marginal notes as you take the necessary action, for example, when you write to the buyer, or amend your abstract. Any matters referred to in the replies, which will need to be taken into account on completion — eg details of the title deeds that will be handed over, a requirement that an outstanding mortgage should be discharged on or before completion, an undertaking of some sort given in replies — should be marked 'Completion' so that when you come to prepare your completion agenda, these matters can at once be picked out, and no further lengthy perusal of the replies will be needed. Better ('one bite at the cherry') complete and mark your completion and post-completion agendas *now*.

When you receive the buyer's requisitions on title, try to be more helpful than 'cagey' in your answers and don't fall into the easy habit of giving stereotyped and evasive replies if you could be more helpful. Don't get 'tough' with a buyer and refuse to answer reasonable enquiries; you are only likely to make the buyer get 'tough' with you, and your unreasonable reticence will delay the matter unnecessarily. On the contrary, when requisitions raise a difficulty that you can't answer easily, it is your job to take immediate steps to find the answer or to rectify the position, if possible.

With the object of saving both delay and waste of time spent on unnecessary letters, in cases where buyers send the draft transfer with their requisitions (the buyer's package) this should be approved and returned with your replies. In going through this document, look at it from the viewpoint of the buyer as well as your own client, and if the buyer's conveyancer has made any slip or omission, put it right; you may yourself one day be grateful for a similar courtesy.

8 Preparation of transfer

Almost every transaction can now be completed by the use of a transfer deed, and this means that the use and the art of preparing a conveyance deed will slowly become obsolete over the next few years. (See head 9 of Chapter 5 above.)

The most simple and straightforward situation is where land is already registered, and in nine times out of ten, a simple pro forma transfer deed can be used to effect the transfer of the interest, whether it be freehold or leasehold. The standard form of transfer simply requires the conveyancer to insert the county and district, the title number, the address of the property, the date, the consideration, the parties to the transaction and any special provisions that might be appropriate should new restrictive covenants be proposed, or should the purchase be a joint purchase.

It is no longer necessary for a deed to be sealed. Quite simply, the parties to a deed should sign it in the presence of a witness, who must be present at the time it is signed, and who must then put his own name, address and occupation.

If the land is unregistered, then it is now common practice to use what is called a 'Rule 72 transfer'.

Clearly, you will not be able to insert a title number but the county and district address of the property, the date, the consideration, the parties and any special provisions as mentioned above can be included in exactly the same way as if the land were already registered. Again, a Rule 72 transfer is equally applicable as between a leasehold or freehold property.

If the transaction is complicated—eg it involves the sale of part of a farm—and there are lots of easements, declarations, covenants, stipulations etc, then it may still be more appropriate to use a conveyance, notwithstanding the fact of first registration. In such a case, a draft conveyance would probably need to be tailor-made, and any precedents held on your firm's word processor may not very precisely fit the particular situation.

In view of the fact that the need to prepare a conveyance is reducing all the time, we will not go into this in detail in this text.

There are just two additional points that should be made. The first is that when a property is subject to restrictive covenants, it is bad practice to burden the title with a fresh covenant to observe them, unless it is really necessary to protect a seller, who will remain personally responsible for their observance. It should not be necessary to take a new and separate covenant. Contest the position relating to positive covenants.

The second point concerns the acquisition of a lease. The seller may seek to make the buyer liable to indemnify him or her in perpetuity, thereby placing the buyer in the same invidious position as the original lessee, who remains liable for the whole of the term of the lease to whomever it may have passed. Therefore, it is appropriate to insert such safeguarding words as:

So long as the buyer shall remain in possession of the lease and shall not have assigned the same.

The issue of 'privity of contract' within a lease whereby the first lessee remains liable throughout the term is the subject of much debate. Legislation to change this may arise.

In the case of a simple transfer, the document is still produced in duplicate and submitted to the seller's conveyancer for approval. However, it has become common practice to say that if the terms of the draft are approved, then the top copy should be retained and used as an engrossment for the purposes of signature. Since the Law of Property (Miscellaneous Provisions) Act 1989 and the introduction of compulsory first land registration throughout the country, there is not so much emphasis placed upon smart engrossments. After all, the purpose of thick engrossment paper was to make it last. Nowadays, most transfer deeds are not required for very long, because the information contained on them is simply transferred onto the Register at HM Land Registry, and the deed then becomes superfluous to requirements. It is acknowledged that this does not apply to the transfer of a new home on a building estate, but then a copy of that document is simply incorporated into the land or charge certificate.

The buyers should sign the transfer deed before the sellers, but if this is not achieved because of shortage of time, it is again becoming increasingly common practice for the buyers to sign after completion. It has to be acknowledged that there is some potential risk attaching to this, particularly where the buyers are covenanting with the sellers, but such risk appears to be part of the price that conveyancers are prepared to pay for working within the commercial pressures in the modern conveyancing market.

If you are acting for a mortgagee as well as for a buyer or borrower, then you prepare the mortgage deed at the same time as the transfer deed.

In preparing a transfer deed, it is important to check whether the buyers are to hold the property in trust for themselves as joint tenants or as tenants in common. There is an official form of transfer known as Form 19(JP), and this caters for a joint purchase. This means that it is necessary only to strike out in the declaration at the top of the second page to the effect that the survivor can (for joint tenancy) or cannot (tenancy in common) give a valid receipt for capital money. If, by an oversight, a transfer is obtained in the simple form of a transfer of whole (Form 19) or of part, all is not lost—the Land Registry cover under which, after completion, you will lodge the transfer and other papers in the appropriate District Land Registry for registration, contains (top of page 2) a declaration as to the right of the survivor to give a valid receipt, similar to that in Form 19(JP). There has however been some debate whether this is sufficient on its own and therefore additional reference to the nature of the purchaser's joint ownership is very important.

The position is a little more complicated in the case of the parties holding as tenants in common. A very short separate 'Declaration of Trust' is required (because such matters cannot be referred to in the entries on the Register) to the effect that the parties hold the property and the proceeds thereof in trust for themselves as tenants in common in whatever proportions may have been agreed between them. The declaration should be prepared in duplicate, so that both parts can be signed by both parties, so that each may hold one part, or leave them with you to hold. Record this in a letter to them.

As mentioned earlier in the text, it is important to proceed with caution when acting for joint buyers. Make sure they are both instructing you, and in all correspondence and communications, contact them both.

9 Licence to assign a lease

Short-term leases, if they don't contain an absolute bar to assignment, commonly contain a covenant by the lessee not to assign the lease without the lessor's licence, and usually provide that such licence shall not be unreasonably withheld—if such proviso is omitted, then acting for a prospective lessee you should always insert it in the draft.

Long leases, on the other hand, rarely have any such clog on the right to assign, mortgage etc, and in general ought not to; in the event of a draft lease (when acting for the original lessee) you should *always* delete the offending provision should it occur, and always have it in mind when perusing the draft. If the conveyancer for the lessor refuses to delete it, or if you act for a purchaser of an existing lease that includes such a provision, you should *always* explain to your client the nature of the provision, its unusual nature and its disadvantages (putting off a subsequent prospective buyer or mortgagee, delay and expense in taking up references and obtaining the licence). If despite your gloomy forebodings your client nevertheless instructs you to proceed, confirm your advice and his instructions by letter, and advise your client's mortgagees, if you act for them, or if not, advise their solicitors of the provision and don't agree the draft until you know that the term is acceptable to them, too.

There's one case, however, where a buyer can be told at the inception of a matter that the lease will provide that it can't be assigned without the lessor's licence: the Ecclesiastical Commissioners and one or two other bodies insist on such a covenant in all their leases. The client should be advised of this, and at the same time that it is an undesirable feature of a leasehold estate: then it's for the client to decide whether to proceed.

10 Report on title

As soon as you receive replies to requisitions, you should be in a position to prepare a report on title for any mortgagee for whom you act, as is commonly required by any but a private mortgagee; you can't usually do so before, because until you have had satisfactory replies you can't certify that the title is good. In such a case your report should be prepared at once, and the original instructions and any other documents sent to you by your mortgagee client, as well as your notes on title and the replies to requisitions, should be carefully perused.

Building societies and banks all have their own forms of report, but in case you need to prepare your own form base this on the printed forms of such bodies. Or sometimes you can report informally by letter: 'we have investigated the title to the above property, which we find good and marketable.'

Chapter 7

Access to Neighbouring Land Act 1992

You are invited to note the following points about this comparatively recent piece of legislation:
(1) The applicant need not be the owner.
(2) The works necessary must be for the preservation of the whole or part of the dominant land which cannot be carried out or which would be substantially more difficult to carry out without the necessary entry.
(3) The right relates to basic preservation work: it does *not* extend to improvements or development work unless incidental or consequential on preservation works.
(4) The Act does not permit the granting of a permanent easement.
(5) The dominant land (benefiting from the right) can be commercial or residential: if commercial, as well as compensation being awarded to the owner of the servient land (discretionary) the court can order the payment of a premium.
(6) The servient land includes land or buildings but not highways.
(7) Application is made to the county court for an access order: detailed notes specify the information required in the application. The access order is registrable as a writ order affecting unregistered land and as a pending action before the order is made. It is also registrable as a caution or notice. It is *not* an overriding interest.
(8) The benefit of an access order will not pass to successors in title to the dominant land.
(9) The applicant can be required to provide security for financial liability and insurance.

Chapter 8

The National House-Building Council

As a measure of protection to buyers and the owners of dwellings, the Defective Premises Act 1972 was passed; 'an Act to impose duties in connection with the provision of dwellings', including a duty to build dwellings properly, 'in a workmanlike or . . . professional manner, with proper materials and . . . fit for habitation'; a similar duty is imposed on a builder who does work of construction, repair, maintenance or demolition. Liability isn't abated by disposal of the premises.

But this does not cater for builders' disappearance or insolvency. Some years before the Act was passed, to provide buyers and their mortgagees with protection against just such widespread hardship, an organisation now known as the National House-Building Council ('NHBC') was formed.

The NHBC is an independent, non-profit-making body, including amongst its members representatives from the Building Societies Association, the Law Society, building employers' organisations, the Royal Institution of Chartered Surveyors, the Royal Institute of British Architects, building trade unions, and consumer interests. Observers from the Department of Environment attend meetings of the Council and some committees. The main purpose of the NHBC is to protect buyers and their mortgagees from the hardships they might otherwise suffer because of poor quality workmanship by builders, and the losses that might otherwise be suffered because of the vagaries and hazards of litigation should in fact a particular dwelling not meet those standards. To achieve this purpose the NHBC operates a scheme that:

(1) requires developers and builders to become members;
(2) requires members to attain certain standards of quality in building work;
(3) inspects dwellings in the course of their construction; and
(4) provides insurance cover for buyers and subsequent buyers should, in fact, defects arise during the first ten years after the dwelling is completed.

92

The scheme, and the effect it has had on the quality of building and the protection of buyers, constitutes a major revolution in domestic conveyancing. How effective it has been may be judged from the fact that some 26,000 builders are now registered with the NHBC and bound by its rules, with all that implies for quality of methods, materials and workmanship; and the fact that the Building Societies Association has recommended its members to lend to buyers of new houses, purpose-built flats and maisonettes only if they have the protection of NHBC cover—a powerful incentive to most builders to qualify for membership. With more and more properties protected by the scheme, it behoves conveyancers to be familiar with its operation, whether acting for sellers or buyers.

There have been many changes in the NHBC scheme since its beginning. As from April 1989 there are two schemes in everyday use. The first, called in this book the Buildmark scheme, which is important to first buyers and subsequent buyers of all homes registered with the NHBC on or after 1 April 1988. Secondly, the scheme in operation before April 1988, called in this book, the pre-1988 scheme. This is important to the owners and subsequent buyers of homes registered with the NHBC in the period from 1 April 1979 to 31 March 1988. I call it pre-1988 because most dwellings registered in the first three months of that year were later reregistered under the Buildmark scheme. These two schemes will run side by side until the dwellings registered under the pre-1988 scheme are no longer covered on expiry of the ten-year period. The count-down for the end of the pre-1988 scheme has already begun.

By April 1989, the guarantees issued under an older scheme for homes registered with the NHBC before April 1979 expired; for further information as to pre-1979 schemes, see p 238 of the 10th edition of this book.

1 The Buildmark scheme

The NHBC maintains a register of house-builders and developers, which is open to inspection at its offices in Amersham, Buckinghamshire. Before accepting a person's name for entry on the register, the Council must be satisfied as to various matters such as the applicant's credit-worthiness and ability and commitment to construct or to arrange for the construction of dwellings in compliance with the NHBC's requirements. Registration with the NHBC will lapse immediately upon the bankruptcy or liquidation of the house-builder or developer or the appointment of a receiver in connection with the business.

The NHBC may also remove names from the register if, for example, builders have committed a breach of its rules, or conduct themselves in a manner likely to bring the NHBC into disrepute, or fail to pay their annual subscriptions.

The scheme is intended to cover homes (whether houses, bungalows, maisonettes or flats) built by registered house-builders and sold by them or by registered developers. The distinction is made between house-builders and developers because the latter may know little, if anything, about building techniques. A registered developer must not act as a house-builder unless registered with the NHBC as such. Neither a developer nor a house-builder is permitted to employ as main contractor any person other than a house-builder registered with the NHBC. A home being sold by an unregistered developer may have NHBC cover if it was built by a registered house-builder and prior approval is obtained from the NHBC; such approval will be given only for estates of nine homes or fewer. If there are more than nine the developer must apply to become a member.

The scheme does not apply to homes made by the conversion of existing buildings. However the NHBC have now provided a special register for builders and developers who convert and renovate old buildings with insurance cover in respect of defects arising within the first six years after the conversion or renovation was completed to the satisfaction of the NHBC. The NHBC must be satisfied that, at the very least, the work complies with the standards laid down for an improvement grant; at their discretion they may ask for more work to be done.

This chapter deals only with the main schemes for new dwellings. For the sake of simplicity it is assumed that there is no separate developer, and therefore the house-builder is intending to sell direct to the public.

The house-builder must make an 'Application for Inspection' of the home and pay a registration fee at least 21 days before beginning construction. If the home is to be built on a hazardous site (eg on land affected by landslip, or in a mining area, or liable to flooding), the house-builder must notify the NHBC of the particular hazard at least eight weeks before building commences. The application for inspection registers the intended new dwelling with the NHBC for cover under its scheme.

The home must be designed and constructed in accordance with the NHBC requirements in force when the concreting of its foundations was begun. The house-builder must also provide the NHBC with certain plans and all facilities necessary for inspecting the building at various stages. Ultimately a final inspection will be made. If at that stage the NHBC is satisfied with the quality of workmanship etc, it will (by later documentation, see below) issue its insurance cover for that home for a period of ten years from the date of the final inspection.

Insurance benefits enjoyed by buyers

Compensation may be accorded to a purchaser in respect of three periods named (conveniently) Section 1, Section 2 and Section 3. There's also a Section 4, applicable in those cases where compliance with buildings regulations was supervised by the NHBC Building Control Services Ltd. The extent of the benefits is very clearly and fully set out in the documentation the first buyer will receive (see below, the Buildmark booklet, Form BM3). What follows is a short, non-exhaustive summary.

Section 1 covers the period before the final inspection of the home and covers losses, not exceeding £10,000, caused because the house-builder fails, whether because of insolvency or fraud, to complete the dwelling in accordance with the NHBC requirements.

Section 2 covers losses suffered during a period called the 'initial guarantee period'. This is defined as the first two years of the ten-year period *or* a period of one year from the date of first sale *if* the home was unoccupied and unsold during the first 12 or more months after the ten-year period began. During the initial guarantee period, house-builders must put right any defect caused by any breach of the NHBC requirements *provided* it first appears and is reported to them in writing within that time. If the buyer fails to obtain satisfaction from the house-builder, the NHBC will pay compensation *provided*:

(1) the buyer reported the defect to the house-builder within a reasonable time and before the expiry of the initial guarantee period; and
(2) gave notice in writing as soon as possible to the NHBC; and
(3) pursued the house-builder to judgment or an arbitration award (unless the NHBC waived this requirement on being satisfied that the house-builder was insolvent and that therefore no useful purpose would have been served by litigation or arbitration).

One difference between claims against the house-builder and claims against the NHBC scheme is that the scheme covers only the costs or damages arising directly from breaches of the NHBC requirements. It doesn't cover, for example, damages for distress or inconvenience.

Section 3 covers losses suffered during the period called the 'structural guarantee period', which is defined as the period from the end of the initial guarantee period until the expiry of the first ten years after the final inspection. During this period the NHBC will pay the cost of putting right any 'major damage' (defined to include damage necessitating

complete or partial rebuilding, extensive repair work and damage classified as severe or very severe in certain scientific tables) if the damage was
caused by a defect in the structure or by subsidence settlement or heave
affecting the structure. The NHBC will also pay the cost of putting right
the defect or the subsidence settlement or heave. If repair work necessi-
tates the occupier vacating the home for a period the NHBC will also pay
reasonable costs incurred for removal, alternative accommodation and
storage.

During the structural guarantee period claims can be made directly to
the NHBC. The aggrieved buyer needn't pursue the house-builder
first—although, of course, this may be done if desired.

The cover is subject to some exclusions; for example the NHBC
won't be liable for any major damage of which written notice was or
could reasonably have been given to the house-builder during the initial
guarantee period. The cover also excludes liability which is covered by
any other insurance policy; for example subsidence and heave are
usually covered by ordinary house-owners insurance. If buyers can
claim on that, they can't also claim from the NHBC.

There are also certain limitations on the amount of compensation
payable under Section 2 and Section 3. For each home the amount of
compensation is limited to the 'maximum insured value as increased';
this is a sum equal to the purchase price (or three times the national
average purchase price for a new building, if less) inflation proofed by
increasing that figure in line with the Housing Cost Index up to a limit
of 12% per annum compound. There's also a limit on the total sums
payable in respect of all homes registered with the NHBC in a particular year. This limit, which is counted in millions, has never in previous
years led to any buyer suffering reduced compensation.

The documentation

NHBC will send the following documents to the house-builder who
registers a new home:
(1) An Offer of Cover: Form BM1.
(2) An Acceptance Form: Form BM2.
(3) The Buildmark booklet: Form BM3.

The first two documents, which are attached together, state the
'Buildmark number', the address of the home and the name and membership number of the registered developer or registered house-builder
as the case may be; the documents all refer to this person as 'the builder'.

The booklet describes, in admirably plain English, all the insurance
benefits summarised above. The booklet is aimed at the buyer in person
rather than the buyer's solicitor or mortgagee and includes colourful pic-

tures of smiling people and some handy hints on 'DIY' jobs such as how to change tap washers.

The builder should deliver these documents to the first buyer when contracts for the sale of the dwelling are exchanged.

By the offer of cover, the NHBC and the builder offer the first buyer of the home and all subsequent buyers the protection set out in the Buildmark booklet. The term 'buyer' is defined to cover only persons taking the freehold or a long leasehold interest (or a share therein) and who are acquiring the home for residential use by themselves, their tenants or licensees; this definition therefore excludes, for example, any developer or speculator purchasing merely for resale.

The buyer should sign the acceptance form and return it forthwith to the NHBC. Assuming all is well, the NHBC will send to the buyer two copies of a Ten-Year Notice (Form BM4). This notice confirms, amongst other things, that the home is within the scheme and it states the commencement date of the ten-year period and the maximum insured value. In the case of a flat or maisonette the buyer will also receive two copies of a Common Parts Ten-Year Notice (Form BM5). Marginal notes in various documents ask the first buyer to keep the offer of cover and the ten-year notice(s) in a pocket at the back of the Buildmark booklet. The duplicate ten-year notice(s) is intended for onward transmission to the buyer's mortgagees.

Acting for the first buyer

When acting for first buyers you must do the following things:
(1) Be ready to explain the scheme to them. In particular, whether you are asked or not, explain how the ten-year period is calculated. It runs from the time the home is completed to the satisfaction of the NHBC; that time will not necessarily coincide with the date the buyer first owns the property. Give as an example the case of a new estate of houses. The ten-year periods for the houses may all commence within a few weeks of each other and therefore, later, will elapse within a few weeks of each other. However some of the houses, especially the show-house, may not be sold until several months, and often years, after the ten-year period began. Unless they are given such an explanation, some buyers will assume, wrongly, that the cover on their new home runs from the date of purchase. It doesn't. Its purpose and function is quite different from, for example, the guarantees given on the purchase of new cars or washing machines.

Another point to stress, whether asked or not, is the heavy obligation on the buyer to report in writing any defects promptly both to the builder and to the NHBC itself. Thirdly, make sure you tell the client that the details of what is and isn't covered by the guarantee are all explained fully in the Buildmark booklet, which must be read. Any attempt by you to explain what is already clearly explained in that booklet is unnecessary.

(2) Ask the seller's conveyancer by way of practical enquiry when the dwelling was completed to the satisfaction of the NHBC. This is the date which will later be stated in the ten-year notice(s).

(3) Strive for a special condition in which the seller undertakes to deliver the documentation immediately upon exchange; a convenient form of wording to use is as follows:

> The seller undertakes to deliver to the buyer forthwith the Buildmark offer of cover (Form BM1) plus the attached acceptance form and the Buildmark booklet (Form BM3).

Alternatively, insist upon an undertaking by the seller's conveyancers that they now have in their possession that documentation and will deliver it together with the contract signed by the seller.

(4) On exchange of contracts ensure that the seller's conveyancer hands over the offer of cover, the acceptance form attached, and the Buildmark booklet.

Always check that the correct documents have been supplied, ie that they state the correct address or plot number. This information together with the Buildmark number and the name of the builder, etc, are all printed in the documents by the NHBC. However, there are separate documents for each and every home in the estate. Unless care is taken mistakes can be made in the builder's office or in the builder's solicitor's office and the buyer of one home may be handed the documents appropriate for a different home.

(5) Complete the acceptance form, get it signed by the client and send it off to the NHBC as quickly as possible.

If the ten-year notice(s) is not received within the next few weeks contact the NHBC to find out why. It may be because the acceptance form has been lost. Alternatively, it may be because there are outstanding defects that prevent the issue of the notice. In the latter case prepare to advise the client about making a claim under Section 1 of the insurance benefits.

(6) On receiving the ten-year notice(s) check that it is correct, send the top copy to the client for inclusion in the Buildmark booklet and retain the duplicate for later delivery to the mortgagees.

Acting for subsequent buyers

(1) Raise the enquiry that asks for copies of the documentation and asks whether any defects have arisen and if so, whether they have been reported as required.

(2) Check carefully any survey report obtained on behalf of your client and insist that the seller reports any defects revealed by that survey.

(3) Insist upon a special condition requiring the seller to hand over the original documents on completion.

(4) On completion receive the original documents and check that they are correct.

It is not now common practice for the seller to assign to the buyer the benefit of the NHBC scheme, and therefore it is no longer the practice for the new buyer to give notice of assignment to the builder or to the NHBC. Since April 1979 the NHBC scheme has defined the term 'buyer' to include subsequent buyers. Case law has held that this will mean the rights are impliedly assigned whenever the land is sold. Moreover, since 1979, the NHBC rules have included a rule that seeks to prohibit builders or developers denying liability on the basis that the agreement has not been assigned.

2 The pre-1988 NHBC scheme

The Buildmark scheme covers all dwellings first registered with the NHBC after April 1988 and also, by way of transitional provisions, many dwellings that were first registered after April 1987 but later re-registered under the Buildmark scheme. The pre-1988 scheme covers all dwellings registered before April 1987 and those dwellings registered in the year April 1987 to March 1988, which were not reregistered under the Buildmark scheme. Details of the old scheme remain important in respect of any claims made on the insurance benefits and also in respect of sales of the dwellings at a time before the insurance cover has expired. For most purposes the scheme will finally disappear sometime after March 1998. The two schemes are very similar both as to the obligations they impose on the house-builder and as to the insurance benefits they give to buyers and subsequent buyers.

There are however some differences. Under the Buildmark scheme the insurance benefits available are in three respects significantly improved. Under the old scheme there is a 10% excess clause payable by the buyer in Section 1 and Section 2 claims. Also, the builder's liability in respect of central heating boilers, air conditioning units and waste disposal units covers a period of only one year (not two years as under the Buildmark scheme). Lastly, the old scheme excludes all liability in respect of professional fees; this exclusion is modified under the new Buildmark scheme.

Between the old and the new, there is also a substantial difference in documentation. Under the pre-1988 scheme for 'Offer of Cover' see 'The House Purchaser's Agreement'; for 'Ten-Year Notice' see 'Notice of Insurance Cover'; for 'Buildmark booklet' see 'Insurance Policy'.

3 Making a claim

The NHBC require a fee to be paid before they will investigate a claim. They also encourage complainants to settle disputes directly with the builder, assuming he is still in business.

4 The alternatives

If there is no NHBC cover an architect's certificate may be offered instead. Check this carefully and in particular that it is acceptable to the buyer's mortgage lender.

Thre is at least one insurance based scheme offered by a major developer similar to the NHBC. This is equally as good and offers 15 years cover.

Chapter 9

'Right to buy' conveyancing under the Housing Act 1985

The Housing Act 1980 as amended by the Housing and Building Control Act 1984, now consolidated by the Housing Act 1985, gave a new dimension to conveyancing. For a summary of the 1984 Act see an article by P W Rhodes in [1984] *Gazette* 7 November, 2100. Council and some other tenants have now the inalienable right, of their own choice, to buy the freehold or a long lease of their homes on very favourable terms, both as to price and mortgage finance. References to sections below are to the 1985 Act.

1 Who has the right to buy?

A secure tenant (defined by s 80(1) of the Act) of a flat or house occupied as his or her only or principal dwelling-house held of a local or other authority as defined below, who has been a secure tenant for not less than two years, or for periods amounting together to not less than two years. But neither the landlord nor the dwelling-house (the term includes flats and maisonettes) need have been the same during the whole of that period.

A joint tenant who has occupied a dwelling-house as his or her only or principal home shall be treated as the secure tenant, and where the secure tenancy is a joint one that condition need be satisfied as to only one of them (s 118(2)). Where the secure tenancy is joint, the right to buy and to a mortgage belongs to them all jointly, or to such one or more of them as they may agree (s 118(2)).

When exercisable, the right is to acquire the freehold, if the dwelling-house is a house; if it's a flat the right is to a long lease of not less than 125 years at a rent not exceeding £10 per annum. In either case, the purchaser has the right to leave the whole or part of the aggregate purchase money on the security of a first mortgage (s 132(1)).

These provisions in the Act relate only to freehold property owned by the landlord, but by s 118(1) of the Act if the landlord (local or other authority) has only a leasehold estate, it is possible, if it is long enough to allow it, to grant a lease of at least 21 years of a house or 50 years of a flat.

Land that has been used for the purpose of the dwelling-house is included therewith if the tenant serves a notice requiring this and it is reasonable to do so.

The right to buy can't be exercised by tenants who: (1) are bankrupts, or against whom bankruptcy proceedings are pending; (2) are or will be obliged to give up possession under an order of the court; or (3) have made a composition with their creditors the terms of which have not been fulfilled.

Nor can the right be exercised if applicants move to another home that they have bought, even if they move only after serving notice—by the move they cease to be secure tenants (*Sutton London Borough Council v Swan* (1985) *The Times*, 30 November). And the landlord can at any time up to completion seek a possession order by giving notice thereof even, again, although notice claiming the right to buy has been given and accepted by the landlord (*Enfield London Borough Council v McKeon* [1986] 1 WLR 1007). The right to buy, the Court of Appeal found, is exercised every time tenants take steps in the process, and a possession order made before completion destroys their status of secure tenants.

Previously debarred from purchasing their homes because living in special housing, the disabled may now buy (Housing Act 1988, s 123).

2 Children

When a secure tenant dies or otherwise ceases to be such, and thereupon a child of that tenant who occupies the dwelling-house as his or her only or principal home becomes the secure tenant ('the new tenant') the landlord *may*, if it thinks fit, count the whole or part of any period or periods of occupation by the new tenant towards qualifying for the right to buy and for the discount if the new tenant occupied the dwelling as his or her only or principal home after attaining the age of 16 immediately after his or her parent was a secure tenant (s 15).

3 Family problems and the lawyer

Often the tenants who seek your help under the Act are inexperienced in matters of property, never before having owned their homes, innocent in its problems and pitfalls. They may never have made a will, be a little fearful of contemplating their own death and its family consequences. Your duties are correspondingly onerous.

Taking their instructions, of course, is the opportunity for gently leading them to consider what will happen when the client, or when one of two joint tenants dies? What happens when the survivor dies? What children have they, what are their ages and needs? What will the children's legal rights to the property, if any, be after the parents' death? What about that will? And the declaration of trust between joint tenants? All these questions, and more, are a challenge to your compassion and to your ability for simple explanation of legal complexity.

4 Shared ownership

Shared ownership—joint tenancy—was excluded from the 1980 Act, which provided for selling or letting to an individual tenant. The right for joint tenants to buy a lease (not a freehold) is now conferred by ss 143–147 and 150–152 of the 1985 Act on certain conditions: a deposit of £100 returnable on completion of the sale, must be paid; the right to buy has been established; notice requiring the lease has been served; when the landlord is a housing association, the Housing Corporation has been notified by the authority and has served on the tenant notice of any variation that it considers should be incorporated in the mortgage. Elaborate provisions are contained in ss 144–147 and 150–152.

See head 2 of Chapter 2 above as to the importance of taking instructions on the terms of every joint purchase.

5 Bodies to which the Act applies

(1) A local authority, ie a London borough council, a district council, the City of London, the Isles of Scilly Council;
(2) the Development Corporation;
(3) an urban development corporation within the meaning of the Housing Act 1985;
(4) the Commission for the New Towns;
(5) a county council;
(6) the governors of an aided school; and
(7) the Development Board for Rural Wales (Sched 2, Pt I, Ground 7 of the Act).

Excluded from the list are one of a group of dwelling-houses for persons suffering from a mental disorder, and one of a group of dwelling-houses for persons of pensionable age for whom services are provided.

If a landlord falling within one of the above classes disposes of his or her estate subject to an applicant's lease, the new reversioner is subject to the same obligations as the local authority or other predecessor (Housing and Planning Act 1986).

6 Acquisition from housing associations

Secure tenants have the right under the Act to purchase their houses from a private housing association but not from a charitable one. The Act does not give tenants the right to buy their homes, but it allows them to buy another dwelling-house and to be granted towards its purchase a discount appropriate to their housing association home. The procedure is somewhat complicated.

First, the housing association must be involved in the purchase and in the processing of the procedures, which are, briefly, that the new home is bought in the name of the housing association who then, in the same breath, transfer it to the tenant by subsale for the price paid for it less the discount calculated on the previous home. Alternatively, the authority may take a shared ownership lease with the buyer. The authority does not itself have to investigate title, make searches etc, but may leave this to the tenant's conveyancer; but the consent of the Housing Corporation must be obtained, and tenants should never commit themselves to a purchase until both the housing association and the Housing Corporation have agreed the terms of the transaction. The wisest course is to make the housing association party to the agreement to purchase.

For a consideration of the subject and precedent of a contract for purchase in which both tenant and association join see an article by W H W Buckell and T P Baker in [1985] *Gazette* 5 June, 1631.

7 The price

The price for a freehold or leasehold dwelling-house is its value on the open market with vacant possession. For the grant of a lease it is assumed that the seller is granting a lease of 125 years at a ground rent not exceeding £10 per annum. In both cases the sale is with the same rights and subject to the same burdens as are specified in the Act (s 127).

8 The discount

A person exercising the right to buy is entitled to a discount equal to:
(1) if the period to be taken into account is less than three years 32%; and
(2) if that period is three years or more, 32% plus 1% for each complete year by which the period exceeds two years, but not together

exceeding 60% (s 129 of the Act), or 70% for a flat (Housing and Planning Act 1986). But the discount must not be such that the price would be less than the cost to the council in the previous eight years (Housing Act 1988).

If the right is exercised by joint tenants, the section shall be construed as if the one whose substitution would procure the largest discount were the secure tenant (s 129(3) of the Act).

9 Resale

If the dwelling-house is sold, or a lease granted exceeding 21 years otherwise than at a market rent, within three years, the discount or a proportion thereof must be repaid; but the amount to be repaid is reduced by one third of the discount for each complete year that has elapsed between the dates of completion of the purchase and the resale (Housing and Planning Act 1986).

An exemption is made in the following cases:

(1) If the new buyer or lessee is a qualifying person.
(2) If it is a vesting of the whole of the dwelling-house in a person taking under a will or an intestacy.
(3) If it is a disposal pursuant to an order under s 24 of the Matrimonial Causes Act 1973 or s 2 of the Inheritance (Provision for Family and Dependants) Act 1975.
(4) A disposal under a compulsory purchase order.
(5) If the disposal is to the person or one of the persons by whom it is made.
(6) To a spouse or former spouse.
(7) To a member of the family who has resided with the seller for 12 months ending with the date of disposal (s 160(2) of the Act).

The discount provisions are entered as a charge at the time of first registration of the buyer's acquisition.

10 The right to a mortgage

A buyer has the right to a mortgage from the selling authority towards the purchase.

The amount that secure tenants, exercising the right to a mortgage, are entitled to leave on mortgage, or to have advanced to them, is the aggregate of:

(1) the purchase price;
(2) such costs of the landlord or the Housing Corporation as are chargeable to the tenant under s 178, which entitles the landlord

or, as the case may be, the Housing Corporation, to charge the costs incurred in connection with the mortgage;

(3) any costs incurred by the tenant and defrayed on the tenant's behalf by the landlord or the Housing Corporation (s 133).

Regulations can be made by the Secretary of State limiting the amount available on mortgage having regard to the tenant's available income (s 133).

The provisions that the mortgage deed must include are set out in Sched 7—provision for repayment by equal instalments of principal and interest combined; the period of repayment (25 years, unless the tenant opts for a shorter period); other terms agreed between the parties.

The right conferred by the Act relates only to the selling authority. If, however, the buyer wishes to borrow from another source (eg a building society), by regulations made under the Act, the authority may contribute to the costs of such a mortgage up to a maximum of £200 (Housing (Local Authority Contributions towards Mortgage Costs) Order 1984 (SI No 174)).

Procedure in the case of a local authority mortgage is somewhat simplified compared with a building society or other mortgagee—there will be no special conditions of advance common in building society mortgages, and although title may be deduced to the mortgage department of the council there will normally be no requisitions and the council will collect direct the mortgage advance, giving credit for this on the completion statement; and the legal department of the council will attend to all formalities of completion such as stamping and denoting documents, registering title, etc. To this extent, therefore, the work of a buyer's conveyancer is greatly reduced.

11 The machinery of purchase

Tenants claiming the right to buy either freehold or leasehold must serve on their landlord a written notice claiming that right—form obtainable from the landlord.

The landlord must within four weeks (within eight weeks if the period counting towards the three years includes a period when the present landlord was not the tenant's landlord) serve on the tenants a notice either (i) admitting, or (ii) denying the tenants' right to buy, stating reasons if the right is denied (s 144).

When the secured tenants' claim to exercise the right to buy has been established, the landlord must serve on them, as soon as practicable, a notice describing the dwelling-house, stating the price at which, in the opinion of the landlord, they are entitled to the freehold or leasehold

interest, and the provisions that the landlord considers should be incorporated in the conveyance or grant (s 125(1)–(3)). Such a notice follows
a valuation of the property by the district valuer for the authority.

The notice must state:

(1) the value at the relevant time;
(2) the discount to be allowed, stating the period to be taken into
    account under s 7(5);
(3) the improvements disregarded pursuant to s 127.

The notice must also inform tenants:

(4) of their rights to have the value determined by the district valuer;
(5) of their rights to a mortgage;
(6) of the effect of ss 134–135 and 142(1)–(2). Sections 134–135
    provide that tenants must exercise their right to a mortgage by
    notice served on the landlord within three months from service of
    the landlord's notice (the period can be extended). Section
    142(1)–(2) gives tenants the right to defer completion if they have
    claimed the right to a mortgage.

The landlord's notice must be accompanied by a form of notice to be
used by tenants if they require a mortgage.

If the tenant delays completion after all outstanding matters have been
determined, the landlord may serve notice requiring completion in not
less than 56 days; if by the expiration of that notice completion has not
taken place, a further notice, again for not less than 56 days, may be
served, and if not complied with the right to buy shall be deemed to be
withdrawn.

The Act specifies terms that must be included in transfers and leases.

12 Appeals

Tenants may require the value of their dwelling-house to be determined or redetermined by the district valuer not later than three months
after service on them of the landlord's notice under s 125, except that if
proceedings are then pending between the landlord and tenants for the
determination of any other question under the Act, the notice may be
served within three months of the final determination of the proceedings.

The landlord may, within four weeks after such final determination of
proceedings, require the district valuer to redetermine the value of the
dwelling-house at the relevant time.

Before making a determination or redetermination, the district valuer
shall consider any representation made to him or her by the landlord or
the tenant within four weeks from service of the tenant's or landlord's
notice (s 128).

13 Completion

When a secure tenant's claim to the right to buy has been established, the landlord is bound to make the tenant a grant of the freehold for an estate in fee simple, if the dwelling-house is a house; or, if a flat, a lease for a term of not less than 125 years as soon as all matters relating to the grant and mortgage have been agreed or determined (s 140). Completion is normally by bank draft sent through the post—most local authorities have no facilities for completion by credit transfer.

If tenants fail to complete, the landlord can serve on them a notice requiring them to complete. (See head 11 above.)

14 Registration of title

When the title is unregistered, the buyer must register the title (s 154).

To facilitate registration and to eliminate the strict investigation of the unregistered title, the Act provides that the landlord shall give the tenant:

a certificate stating that the landlord is entitled to convey the freehold or make the grant subject only to such incumbrances, rights and interests as are stated in the conveyance or grant or summarised in the certificate. (s 154(6))

The certificate is in a form approved by the Chief Land Registrar and must be signed by such officer of the landlord as he or she may approve. The Chief Land Registrar shall accept such a certificate as sufficient evidence of the facts stated in it, but the landlord shall indemnify him against any claim under the Land Registration Acts (s 154(4) and (5)).

15 Common provisions in the purchase documents

The conveyance or grant shall not exclude or restrict the general words implied under s 62 of the Law of Property Act 1925 (Sched 6, PtI, para 1).

The transfer or grant shall include all such easements and rights over the property, so far as the landlord is capable of granting them, as will put the buyer in a position similar to what it was under the tenancy. The assurance shall also contain such easements and rights for the benefit of other property as were available against the tenant under the former tenancy.

The transfer shall also include such rights of way as may be necessary for the reasonable enjoyment of the dwelling-house, and shall contain such provisions as may be necessary for the reasonable enjoyment of other property (Sched 6, PtI, paras 2 and 3).

In practice, both drafts and engrossments of transfers and leases are prepared by the landlord.

Part II of Schedule 6 lays down provisions to be in the assurance of freeholds.

A conveyance shall not exclude or restrict the 'all estate clause' implied under s 63 of the Law of Property Act 1925.

The conveyance shall be for an estate in fee simple subject (but otherwise free from incumbrances) to: (i) the tenant's incumbrances; and (ii) the burdens in respect of the upkeep or regulation for the benefit of any locality of any land, building, structure, works, ways or watercourse.

The conveyance shall be expressed to be made by the landlord as beneficial owner.

Part III of Schedule 6 lays down provisions to be in leases.

Where the tenant has enjoyed facilities or services under the tenancy, the lease shall include similar rights (para 13).

By virtue of the Schedule there shall be implied the following covenants by the landlord:

(1) To keep in repair the structure and exterior of the dwelling-house and of the building in which it is situated;

(2) To keep in repair any other property over or in respect of which the tenant has any rights by virtue of the Schedule;

(3) To ensure, so far as practicable, that any services to be provided by the landlord and to which the tenant (alone or with others) may be entitled are maintained at a reasonable level and to keep in repair any installation connected with the provision of those services (Sched 6, PtIII, para 14).

Note that some clauses that a lessee would normally require, such as a covenant by the landlord to enforce covenants by the lessees of other flats, are not included in the statutory lease.

16 Prudent advice to buyers

Maintenance

The landlord's covenant to keep the structure, etc, in repair is qualified under the heading 'Avoidance of certain agreements' in Schedule 6, the effect of which, in somewhat tortuous language, is that a provision is not void by virtue of the terms of para 17 'so far as it requires the tenant to bear a reasonable part of the costs of carrying out repairs not amounting to the making good of structural defects or of the costs of making good any structural defects falling within para 18 below'. A structural defect falls within para 18 if:

(1) the landlord has notified the tenant of its existence before the lease was granted; or

(2) the landlord does not become aware of it earlier than ten years after the lease is granted.

The result of the above provision is that a buyer may be confronted, after completion, with a massive and wholly unexpected bill for 'repairs not amounting to the making good of structural defects' both of the buyer's own home and 'the building in which it is situated'. Such a bill can be a financial disaster for a former council tenant who is quite unable to meet it—a bill that, if continuing as a secure tenant, the buyer would never have been asked to pay. See letter to seller (Appendix II).

The position is exacerbated by the question 'When do repairs amount or not amount to the making good of structural defects?' This is a grey area, which has not yet been fully clarified by the courts. See head 3 of Chapter 32 as to repairing covenants in leases.

In order to safeguard a 'right to buy' buyer against this financial landmine, therefore, the buyer's conveyancer should in all cases write a letter (see Appendix II).

There are some remedies. In some cases of defective dwellings, an aggrieved buyer may require the seller to re-purchase the buyer's home (Housing Act 1985, PtXVI and Sched 20). For an article on the conveyancing aspects of repurchase of defective dwellings by Mark Turnbull see [1987] *Gazette* 30 September, 2754.

Under the Housing Act 1988, a local authority is obliged to itemise the works of maintenance anticipated in the period of five years from the date of an application to buy, must cost the same and notify the prospective buyer. This information is often set out in the offer notice. Thereafter the authority may not for the next five years charge the buyer with a proportion of the cost of maintenance exceeding their estimate for the next five years.

Public to private

As well as the need to be wary of large-scale maintenance works contemplated by the landlord or in progress, would-be buyers need to consider, and to be advised upon what will be their position after their purchase. They will then have moved from the public to the private sector, and instead of having a landlord (albeit perhaps a tardy and bureaucratic one) responsible for future maintenance, as private owners they'll be responsible for their own repairs and maintenance. No comeback on the seller—the maxim *caveat emptor* applies as it does in the case of a private sale and purchase.

As in that case, the safeguard lies in the buyers satisfying themselves by the professional advice of a surveyor as to the condition of the property before they finally commit themselves to its purchase.

Here it must be remembered that if the buyers obtain finance from a building society they can, for a small additional sum, have the benefit of a report from the society's chosen surveyor instead of the expense of a survey by another surveyor; if they avail themselves of the statutory right to a mortgage advance by the local authority it is unlikely that they'll make such a survey, or if they do that they will make the report available to the buyers. So it may pay them to seek building society rather than local authority finance. It does not now cost the buyer much if anything to obtain a building society mortgage—since 26 August 1984 a local authority has the power to contribute to the cost of obtaining a building society mortgage up to a maximum of £200 (Housing (Local Authority Contributions towards Mortgage Costs) Order 1984 (SI No 174)). Whichever course they adopt, your clients ought to have that survey. How can they know whether the foundations are slipping or subsiding? That there's evidence of past heave? That the roof is likely to take off or fall in? Advise your clients firmly and clearly.

Chapter 10

Preparing for completion—seller

You ought to see the client for the signing of documents and final instructions as to keys, etc.

Whichever side of the transaction you represent, as soon as you've dispatched or received replies to requisitions (you can't do so before, because you won't know what the other side wants or is able to give on completion), complete the three agendas 'before completion', 'completion' and 'after completion'. These include standard items applicable to both a sale and a purchase, and those that are inapplicable to your side of a particular transaction should, of course, be deleted; if you run quickly through the agendas this will be enough in most cases to remind you which items should stand and which should be deleted.

Run through the papers in your file, including the subfile of any mortgage a buyer-client may be obtaining, to ensure you haven't missed anything.

From the moment you prepare your agendas the conduct of the matter pivots on them. Take your time preparing them, free from telephone calls and interruptions, so that you can look at the whole matter thoughtfully. You'll find that in a simple case no more than a few minutes are required. A systematic method of conveyancing, time and labour-saving as well as relatively foolproof, can be built on the framework of these three agendas: 'before completion', 'completion' and 'after completion'.

The 'before completion' agenda (Appendix III, Form 2) is divided into two sections, one for a seller, mortgagor or lessor and the other for a buyer, mortgagee or lessee; you can thus strike out whichever section doesn't apply without wasting time on it.

Here are some points on this agenda when you act for a *seller, mortgagor or lessor*.

1 Preparing a completion statement

(1) *Deposit(s) paid*. This comes first on the agenda as a precaution against overlooking it on exchange of contracts, and as a reminder,

when it's paid to the selling estate agent, to get a release of deposit on completion. Not that you're likely to need it: they're usually only too willing to release it on hearing of completion because then, with the balance of their commission, it can be used by them.

(2) *Last receipts etc.* This is a reminder to obtain from your client (if you haven't already done so) the last receipts for ground rent and service charges, which you will require in preparing the completion statement.

(3) *Discharge of mortgages.* A reminder, when your seller-client is subject to a mortgage, to arrange for this to be discharged on completion. Immediately contracts have been exchanged the exact redemption figure should be obtained from the mortgagee. In the case of a building society mortgage, it may be useful to ask for a 'daily interest rate' in case there's some slight delay in completion; this will save writing another letter, and will enable you in such a case to disburse and account for the completion money as soon as you receive it. This won't be necessary in the case of societies that give you one redemption figure applicable whenever the mortgage is redeemed during the month for which the figure is given.

(4) *Agent's fees.* Immediately contracts are exchanged on behalf of a seller, telephone the estate agent and ask for an account. Upon receipt, check that it is acceptable to your client and if so, include it in the arithmetic on the completion statement that you must prepare for your client and dispatch to him or her for agreement prior to completion.

(5) *Bill of costs.* It is also appropriate to prepare your own bill immediately after contracts are exchanged. Disbursements should be separately included on the completion statement. The information contained above should enable a completion statement to be prepared, and if there is a simultaneous sale and purchase, one completion statement should suffice for both, indicating whether there is a balance required from the client in order to complete, or whether there is a balance returnable to the client upon completion. Generally, much will depend on whether the client is buying up-market or going down-market and also whether the client is raising a mortgage.

2 Completion documents

This lists the documents that you'll need on or shortly before completion, acting for a seller or mortgagor. As you go through your papers preparing your agendas, add any other documents that may be needed.

(1) *Unregistered title*. When the title's unregistered, a schedule of documents will be a standard requirement and can be prepared now, unless the title deeds are in the hands of the seller's mortgagee for whom you don't act, in which case his or her solicitor will prepare the schedule, not you, and you can strike it out of your own agenda.

(2) *Registered title*. Clearly, upon the completion of the purchase of a registered title, the main task is to collect the charge or land certificate of the seller, together with a signed transfer deed. There will commonly be ancillary documents, such as NHBC documentation, but otherwise the completion procedure is very simple. The receipted Form 53 is likely to follow a little while later, and the undertaking in respect thereof will have been given in replies to requisitions on title. The new Protocol form makes this position very clear.

(3) *Undertakings*. When giving an undertaking, remember that unless you make the contrary very clear you will be *personally* responsible for carrying out its terms if your client fails to do so— see the pronouncements of The Law Society published in the *Law Society's Gazette* at various times over the years. This isn't to say that you ought not to give such personal undertakings; on the contrary, unless you have reason to distrust your client, you should be prepared to take this very small risk to facilitate completion. But don't commit yourself unwittingly to any liability exceeding a few pounds. And see the warning in head 2 of Chapter 16 on undertakings to discharge mortgages.

Most building societies refuse to execute a discharge of their mortgage until they have actually received the redemption money; ie *after* completion has taken place. In such a case when you act for a building society-mortgagee, therefore, you will undertake to the buyer's conveyancer forthwith to redeem the mortgage and to send the redeemed mortgage or (as the case may be) LR form 53 to the other side.

The following, recommended by The Law Society, is often used:

In consideration of you today completing the purchase of   we hereby undertake forthwith to pay over to   Building Society the money required to redeem the mortgage/legal charge dated   and to forward the redeemed mortgage/legal charge to you as soon as it is received by us from the   Building Society. ((1971) *Gazette* January, p 12.)

For a somewhat abridged form suggested by D S Wellhamser see [1984] *Gazette* 14 November, 3140.

In the case of a registered title, of course, you would undertake to forward LR form 53, the charge certificate having commonly been handed over on completion. And see below as to the new practice whereby a Form 53 duly executed by a building society may be available on completion.

At one time a number of societies have adopted the practice of sending their solicitor a sealed Form 53, in the case of registered property, in anticipation of redemption, in which case no undertaking is required, the form being handed over on completion.

If you are acting for a builder-seller selling a new dwelling and the builder is on the National House-Building Council's register (see Chapter 8), you may not, unless the property is completed some time before completion of the sale, have received the standard notice of insurance cover to hand over, in which case you will give an undertaking to do so as soon as it comes to hand.

Lastly, if any other undertaking is required from a seller on completion, make a note of it here and prepare it now. As part of modern file management, it is a good idea to put red warning stickers on the outside of those files where you have given an undertaking.

(4) *Receipts for outgoings*. It is no longer common practice to hand over receipts for the payment of rates and other outgoings relating to the seller's occupation of the property. In practice, most sellers of a freehold will make arrangements directly with the authority concerned, and arrange to pay their bills up to the date of completion. After all, such bills are personal to the seller, and they are not a charge on the property.

It is, however, necessary to hand over a receipt for the last rental instalment in respect of the assignment of leasehold property. Such a receipt, if clear, indicates that there is no outstanding breach by the tenant of any covenant contained in the lease.

When dealing with leasehold property, it is also necessary to deal with the apportionment of any service charge liability. Sometimes service charges will have been paid on account in advance, and sometimes the 'service charge year' will be only halfway through and a balance will remain payable by the seller to the landlord or management company and the precise amount will not be ascertainable as at the date of completion. In these cases, it is necessary to prepare apportionments, but for freeholds apportionment of the outgoings has been discontinued.

(5) *Receipted mortgages.* Unless the mortgagee has his or her own solicitor, it is for the seller's conveyancer to prepare and obtain the discharge of any mortgage over the property, and this is a reminder to prepare, in the case of a registered title, the discharge of registered charge (LR form 53), or in the case of an unregistered title the usual statutory receipt endorsed on the original mortgage. If you don't act for the mortgagee, you should now write to the mortgagee or the mortgagee's solicitor, asking for a redemption figure as at completion date. Most banks have their own printed form of discharge on Form 53.

In the case of a registered title, a charge may have been secured by the less formal method of giving notice to the Land Registry of 'Notice of Deposit' (or 'Intended Deposit') of the land certificate, and in such a case the appropriate document is the 'Withdrawal of Notice', which is endorsed on the back of the official receipt of notice of deposit. If the sale is of *part only* of the land affected by the notice of deposit, a simple letter of consent to the transaction from the bank or other person protected by the notice, addressed to the Chief Land Registrar, is sufficient; but some banks have their own form, which they like to use in such cases. Your client's bank manager will tell you the bank's favoured procedure.

(6) *Special notices relating to leasehold property.* When a property is sold subject to tenancies, the seller's solicitors should prepare and hand over on completion an authority to each tenant to pay future rent to the buyer; without such authority the tenant cannot be expected to recognise the change of landlord.

The form of your letter to a tenant (left undated until completion) could be:

re Blackacre

The above property has today been sold by our client, Mr Jones, to Mr John Smith of Whiteacre, to whom all future payments of rent should be made.

Yours faithfully
Solicitors for Mr Jones.

Acting for a seller of leasehold property, it may be that your client, as lessee, for instance, of a flat in a large block, holds a share in a management company that looks after the maintenance of the building, etc (see Chapter 32 on leases). Since you will hold the seller's share certificate until you hand it over to the buyer on completion together with a transfer of it to the buyer, it's for you to prepare the transfer, unless you send the certificate to the buyer's conveyancers for them to prepare the transfer. Either way, this is a reminder to attend to it now.

(7) *Company form 395*. On the completion of a new mortgage, the above form must be sent to the Companies' Registry within 21 days of completion.

The Companies' Registry will require sight of the legal charge to which the form relates.

The Companies' Registry will also require a resolution completed by both the mortgagee and the mortgagor.

The above procedure is pursuant to s 395 of the Companies Act 1985, and where a mortgage is taken against a company, it is vital that the above steps are followed.

(8) *Special arrangements for a lender*. This is a reminder when you are acting for a *lender* as well as for the buyer-borrower. Your mortgagee is likely to have a number of requirements that you must comply with, some of which have been dealt with above. These may include, for example, getting certain undertakings signed by the borrower (eg as to repairs) within six months, giving banker's orders for future payment of instalments of interest and capital etc. There may also have been certain *conditions* of the advance (eg that a woodworm infestation shall be treated before completion, that certain repairs shall have been carried out or a deduction made from the mortgage loan until they have been). This is a reminder to go through your papers, particularly the *offer of advance* by a building society if this is on your file and requisitions on title, to check that by the time you go to completion you can satisfy the mortgagee on every point he, she or it has raised. Remember to search in the Land Charges Department against the borrower, whether or not the title is registered, for possible bankruptcy, and also, for the same purpose, against any guarantor of the loan: a bankrupt surety wouldn't be much help to anyone.

3 Signing of documents by client

In due course the transfer (or in the case of a mortgagor, the mortgage), and possibly other documents as well, must be signed by the seller. They can all be signed by the client on one visit to your office. Some of the documents are those listed above for preparation by the seller's conveyancer; some will be those received from the buyer's conveyancer.

You can send the transfer or the documents by post to your client for signing, and if you do, you can enclose the printed directions, which can be bought from your law stationers as to how to do this, or describe this yourself. But as already stressed, you really should see the client yourself. Note that when you are acting for a *seller* of registered land (unlike unregistered), the plan attached to the transfer *must* be signed by the seller alone, and not by the seller's agent—not even by the seller's conveyancer as you can for a buyer. So unless your client lives and works a considerable distance from your office, or is unwell, it's best for your client to come to you to execute the documents. It's surprising how many mistakes an otherwise intelligent person can make when left to execute a document unaided.

As stipulated above, if a property is being sold subject to and with the benefit of existing tenancies, instead of vacant possession of the whole property being given, the buyer will require an authority addressed to each tenant signed either by the seller-landlord or by his or her solicitor notifying the tenant of the sale and authorising the tenant to pay future rent to the buyer (see head 7 of Chapter 12). Remember that under the Landlord and Tenant Act 1987 the lessee is entitled to notice of the full name and address of the lessor, so ensure that this is given in your notice.

In the case of a sale of leasehold property where the lessor's licence to assign is required, the form of licence sometimes requires signing of a counterpart licence by the seller, and frequently by the buyer too, whereby the latter explicitly becomes responsible for the tenant's covenants in the lease; this is a reminder in case the seller must execute the document.

4 Completion

Lastly, arrange with the buyer's conveyancer the manner of completion—whether by post or by credit transfer or by CHAPS. Make final arrangements in good time with your client.

As soon as you've completed your pre-completion agenda you should proceed to prepare *all* the documents listed under head 2 above. Don't be tempted to put off dealing with any items because of pressure of time; in the long run of the whole transaction you will *save* time, and possible error too, by preparing all the documents at once, whilst the matter is fresh in your mind.

Chapter 11

Preparing for completion—buyer

Reminders of all the matters to be dealt with on behalf of a buyer before completion are itemised on the pre-completion agenda (Appendix III, Form 2) with any items added that are peculiar to a particular transaction. The following observations follow those on the agenda, and of course will be dealt with together at the same time so far as possible.

1 Searches prior to completion and replies

It isn't enough to make searches; you must deal intelligently and adequately with the replies you receive. It's important to establish the invariable habit of going through replies to all your searches (the same principle applies to the property information and requisitions on title), ticking each one *after you have considered it and found it satisfactory*; if the contrary is the case, or if, for example, some information is disclosed that ought to be passed on to your client, mark it accordingly, and thereafter tick it when you have dealt suitably with the item.

2 Check formalities correctly negotiated to date

(1) This includes: contracts properly exchanged.

(2) Check references taken up appropriately on leasehold property.

(3) Remember to examine deeds. In appropriate cases, examine and mark your abstract of title against the deeds in the case of an unregistered title. The same applies to death certificates, probates and marriage certificates.

(4) Remember to prepare and send to the other side for approval the draft transfer in duplicate. Prepare it with any additional requisitions, whilst the title is still fresh in your mind and remember to make a third copy when you don't act for your client's mortgagee. Remember that a transfer to *joint tenants*, such as a man and his wife, on the form of transfer appropriate to such a transaction

119

(19(JP)), requires execution by the transferees as well as by the transferor, because it contains a declaration that the survivor can (or cannot) give a valid receipt for capital money arising on a disposition of the land. In the case of a simple transfer have the engrossment executed by the purchasers *before* sending it off.

(5) Consider insurance. A property is not now at the risk of a buyer until completion has taken place. In the case of leaseholds, of course, the property may be insured by the lessor under the terms of the lease. In that case you must obtain particulars of the insurance (additional property information form), transmit the information to your client's mortgagee and satisfy yourself that the property is adequately insured.

3 Obtaining the mortgage advance—mortgagee's requirements

If you are acting for a building society in the transaction, it will have its own form of report on title, which you must complete and submit before the advance can be made to you. Allow sufficient time. This varies but may be assumed to be at least a week.

The report on title must indicate the details of the property to be used as security and generally, details of any endowment policies that will support the mortgage borrowing.

The report on title must be signed and dated and must indicate the completion date.

Sometimes, the mortgage advance will be sent by cheque and on other occasions it may be sent by telegraphic transfer. The latter is becoming increasingly common, but watch for the deduction of the fee (usually £20 or £30).

Before you submit your report on title, it is important to check that all the requirements made by the mortgagee have been satisfied.

In the case of a building society for which you act, you will probably receive a number of forms, which might include instructions to yourself, a copy of the surveyor's report, a copy of the offer to the borrower and a set of schedules for the return of the deeds to the society. It is helpful to keep these together in a folder on your file. It is important to go through these documents in order to check what you have got, so that you will know at which stage they should be completed. In addition to the above forms, you will of course be required to obtain the borrower's signature to the mortgage form and possibly a deed of assignment in respect of any endowment policies.

It is important to treat the mortgage instructions seriously, and not to take them as standard. Sometimes experienced practitioners do not read the conditions sufficiently carefully, and assume that they are simply a standard pro forma. Although produced by computer, the conditions are not always in a set standard form.

Sometimes, it may be wise to arrange for the mortgage advance to come a day or two before completion is scheduled. This will afford the opportunity to clear the cheque, and indeed to make sure that there are no problems caused by postal delays. The only difficulty with arranging for the mortgage advance to come a day or two early is that interest will be charged to the client-borrower a day or two before completion is actually scheduled. Some clients will query this.

4 Preparing a completion statement

Apart from the mortgage money, it may be necessary to obtain the balance from the client in person. You will not know the precise balance until you have prepared a completion statement, and you cannot prepare a completion statement until you have worked out your own firm's costs and disbursements; and indeed until you have taken into account the costs and additional fees or charges that may be relevant to the particular transaction.

(1) *Bill of costs*. Your firm's bill of costs should be prepared in accordance with the quotation that you will almost undoubtedly have given at the commencement of the transaction. The professional charges will attract VAT at the current rate. The total of your bill is one of the expenditures that will then appear on the completion statement that you are about to prepare for your client-buyer.

(2) *Disbursements*. Disbursements include your expenditures for any searches that you have done, or planning permissions that you may have had to obtain. Future disbursements that you must take into account will include stamp duty and a land registration fee. These latter two are incurred after completion has taken place, and should feature on the completion statement.

(3) *Linked transactions*. Where there is a sale and a purchase these can be adequately dealt with on the same completion statement, thereby working out in the relevant income and expenditure columns the balance that will either be due from the client or payable to the client.

(3) *Balance required for completion*. Simple addition of your income and expenditure columns will lead to a balance on either column, which will indicate the ultimate result. It is important to let the client have this information as quickly as possible after contracts

are exchanged. Sometimes, you will be waiting to receive an estate agent's account before you can prepare your final completion statement. It may be a good idea to telephone the agent to find out how much they propose to charge. It is important that you obtain your client's approval of the estate agent's fees before you effect payment of them. Sometimes, disputes can arise and you will seriously compromise your client's position if you pay the estate agent before formal approval to do so has been received by you.

It is also good practice to ask your client to let you have the balance required (if applicable) a few days before completion, because you will need to clear the client's cheque before you use the relevant money represented by it. If the client's cheque is dishonoured, you can cause a serious shortfall in your firm's office account (it is this account that will have to bear the consequences of any dishonoured cheque against which you have already drawn).

Money is at the hub of every transaction, and you must proceed with the utmost care and skill when dealing with it. Most transactions involve substantial numbers of tens of thousands of pounds and whether it is your firm or your employer's firm, you must respect the large sums of money which any conveyancer is called upon to handle in every week of his working life.

5 Documents for completion

This item lists the documents that, as conveyancer for the buyer, you will need to prepare before completion takes place. As when you act for a seller or mortgagor, add any other documents which suggest themselves as the matter proceeds.

(1) *Unregistered land.* Collect the deeds and documents of title, or in a purchase of part, a marked abstract. In either case collect the transfer deed duly executed by the seller. In most cases, make sure that you hold an undertaking in respect of any outstanding borrowing, so that you know that you will receive a receipted mortgage deed as soon as possible.

(2) *Registered land.* You will be expected to collect the land or charge certificate together with the duly signed transfer. There may be additional documents as mentioned above.

(3) *Undertakings.* A variety of undertakings are possible in order to facilitate a completion taking place on the agreed date. The most common undertaking relates to outstanding borrowing on the part of the seller.

However, sometimes buyers can be required to give an undertaking to their building society to effect repairs as mentioned above and otherwise undertakings are used as a device to fulfil a commitment that it was not possible to fulfil before the completion date.

(4) *Receipts*. Again, these have been mentioned in general terms above, particularly in relation to leasehold property.

Traditionally, another form of receipt is possible, although rare. If part of the price is attributed to chattels such as a lawn mower, or curtains, or carpets, then the seller may be asked to sign a separate form of receipt to indicate the sum of money received in order to transfer ownership of the items concerned.

(5) *Leasehold property*. When your client is buying a leasehold property in a case where the lessor's licence to assign is required, the licence (which is always prepared by the lessor's solicitor, who should submit the draft to you for your approval) may require your client's execution of a counterpart of the licence.

Further, when acting for the buyer of a residential leasehold property there will probably be a covenant in the lease to register all transfers, mortgages and other dispositions with the lessor's solicitors and to pay them a fee prescribed for such registration. Notice is commonly given by a printed form obtainable from law stationers in duplicate (the duplicate for receipting and return to you by the lessor's solicitors as evidence that the covenant has been complied with). Generally, a letter will suffice.

Finally, again as mentioned above, a lessee sometimes holds a share in the management company responsible for the maintenance of the building and grounds, which is an advantage to him or her in giving him or her a say in these important matters. In such a case, either you, or the seller's conveyancer will need to prepare a transfer of the share. Both the transfer and the original share certificate should be handed over on completion, and subsequently registered with the secretary of the company.

(6) *Notice to insurance society*. When an endowment insurance policy on the life of a buyer-borrower is to be assigned to that person's mortgagee (commonly building society or bank) notice of the assignment must be given to the insurance society when the policy has been assigned. Most, but not all, building societies have their own printed form of notice, which is always served in duplicate, so that one copy can be receipted and returned to you and lodged with the title deeds, which are ultimately sent back to the lender. Generally, you will be supplied with a third copy for

your file. In the absence of a printed form, a letter giving details of the charge is sufficient. However, always send a copy for receipting and return.

It is increasingly common to dispense with deeds of assignment in respect of endowment insurance policies and simply to have a notice of deposit. The procedure for sending the notice of deposit to the insurance society is exactly the same as that described above.

Some mortgagees are dispensing with the involvement of conveyancers with endowment policies altogether. The policies are simply left with the clients, and if the policy is not maintained, the mortgage will automatically revert to a repayment system. The practice is increasingly variable, hence the importance of reading the instructions very carefully indeed.

(7) *Special arrangements for companies*. The company form 395 has already been mentioned above in the context of acting for a mortgagor. Remember how important it is to register the new mortgage at the Companies' Registry within 21 days of completion. Keep a supply of the relevant forms in your office. Also recall the importance of a company resolution.

6 Final searches

See Chapter 4 as to searches generally. From the date your application for a *title search* is received at the Land Registry, you have 30 working days (ie not less than six weeks) within which period your client has priority over any other person who searches or seeks to register a dealing. So send off this search about a week before completion—you'll still have plenty of time to stamp and register your transfer within the period of priority.

The one search will serve if you act also for a mortgagee, in which case name the mortgagee rather than the buyer, because the priority given to the mortgagee extends to the buyer, but not *vice versa*. Results of searches are normally dispatched by first-class mail the day they are received if the application is received by first post.

With a registered title, this is normally the only final search you make *except* when you act for a mortgagee: then a *bankruptcy search* must be made against the borrower because your title search will not, of course, reveal anything about him or her.

If for any reason you fail to register the transfer etc, within the period of priority, you may apply for one (no more) fresh certificate. Apply before the first priority period has expired. Then your client's transaction will take priority over any other event (such as the bankruptcy of the seller) or transaction (such as a mortgage of the property) of which the official certificate of search did not give you notice.

Note that to retain protection, the transfer etc, must be *lodged for registration* within the period of protection; in the case of unregistered land the transaction need only be *completed* within the period of priority given by your search in the Land Charges Register.

The date to which the period of priority extends is conveniently given on the official stamp on the certificate of search, which will be on Form 94A or 94B, depending on whether you are searching part or all of the land comprised in a title.

In the case of an *unregistered title* you will of course make a full land charges search, and you can include in it the name of any buyer-borrower. You should include in this search *all* names of past owners of the property against whom no search is revealed by the abstract or epitome. The period of priority given by your search is 15 working days for both the bankruptcy and the full land charges search.

In very urgent cases the result of either a full land charges search or bankruptcy search can, for a fee of £2 a name, be telephoned. A search can also be made by fax as described above.

There's one further search that should be made on a purchase or mortgage of *unregistered* land: if the seller or mortgagor is a *limited company*, search the Companies Register to ascertain whether there are any winding up or striking off proceedings or any mortgage.

There is no machinery whereby an official certificate of search will be issued: you must make your own personal search. Simplest procedure is often to employ law agents for the purpose, writing to them some such letter as this:

Messrs Scrivener & Tipstaff,
Law Agents.
Dear Sirs,

        re   Ltd
        Property:

We act for the buyer of the above property, and we should be grateful if you would search the register of the above company to ascertain whether any charges or incumbrances or the appointment of a receiver or other matter adverse to the company's title prior to 1 January 1970 are registered against the said property.

Yours faithfully,

Such a method is now a little laborious and larger firms will be able to obtain a search result by telephone within 24 hours. Some law agents have devised their own forms.

Lastly, whenever you make any search, whether against registered or unregistered land, make a note of the date and nature of every search on your instructions sheet, then you need be in no doubt later, if the reply to a search doesn't arrive in a day or so, as to whether and when you made your search.

Chapter 12

Completion

1 Completion methods

At the same time as you make up your pre-completion agenda the other two agendas ('completion' and 'after completion') should also be prepared.

The purpose of the 'before completion' agenda is to make sure that all action needed before completion is taken in good time; the object of the 'completion agenda' (Appendix III, Form 3) is to ensure that nothing is overlooked on completion itself. Every item on your pre-completion agenda should therefore be ticked as disposed of *before* completion is reached. When completion takes place, each item on *that* agenda will be ticked off as it's dealt with.

Given that preparation, your completion agenda will enable any reasonably competent person in your office to handle the completion of the matter with confidence and efficiency.

There are four ways of completing conveyancing matters.

(1) The traditional and now rare method of a personal meeting between the parties' conveyancers at the seller's office. Sometimes used still, though very largely replaced by methods (3) and (4).

(2) Similar procedure where the buyer attends through an appointed *agent* who will do all that the principal would have done — examine deeds, hand over purchase money etc. Little used now. Useful in a complex matter at a distance.

(3) Completion by post. The buyer takes the first step, writing to the seller's conveyancer with a bank draft (crossed 'a/c payee only' for safety in the post) for the completion money and with any documents executed by the buyer (eg counterpart lease), which should pass on the seller's prior undertaking to send transfer or conveyance with other documents by return of first-class post. Works well, but not much used now — and too slow when there are other dependent sales or purchases.

(4) Direct credit transfer of completion money on prior undertakings by seller to transmit transfer etc, by return of first-class post, and by buyer to do likewise on receipt of seller's deeds if the seller too has anything to transmit. The transfer was until recently made by telephone calls between banks, now almost always by CHAPS (see head 8 below). Good and quick—very suitable for linked sale and purchase or longer chains, now used for all kinds of matters, and profitable for the banks who debit your account with around £20 for the service.

The following are comments on some of the matters arising on completion.

2 Unregistered land

Check that a seller's redemption of the mortgage is dated not later than the conveyance or transfer to the buyer, and that the buyer's mortgage is dated the same day as the conveyance or transfer to him or her. This is the time, too, to check again that all blanks in the mortgage are completed and any alterations initialled in the margin.

On completion you'll hand over or receive all the title deeds and other relevant documents in the possession of the seller or the seller's mortgagee, with the exception of:

(1) a mortgage of the property retained because it relates to other property also of the seller, or in the case of a building society, for indorsement of a statutory receipt below; and

(2) documents relating to property of which only a part is now being sold.

In this case the seller of an unregistered title will endorse a memorandum of the sale on one of the documents. See that you hand over or obtain the deeds, including, of course, the transfer or other document vesting the property in the present buyer. To check the documents that should be handed over you can refer to the relevant requisition and the epitome.

3 Registered land

In a case of the sale of part of land comprised in a registered title, you must ensure that the seller's conveyancer either has, or undertakes to lodge the seller's land or charge certificate at the appropriate Land Registry. When the certificate is deposited at the Land Registry, a deposit number will be allotted. This deposit number will need to be communicated to the buyer's conveyancer, because it must be quoted when the buyer lodges an application for the registration of part (LR form A5).

Otherwise, the position on completion in relation to registered land is similar to that for unregistered land, and even though the land or charge certificate is the key document, it is likely that you will nevertheless receive the bundle of title deeds as well, because it is customary to keep them. However, those deeds, or at least some of them, are bound to have a rectangular stamp impressed on them by HM Land Registry. This stamp indicates that the title has been registered, and prevents a would-be fraudulent seller from passing off unregistered deeds as if they were still in themselves valid title documents. (Hence the importance of an index map search when you are offered an unregistered title.)

4 Discharge of mortgage

This item lists the various discharges of a mortgage or charge over the property to be handed over on completion.

In the case of building societies and other institutional mortgages, it is the practice not to execute a discharge of the mortgage until the redemption money has been actually received by the mortgagee. In such a case the society's conveyancer commonly gives a personal under-taking.

The re-assignment of an endowment policy may be by a separate document, which will be discharged at the same time as the mortgage of the property, but sometimes the charge on the policy is contained in the mortgage itself and then it is usual to have the discharge of the policy endorsed on the original mortgage, even if the title is registered, when the charge on the property will of course be effected by LR form 53 co.

To whatever use the seller may now put the discharged policy, remember that when it was assigned, notice thereof was given to the insurance society, which would operate as a stay on that society making payment under the policy to any but the mortgagee, so the discharge must be produced to them in order to vacate that stay. When the dis-charge is returned by the insurance society it should be kept with the policy as evidence of the discharge.

For a suggested notice of charge or assignment (they amount in this context to the same thing) of a life insurance policy see head 7 of Chapter 13 below.

The last document—consent to dealing—is the document used in the case of registered land when there is not to be a complete discharge of a registered charge or a notice of deposit of land certificate—for example, if a long lease is being granted out of a freehold, the title of which, subject to the lease, will remain charged; then the mortgagee gives written consent to the dealing. There's no specified form: it can be quite informal, in wording such as this:

Title No
Property

We hereby consent to the grant of a lease of the above property to John Smith for a term of 99 years from   free from the charge dated   and registered   of which we are the proprietors.

A similar form can be used when the security is notice of deposit instead of a full mortgage, and part only of the property is being dealt with.

5 Completion of mortgage

If you act either for a mortgagee or for a buyer who is obtaining a mortgage, or for both, this is a reminder to obtain or hand over the security for the advance, the execution of which (if you act for the borrower) you'll have obtained already.

At the same time there will probably be certain other documents to hand over to the solicitor acting for your client's mortgagee (or which you will anyway require if you act for the mortgagee, such as a building society, as well as for the buyer-borrower). These will include a *land charges search* against your client—see head 2 of Chapter 10. If the title is registered, you may be required to hand over a clear *certificate of title search* still within the period of priority that it gives (although the mortgagee's solicitor should make such a search and obtain the priority that it gives: see head 1 of Chapter 11). In addition you'll no doubt be required to hand over a completed form of *land registry cover*, signed by you as the buyer's conveyancer; and lastly, your mortgagee's solicitor will want from you a completed *P D form*, since (s)he and not you will have to attend to this formality because the transfer will be handed to him or her with the mortgage. There may also be an *undertaking* by the borrower to carry out certain repairs to the property required by the building society or an *acknowledgment* that the property will be occupied only by the borrower and his or her family or an acknowledgment by any person over 18 years of age who will be living with the borrowers, including their child, that he or she has no interest in the property ranking prior to the mortgagee. There may also be (head 4 above) a separate *mortgage of a life policy*. When preparing this item on your agenda you need always to refer to the building society's or other mortgagee's requisitions to be sure that you list and obtain every document called for.

6 Marking of documents

A reminder, when the seller is an executor or administrator, to have a memorandum of the transfer endorsed on the probate or letters of administration (if you act for the buyer, you should have made a request for this to be done in your requisitions). It's a similar reminder to that where the sale is of part only of the property of the seller, who will therefore be retaining the conveyance of the property. Here is typical wording of such a memorandum:

By a transfer dated   and made between the within-named   of the one part and   of the other part the property known as   [(being part of the premises comprised in the within-written conveyance)] was conveyed to the said   and his right to the production of the within-written conveyance/probate/letters of administration was acknowledged.

7 Authority to tenant etc

This is a reminder to hand over, or collect: an authority to the tenant of a purchased property (a separate authority is required for each tenant, if there are two or more) to pay future rent to the new owner; the keys of the property; the lessor's licence to assign, in the case of leasehold premises where this is required by the terms of the lease; and the fire insurance policy, in cases where this is to be handed over.

With regard to fire insurance, you'll initially have taken your client's instructions as to this, if you are acting for a buyer, and the question of whether or not the existing policy is to be handed over will have been dealt with on requisitions or the property information form (instructions sheet, and buyer's pre-completion agenda 10, see Appendix III, Form 2); if the policy is to be handed over the premium will have been apportioned on the completion statement. In such a case the seller's conveyancer should arrange an endorsement on the policy; a memorandum that the seller and the seller's mortgagee (if any) are no longer interested in it and that the seller's interest in the policy is now vested in the buyer; the buyer's conveyancer should see that this is done before the policy is handed over

('We hereby certify that the within-named   and   are no longer interested in this policy
Solicitors for the said   ').

Here, too, are listed receipt for the purchase price of chattels when this is appropriate (buyer's pre-completion agenda 11(d), see Appendix III, Form 3); company form 395 (for use when a company is buying and now mortgaging the property, to enable the mortgagee to register the charge on the register of charges on the company's file: see head 2 of Chapter 10); and certified copy resolutions as to borrowing etc (see head 2 of Chapter 10).

8 Concurrent completion of sale and purchase by CHAPS—Clearing House Automated Payment System

Where there's been a concurrent exchange of contracts it will generally be necessary to have both sale and purchase completed at the same time, so that the purchase money received on the sale may be applied towards the purchase, and the party can move out of the old and into the new home on the same day.

This combined operation is relatively simple.

Particulars of the clients' bank accounts for all the conveyancers concerned will have been supplied in reply to the standard printed requisition. Now, if party A is both buying and selling, then (1) A obtains particulars of the bank and clients' account of B (A's seller), by the standard printed requisition; (2) at the same time (more or less) A supplies the buyer's conveyancer, C, with particulars of A's bank and clients' account in answer to C's usual requisition as to these (or if C doesn't suggest this common method of completing, A will receive C's money in the more traditional manner; but assume that all the transactions will be completed by credit transfers).

The CHAPS procedure is as follows:

A, the first seller, arranges with A's buyer, B, to complete by CHAPS on the morning of completion—or better, for payment to be made to A the day before and to be held by A until completion the next day, in order to avoid hassle and timing problems. A arranges with A's seller, D, to complete his purchase by CHAPS transfer on the due completion date. B arranges with B's buyer, C, to transmit C's purchase money by CHAPS—hopefully, again, the day before—when A or C receive the money they undertake that the money will be held by them or by another conveyancer (A) pending completion the next day. B transmits B's purchase money to A by CHAPS and C does likewise to B. A does the same, on receipt of B's money (next day, if A receives the cash the day before the contractual completion date).

Then the postal channels hum with the volume of completion documents flying through them—A sends the transfer, with other title documents, to B; A also sends completion money and any documents required by D, A's seller (eg a counterpart lease); B proceeds in like manner with C, and C responds in like manner.

The banks are together enriched by all this to the tune of about £20 for each transaction. As each bank receives a CHAPS remittance it should report to its customer by telephone (sometimes you will need to chase them). Most large firms now have their own CHAPS terminal.

It's like a mazey country dance, and with a little bit of luck, all comes out right in the end.

The chief problem of completing by telephone (as distinguished from CHAPS) is delay on the part of the paying banks. If conveyancers for both parties bank at branches of the same bank, there's no problem: money can be transferred in a matter of minutes. But if they bank at different banks the transfer must, at present, follow a circuitous route through the clearing houses, and can take hours. This can be harmful for a buyer now that the standard conditions of sale provide that unless the purchase money is received by the seller's bank by 2 pm, completion (with resulting penal interest) will be deemed to take place on the next working day.

Some firms have overcome the problem by opening a clients' account at branches of several banks, supplying a list of these in answer to the standard requisition; the buyer can then match his or her own bank to one of the seller's, thus achieving the speedy transmission of funds by telephone.

9 Delay in completion

Except for the results flowing from failure to comply with a penal notice requiring completion by either a seller or a buyer under one of the standard general conditions of sale, and the further penalising of a buyer by payment of interest for any period of delay, it had until recently been assumed that delay by a seller, which fell short of 'unreasonable', was not such a breach of a contract for sale as gave rise to a claim for damages. As surprising as that assumption was the absence of case authority one way or the other.

The position has now been clarified by the Court of Appeal in *Raineri v Miles and another* (*Wiejski and another, third parties*) [1979] 3 All ER 763, to a seller's disadvantage.

So now *caveat* seller, and sellers as well as buyers should be warned of the possible consequences of delay, whilst their conveyancers owe them a duty to ensure, so far as lies within their power, that sale and purchase are completed punctually.

Although in the *Raineri* case a penal notice had been served (and complied with), this was quite irrelevant to a claim for damages for delayed completion by a seller. A contract is a contract, and any damage resulting from a breach is unaffected by and independent of a penal notice, from which other results flow—for example, a right for the buyer to rescind the contract on non-compliance.

In a chain of transactions, as there was in the *Raineri* case, it might be wise, and helpful in avoiding disputes and claims, if when acting for a buyer you tell your seller how urgent is your client's need to complete on the due date. But you need to be careful, if you advise the seller of the urgency, not to make time of the essence of the contract: that might be disastrous for your client, if your client is delayed completing by a few days. See the suggested paragraph in the specimen letter exchanging contracts at Appendix II. The case does not entitle a buyer to claim damages unless the buyer has suffered loss—as Lord Justice Templeman observed in the Court of Appeal:

In a good many cases a short delay will not cause damage and if sufficient advance warning is given a purchaser will be able to mitigate or prevent any damage and is under a duty to do so.

But the most minimal loss is not excluded.

Condition 6.8 in the standard conditions of sale provides that at any time on or after completion date, a party who is ready, able and willing to complete may give the other a notice to complete. The condition is even handed as between a willing seller and a willing buyer, and after service of the notice, the defaulting party is required to complete the contract within ten working days, excluding the day on which the notice is given. For this purpose, time becomes of the essence of the contract. If the buyer paid a deposit of less than 10% of the purchase price, then on receipt of a notice to complete the buyer is forthwith to pay a further deposit equal to the balance of that 10%. Condition 7.3 further provides that if there is default by either or both of the parties in performing their obligations under the contract, and completion is delayed, the party whose total period of default is the greater is to pay compensation to the other party. Compensation is calculated at the contract rate on the purchase price or (where the buyer is the paying party) the purchase price, less any deposit paid for the period by which the paying party's default exceeds that of the receiving party, or if shorter, the period between completion date and actual completion.

Any claim for loss resulting from delayed completion is to be reduced by any compensation paid under standard condition 7.3. Where a buyer is in occupation of the property, and completion is delayed, the seller may give notice to the buyer before the date of actual completion that the seller intends to take the net income from the property until actual completion. The seller is entitled to both compensation and income from the property in respect of the same period only if the above option is exercised, as set out in standard condition 7.3.4 (as set out above).

How does this case affect the practical, everyday conduct of a conveyancing matter? Acting for either party it underlines the need to deal with every stage as promptly as possible, and the duty to advise the client of the prospect of a claim for interest or damages if there should be delay on the client's part. It also underlines the virtue of the Protocol and the speeding up of the process which that ensures.

Chapter 13

After completion

Some matters can be dealt with only after completion of the sale has taken place; deal with these the day you complete, or the next day if possible. The manner of your dealing with these final formalities may determine whether you take leave of a well-satisfied and therefore a future client, and it also saves time and energy to deal with matters whilst they are fresh in your mind.

Following are some comments on the numbered items on your after-completion agenda (Appendix III, Form 4).

1 Report to client

This is self-evident. Account fully for money received and paid, if you haven't done so before. Transfer your costs to your office account. See specimen letters in Appendix II.

Contact the building society, if they require you to report completion, as soon as possible. Most building societies no longer have this requirement.

The last item in this heading, 're will,' is a reminder to consider whether it would be timely to remind your client to consider the provisions of his or her will if you've not already taken instructions at the inception of the matter (item 1 of your Instruction Sheet). If you think a reminder would be helpful, add to your completion letter such words as 'Lastly, may we remind you to consider whether the sale/purchase of this property makes desirable any change in the provisions of your will' (or 'makes it desirable to make a will').

In a concurrent sale and purchase (two separate files, remember) conclude your letter on the sale, containing a statement of net cash received, as follows:

Cash in hand...............   £39,000.00

We shall account to you for this sum on your purchase of Blackacre, about which we shall be writing you a further letter.

In the final letter to the client reporting completion:

We duly completed your purchase of the above property today when we paid your seller the sum of £41,000 made up as shown on the enclosed completion statement. You will remember (our first letter to you of today) that we already had in hand the sum of £39,000, and out of this money we have paid the balance of purchase money on the above property. We enclose our bill of costs and disbursements on your purchase, for which many thanks, together with our cheque for the sum of £10,911 being the balance due to you. The figures are as follows:

Our bill of costs and disbursements herewith

		£
Money in hand on your sale		
(see separate letter herewith)		39,000
Net building society advance		
(after payment of their costs, stamp duty, etc)		13,761
		52,761
Paid on completion of your purchase	41,000	
Our bill of costs and disbursements herewith	850	
		41,850
Cheque herewith		10,911

Some firms now send out standard questionnaires at the conclusion of any task on behalf of a client. These 'satisfaction questionnaires' set out a series of questions aimed at pinpointing any deficiencies in the quality of service provided, and they are normally accompanied by a self-addressed envelope to the senior partner of your firm, so that the management of your firm can identify any specific weaknesses that need to be discussed with a view to preserving the firm's goodwill for future transactions.

2 Stamp duty etc

This reminds a buyer's conveyancer to attend to stamping when the transfer is for such sum as will attract stamp duty.

The transfer must be marked under the Finance Act 1931 even if the consideration is under £60,000 so that no stamp duty is payable. However, this task is now dealt with by the Land Registry, and so there is no need for the document to be sent to the stamping office separately. A PD form will need to be completed in the same way, but that PD form and the transfer to which it relates are submitted along with any other documents, and the Land Registry form to the appropriate District Land Registry.

Certain documents dated on or after 1 May 1987 are exempt from stamp duty, and will no longer need to be seen in stamp offices, either for stamping or adjudication. These documents are listed in the Stamp Duty (Exempt Instruments) Regulations 1987. The exempt categories are listed from 'A' to 'M' inclusive, and documents falling within those categories must be appropriately certified, and such certification may either be signed by the parties to the documents or the solicitors acting on their behalf.

3 Registration on company file

A reminder to file your company forms in appropriate cases. Although the memorandum of satisfaction of a charge (company form 403a) can be lodged at any time so far as the Registrar of Companies is concerned, this should of course be done immediately after completion. In the case of a new mortgage by a company, remember to file form 395 ('Particulars of Mortgage or Charge') within 21 days of the charge being created. After that period has elapsed it *cannot* be accepted for registration without an order of the court. Moreover, if first registration of the title is to follow completion, the Land Registry will refuse to accept the mortgage for that purpose until form 395 has been filed.

4 Registration with landlord

Whenever you act for the buyer or mortgagee of leasehold property, check the lease for requirements as to registration of transactions with the lessor, and act accordingly. The additional property information form should reveal the solicitors with whom registration should be effected.

5 Registration of share transfer

A reminder to a buyer, when the buyer's seller has transferred a share in a management company, to *register* this transfer by sending the original share certificate and the transfer to the secretary of the company for registration. In due course a new share certificate in your client's name should be issued—make a diary note to confirm this has been done, as under head 9 below.

6 Cancellation of land charge entries

Acting for a buyer, you may have found an adverse entry of a puisne (or second) mortgage on your certificate of search, and will have obtained on completion and must now register cancellation of any entry (Form K11) signed by the mortgagee's solicitor. Recover the fee from the seller.

There may be other land charge entries registered against a seller, which require cancellation. For example, these could include a Class F land charge which would be cancelled by filing Form K13 at the land charges department. An option to purchase may be protected by a Class C(iv) land charge. Here, the new Form K11 should be used for the purposes of applying for a cancellation.

7 Mortgaged life policies

This applies to the conveyancer for a building society, bank, insurance society or other mortgagee whose advance is secured by an endowment assurance policy on the borrower's life, which is assigned to the society as collateral security additional to the mortgage of the property. In such a case, notice of the assignment should be given to the insurance society immediately after completion. The procedure of the building society in this respect should be checked, as some societies prefer to give notice themselves, and many have their own printed form of notice, which should be sent to the insurance society in duplicate, one copy being receipted, returned to you, and then transmitted by you to the mortgagee.

If your office has no favoured form, here's a precedent for one of your own:

NOTICE OF ASSIGNMENT OF LIFE POLICY

To (insurers)
Please take notice that by the assignment described below the under-mentioned policy or policies of assurance and all money thereby secured were assigned to   to secure repayment to the said   of the principal and interest as provided in the said assignment.

Would you kindly (1) return to us one copy of this Notice receipted by you and (2) notify the said   in the event of any premium payments payable under the terms of the said policy or policies being two months in arrears.

Assignment dated   and made between   of the one part and   of the other part of Endowment Assurance Policy or Certificate No   in the name of

8 Insurance

When a purchaser takes over an existing insurance policy (commonly in the case of leaseholds) write to the society with the policy duly endorsed (post-completion agenda 11) if the policy has been handed over for the memorandum endorsed on the policy to be registered in the society's books. Similarly, if you act for a mortgagee who's taking over an existing policy you should write to the insurance society informing it of this, enclosing the policy for suitable endorsement to be made on it recording the position. Typical letter to the insurance society for this purpose:

re Blackacre
Policy No

We act for Mr John Brown, now of 'Blackacre', who has purchased this property from Mr Smith and has taken over the above policy, which we enclose herewith.

Would you kindly note that Mr Brown and also the   Building Society are interested in the policy, as lessee and mortgagee respectively, and return the document to us suitably endorsed?

Yours faithfully,

When, as often happens in the case of leaseholds, the landlord insures the whole block, the policy will not be available; then you simply write a similar letter, but without enclosing the policy, asking the insurers to receipt and return the copy of your letter which you also enclose.

Some block policies now provide that they are for the benefit of all the owners and mortgagees of the flat without need to register, this to save paperwork. Peruse the policy for such a provision (a copy of which you must have obtained early on in the transaction).

This item is also a reminder to a seller's conveyancer when the buyer is *not* taking over the policy, in which case the policy should be surrendered and any rebate of unexpired premium recovered for the seller.

It is common practice nowadays, when a *freehold* is being transferred, for the buyer to insure afresh (buyer's pre-completion agenda 10).

In matters of insurance be alert for the buyer to see that the property is not under-insured. Check, and advise the buyer whether the policy is index-linked, as many are.

9 Filing

After a matter's completed, the file should be left in good order so that on any further reference to the matter you will know exactly where to find whatever information you require. Most firms will keep a conveyancing file for at least six years after the date of completion of the transaction. Queries often arise with regard to that file. In addition, many clients will want to sell the property they have just purchased, and it is often useful to be able to refer to the old purchase file when dealing with a buyer's enquiries and requisitions.

Most firms have a card index system so that old files are easily located. Some firms record old files on computer, so that all the salient details can be appropriately stored in order to assist with appropriately targeted marketing exercises in respect of the clients who have recently used the firm for the provision of legal or conveyancing services. The storage of client information in this way is a very valuable asset to any given firm in this modern commercial world.

10 Title deeds

Make a note to whom the certificate should be sent (buyer, bank, mortgagee etc) when it's issued. When you do finally dispatch the certificate, make sure that neither in your file nor elsewhere are there any other documents, such as obsolete deeds, which can be got rid of at the same time.

In the case of title documents prior to the root of title (unless they may be of any possible relevance, when they should be kept amongst the title deeds) you can send them to your client, to whom they may be of interest. Certainly any really old deeds, such as parchment skins, should be dealt with in this way. It is unfair to building societies to send them obsolete deeds: they have their storage problems, too. The Building Societies Association has made a plea not to be lumbered with documents of title not retained in the Land Registry on first registration, although societies will accept those not completely obsolete. For The Law Society's endorsement of this attitude and their recommendations see a note in [1977] *Gazette* 20 April, 326.

Chapter 14

Solicitors as property sellers

1 Introduction

Over the last few years, it has become possible for solicitors to set up to sell property as well as to deal with the legal conveyancing. At one time, the business of an estate agent was seen as a highly lucrative business, and it was anticipated that many solicitors would wish to open their own property display centre to offer property for sale. However, the recession, coupled with reality of the significant investment required to set up a property selling business has meant that there are very few solicitors' firms acting as property sellers.

Where a solicitors' firm does opt to make this investment and to proceed down this route, there are certain rules which govern the way they may proceed, not least of which is the rule preventing them from selling a house and acting for the buyer on the conveyancing.

A solicitor is still acting in his capacity as a solicitor, even is he opens a property selling outlet. He is therefore governed by the Solicitors Practice Rules 1990 and he must account for the income earned through his property selling centre in his return. The property selling venture must prominently display the full name of the solicitors' firm, and it is not possible to embark on some of the more extravagant descriptions that other estate agents may employ in order to describe their venture.

2 Setting up a property selling centre

Significant capital investment is required in order to establish a new property centre. One of the key forms of expenditure for this work is the advertising. Indeed, it is also difficult to get a number of properties onto your books in order to make a reasonable display in the early days.

It is important to recruit the appropriate sales staff. The actual job is not one that is well undertaken by a solicitor in person.

A non-solicitor property seller cannot enter into partnership with the solicitor and must therefore be paid as an employee. Commission arrangements are possible pursuant to Rule 7 of the Solicitors Practice Rules 1990.

In order to establish a property selling centre, freedom to advertise is important, but in the case of a solicitor, it must comply with the Publicity Code 1990. To all intents and purposes, solicitors can act as freely as estate agents, although unsolicited visits and phone calls are restricted to commercial property.

3 Supervision

A 'Property Display Centre' is regarded as a separate office for the display of the solicitor's property for sale. It needs to be supervised by the solicitor, but Rule 13 of the Solicitors Practice Rules 1990 does not apply. This is because it does not have 'clients' as such, and therefore falls outside the definition of an 'office'. A good sales manager or property negotiator should require minimal supervision, and most solicitors would expect to let them get on with the job for which they are employed.

4 Arrangements for payment

A solicitor acting as property seller will be paid as an ordinary estate agent (ie upon completion of the sale). Again, as is common practice with estate agents, a written agreement needs to be set up between the solicitor and the prospective seller, setting out the amount of the commission payable and when it is payable. Such ageement must contain other standard details such as the price, the address, whether or not this is to be a sole agency and whether the amount of commission is inclusive or exclusive of VAT, and finally, whether costs (eg special advertisements) ae to be separately charged.

5 Controls on a solicitor acting as a property seller

The Estate Agents Act 1979 does not apply, but the Property Misdescriptions Act 1991 does apply. The usual rules of professional conduct and in particular those relating to conflict of interest apply to solicitors acting in this role. The rules relating to the solicitor's handling of client's money also apply.

6 Summary

A solicitor is able to compete with estate agents on slightly more limited terms. A solicitor entering into this business will have to give serious thought to the effect that it will have on his firm's relationship with other firms of estate agents. As emphasised above, the costs of establishing a property selling operation is not insignificant, and needs to be carefully weighed against the potential gain.

The decision is often finely poised, and is all the more difficult with a recessionary market in house sales.

Part 2

Mortgages and the provision of financial services

Chapter 15

Acting for lender and buyer

1 Introduction

Many building societies and banks maintain a panel of authorised conveyancing practitioners to act on their behalf in any conveyancing transaction. Some building societies will not allow sole practitioners to act on their behalf, and lending institutions require a minimum of three partners. Other institutions are more relaxed, and the possession of a practising certificate suffices for their purposes. In any event, it is important to ensure that you are authorised to act on behalf of the institution from whom your proposed client intends to borrow money or with whom he intends to redeem a mortgage.

2 Conflict

In a majority of cases, you will be instructed to act on behalf of a buyer as well as the buyer's mortgagee. This is common practice, but instructions may not be accepted if a conflict might occur (for example, unreasonable mortgage conditions, or where there is a private mortgage at arm's length. In such cases it is imperative that each party is represented separately.

Strictly speaking, mortgage loans between members of the same family do not require separate representation, but it is wise to be cautious in this respect and to suggest that different family members obtain independent advice about the terms of any proposed mortgage document.

3 Forms of mortgage

Building societies, banks and the other institutions have their own forms of mortgage which will be sent to the conveyancer with mortgage instructions. It is important to read the terms proposed, with particular regard to unfamiliar standard mortgage forms. It is your duty to explain to the purchasing client the provisions of the mortgage deed. Such explanation must be sufficiently comprehensive to enable the purchaser to understand the effect of the mortgage. Many lending institutions require the signature of the borrower to be witnessed by a solicitor or a legal executive, to certify that an explanation has been provided prior to signature. It is common practice for many institutions to provide a short form of mortgage, incorporating standard conditions or special conditions booklet. Such a booklet should be brought to the client borrower's attention.

4 Mortgage conditions

It is crucial to pay close attention to the detailed special conditions attached to the mortgage instructions and the offer. Such conditions tend to become increasingly lengthy, and often represent the practical observations of the surveyor. Conditions which either do not apply to you as the conveyancer or which have been complied with already should be marked. The title may need to be checked, or planning permissions may need to be carefully examined. It is important to obtain the insurance policy/ies required by the mortgage conditions, particularly where such insurances already exist or are not being organised by the lending institution. In general, it is a precondition that such policy be produced prior to completion. Watch this carefully.

Sometimes, mortgage conditions cannot be complied with. In such a case, it is important to secure the agreement of the lending institution to waive that condition and this should be done prior to an exchange of contracts.

5 Signing formalities

When examining the offer and conditions, ascertain that the price is correctly stated. If not, the lending institution should be notified forthwith. In preparing your mortgage deed, it is important to keep a draft copy on file, so that you can make up that draft on completion.

As intimated above, sometimes it will be necessary for your client to attend the office in order to sign the mortgage. At other times, the mortgage will be sent by you to the client to be signed at leisure. Where this is not stipulated by the mortgage conditions, it is important to exercise your discretion carefully; for example, it may be appropriate to meet first-buyers in order to explain the contents of the mortgage carefully, whereas when dealing with experienced purchasers of whom you have knowledge over many years, it might be appropriate to commit the deed to the post with a request that they sign. However, even in this case, it is important to provide a comprehensive summary of the mortgage deed in your accompanying letter. Clients should be invited to contact you if they have any queries concerning the contents of the mortgage or your explanation of its content.

6 Drafting a mortgage deed

The actual drafting of a mortgage deed is likely to apply only when acting for a private lender. There is a statutory form of registered charge, and although it is extremely simple, it probably suffices for most situations, bearing in mind compulsory registration.

Individual mortgage documents can be drafted, if preferred. Many firms have their own precedent on computer disk and virtually every firm has its own Encyclopaedia of Forms and Precedents.

7 Searches prior to completion

The searches previously described in this book are equally applicable in order to fulfil the conveyancer's instructions to the lender and to the buyer. It is important to note that when undertaking a Land Registry search on form 94A or 94B the search should be done in the name of the lender, rather than the buyer. Where the land is already registered at the Land Registry, it is important to undertake a bankruptcy search in respect of the proposed borrower.

8 Additional security

A mortgage lender may require additional security, and this might take one or more of the following forms

(1) *A Guarantee*. A third party guarantee may be sought. This would apply where a retired person purchases a former council house and a son or daughter of working age is asked to guarantee the repayments. Such deeds of guarantee are common in a variety of different family situations.

(2) *Endowment mortgages*. Although less common than in previous years, endowment mortgages enable the buyer to pay interest only to the mortgage lender on condition that the endowment policies are maintained throughout the term of the loan. At the end of the term of the loan the policy will then be used to discharge the outstanding principal. Such endowment policies have

a guaranteed death benefit and the mortgage lender will require that this is at least the amount of the outstanding principal.

Mortgatge lenders vary in terms of their procedures with regard to endowment policies. Some still require a deed of assignment and a notice of assignment to be served upon the relevant insurance company upon completion. Others simply require a deposit of the policy with them and a notice of deposit to be served upon the relevant insurance company. Others require no formalities at all, and after having sight of those relevant policies, will return them to the borrower for safe keeping.

In general, mortgage lenders are more relaxed about endowment policies than was once the case. However, a borrower paying interest only must maintain the policy premium. If it transpires that this is not the case, then the mortgage lender will change the monthly instalment repayments as if it were an ordinary repayment mortgage.

(3) *Pension policies*. Because of favourable income tax treatment of contributions to pension policies, it has become increasingly common for these to be used as part of the security arrangements for mortgage lending. It is not strictly possible for such policies to be assigned in favour of the mortgage lender, but the deposit of an appropriate policy is a likely requirement.

(4) *Personal equity plan mortgages*. These are also quite common because of the taxation treatment of the contributions. Here an agreement is generally drawn up between the morgage lender and the borrower, whereby the mortgage lender promises to maintain the subscription payments on the plan. Such a mortgage will be backed by term assurance in order to ensure sufficient money is available to discharge the principal of the mortgage loan, should the borrower die before the end of the mortgage term.

(5) *Repayment mortgage*. A term policy willl be required to protect the outstanding principal in the event of the death of the borrower before the expiry of the term.

(6) *Mortgage guarantee policy*. Where a significant percentage of the value of the property is raised by mortgage, a single premium policy will be required to guard against any shortfall on an early sale. This enables the lender to be sure of recouping its loan.

In all of the above cases, it is important to ensure that the necessary deeds and documents, notices and other details are dealt with prior to the submission of the report on title to the mortgage lender in anticipation of the appropriate completion date. Where formalities are not attended to properly it can cause delay.

9 Report on title

A report on title form will be dispatched to the conveyancer with the mortgage instructions. This takes a different format, depending on the mortgage lender. It is only when the mortgage lender is satisfied with the provisons of this form that it will release the completion money.

Practice varies as to whether the mortgage money will be sent by cheque from the mortgage lender or by telegraphic transfer. It sometimes depends on the speed with which the matter has to proceed or the amount of the mortgage advance.

The mortgage advance should be completed only when all the conveyancing formalities are satisfactorily concluded. It is important to maintain a checklist for completion day in order to ensure that all is in order before parting company with the mortgage money.

10 Completion

It is not always necessary to advise the mortgage lender of completion. Once the cheque is banked, they will take it for granted that completion has taken place within one or two days of receipt. It is only if completion does not proceed as envisaged that it is important to report to the mortgage lender at this stage. On completion the mortgage deed should be dated and you should take delivery of the completion documents from the vendor's solicitors as quickly as possible. A notice of assignment of the policies needs to be sent off as described above, and the completion formalities described elsewhere in this book must be attended to in order to protect the position of the mortgage lender, as well as their buyer.

11 Land registration

Where a new mortgage is created upon completion of a mortgage advance, Scale 1 of the Land Registration Fees Order 1994 applies. The fee will not be separately assessed on the mortgage, but on the purchase price as in the transfer deed. The new mortgage is to be sent to the Land Registry with the other purchase documents; the correct procedures are described elsewhere in this book. If a new mortgage is created other than on a purchase, Scale 3 of the Land Registration Fees Order 1944 applies. In such an instance, the value or amount of the mortgage advance will determine the fee.

12 Re-mortgaging

In cases where the borrower is re-mortgaging his property, there will be no simultaneous purchase. Re-mortgaging is becoming increasingly common as lending institutions vie with one another for the available business in a contracted housing market. All sorts of offers are made available to existing borrowers in order to encourage them to re-mortgage. Unless instructed otherwise, a local authority search should be done in every re-mortgage. This would not apply, should there be an existing local authority search three months old or less. Other searches relevant on a purchase are also necessary. These vary from one property to another. The creation of a new mortgage does not, in its own right, require first registration in respect of an unregistered property. However, the arrangements for completion are the same as those described above.

Chapter 16

Acting for a mortgage lender and seller

Dealing with the redemption of an existing mortgage is generally very simple. Notwithstanding this, it is most important to obtain a redemption statement early on. In these days of negative equity, one can never be certain that there will be enough money yielded from the proceeds of sale to discharge the subsisting borrowing.

It is important to discuss with the seller at the outset of a transaction whether or not there is likely to be sufficient money to discharge the subsisting borrowing on completion. Lending institutions vary in the arrangements they offer in order to deal with negative equity situations. Generally, they are helpful. This is particularly the case where a seller is also buying. Sometimes, a separate loan account will be opened for the balance, and arrangements will be made for the vendor to pay off such an account at an affordable monthly rate. It is very important to check with the relevant lending institution what arrangements have been made to deal with any shortfall.

1 Subsequent mortgages

Upon receipt of the deeds packet from the lending institution, look through it in order to see whether there is notice of any second or subsequent charge. If there is such a mortgage in existence, then make contact with the lending institution in order to ascertain the arrangements that will prevail upon redemption of the first mortgage.

2 The formalities

These will vary depending on whether the land is registered or not, and whether there are policies to be re-assigned or not. For unregistered land, a receipt on the back of the existing mortgage will suffice. For registered land, a Form 53 is required. This will generally be prepared by you as a conveyancer—sometimes a standard form will be supplied by the mortgage lender.

153

With regard to the subsisting endowment policies, it is important to obtain a re-assignment of the deed of assignment. Once this is received, notice of the assignment must be given to the insurance companies.

Undertakings have been discussed above in this book, and they are invariably required on a redemption of a mortgage. They are required for generally sealed Forms 53 and completed deeds of re-assignment will not be provided until the loan account is redeemed. When giving an undertaking, be careful to state specifically which mortgages you are undertaking to redeem. It is important not to give a blanket commitment to redeem subsisting borrowing, just in case there is something unknown to you.

Chapter 17

Mortgages—some common problems

1 MIRAS tax relief

It is important to note that this is available only in order to assist with the purchase of a first residential property. A second property will not qualify. If the property is first purchased and then mortgaged later, then MIRAS tax relief will not be available, unless the subsequent borrowing is linked to another mortgage which was used to assist with the purchase itself. This situation does sometimes occur, and the client must be carefully advised.

The preservation of the entitlement to MIRAS tax relief must be considered carefully on a re-mortgage. It will be available where the new loan replaces an existing loan taken out to acquire the property.

2 Separate representation of the mortgage lender

The mortgage lender will sometimes be represented by an in-house legal department, or by a firm of solicitors acting for a local building society which operates a restricted panel.

Where there is separate representation, two things must be allowed for; extra legal charges being incurred which may affect the quotation you provide at the start of your instructions, and extra time being required, because effectively all the formalities have to be repeated twice in order to satisfy the mortgage lender's legal representatives in addition to yourself. This does increase costs, and does lengthen the time the conveyancing transaction takes to conclude.

When giving a quotation, ask from whom the buyer proposes to raise a mortgage.

3 'Flying freeholds'

Beware of the 'flying freehold', that is a freehold flat which is an anathema to most conveyancers. It can be achieved by complex cross-covenants, but except in the case of leasehold property, positive covenants cannot be enforced and therefore building societies, banks and other mortgagees refuse to lend on them, and prospective buyers will refuse to buy. One still sometimes meets flying freeholds from a time when attitudes had not hardened, but in any such case you should advise a buyer or a mortgagee against buying or lending.

A freehold flat on the ground floor is not strictly a flying freehold, but its owner suffers the same disadvantage of the unenforcability of positive covenants in the other flats.

When you act for a mortgagee of leaseholds, you will have the same concern as the lessee to see that the terms of any lease offered as security to your client are fair and reasonable, because in the extreme case the lender may be forced to sell the lease under a power of sale, and any defect in its terms might prejudice the sale. In this respect the interests of the mortgage lender and the buyer are identical, the mortgage lender being sometimes a little more intransigent than a proposed tenant. Check the terms of the lease thoroughly. If a proposed security for your client's loan is a new lease, you may be able to suggest amendments to it. If, however, it is an existing lease that is being purchase, don't be too pedantic except over really essential matters.

When, as happens fairly often, a lease provides that the lessee, in common with other lessees in a block of flats shall hold a share in a management company, provision should be made in the lease for the assignment of that share to any buyer from the lessee or the lessee's successors. This poses a problem for a mortgage lender who, in the event of later selling the property under a power of sale, will need to assign the share, too. It is solved by the borrower executing a power of attorney in favour of the borrower's mortgage lender, irrevocably appointing him or her attorney to sell the share in the management company to any buyer of the flat. Both the share certificate and the power of attorney are then lodged with the mortgage lender as part of the security for the loan.

Chapter 18

The provision of financial services

1 The Financial Services Act 1986

Many firms of solicitors have supplemented their private client and conveyancing activities with the provision of a wide range of financial services. The 1986 Act regulates such activities.

Where solicitors provide investment business as defined by the Act a certificate must be obtained from The Law Society, which is then renewable each year. Requirements as to record keeping are imposed, and the requirements of the Act must be carefully followed in order to avoid the commission of a criminal offence.

If the solicitor provides 'discrete investment business' (eg giving advice about appropriate investments) then additionally, the solicitor must comply with the Solicitors Investment Business Rules 1990. Most firms have a standard pro-forma client agreement which clients must sign in order to enable the firm to carry out work for them falling within this category. The form encompasses the payment of commission.

2 Exemptions

Notwithstanding the above requirements, a solicitor who gives general advice, but does not give specific advice such as where to invest the money, is acting outside the scope of 'investment business' and thus is exempt from the provisions of the Financial Services Act 1986. Similarly, referring clients to a third party falls outside the Act. Additionally, basic advice about bank and building society accounts or property insurance does not constitute investment business within the Act.

The following are further specific examples of financial advice not classified as investment business:

(1) Advice, in general terms about a life policy in connection with a client's purchase of land.

157

(2) Introduction to a third party to arrange a life policy.

(3) Where a solicitor considers third party advice in relation to a life policy to be wrong, he should advice the client accordingly and suggest he takes further independent investment advice.

(4) A solicitor acting as an executor or trustee is exempt, as long as he is acting as a principal. If a solicitor is conducting such business on behalf of trustees or executors, then such buying and selling of investments falls within the Act.

3 The provision of financial services—a business decision

Solicitors running a large conveyancing department must carefully reflect upon the wisdom of having their own separate financial services activities. The provision of such services is commonplace within firms of estate agents, banks, building societies—and this is quite apart from the many brokers. Many of these people are important work referrers in their own right, and solicitors who do not provide their own financial services may be at an advantage in terms of work referral.

For the above reason, some firms are moving towards the provision of stock-broking services more closely allied to private client trust and probate work, rather than services related to mortgages and the policies of insurance that go with them. Perhaps the provision of financial services is more appropriate for firms of solicitors who opt to sell property themselves.

4 Solicitors Financial Services

This company is controlled by The Law Society. It provides help and advice to solicitors, relieving them of many of the obligations of providing such services themselves. It might be particularly helpful for smaller firms of solicitors without the resources to provide their own back-up staff.

Part 3

Conveyancing and the rules of professional conduct

Chapter 19

The Rules of Professional Conduct

The practice of conveyancing is guided by the Rules of Professional Conduct, some of which relate uniquely ot the property transaction.

It is important to observe the Rules of Professional Conduct at all times. In practice there is often the temptation to act for both buyer and seller, particularly where one does not wish to lose contact with a good client. In those cases which do not fall within the exemptions to Rule 6 of the Solicitors Practice Rules 1990, it is of crucial importance not to be tempted to act for both sides in contravention of that rule.

1 Acting for buyer and seller

In most cases, a conveyancer should not act for buyer and seller unless:

(1) both parties are established clients;
(2) both parties are related by blood, adoption or marriage or;
(3) the parties are associated companies or;
(4) the price of the land is less than £5,000.00 or;
(5) there are no other solicitors in the vicinity whom either party can reasonably be expected to consult or;
(6) two offices of the same firm are acting for the parties, so long as:
   (i) the offices are in different localities;
   (ii) neither party was referred to the office acting for him from another office of the same firm, and
   (iii) the transaction is dealt with or supervised by a different solicitor in regular attendance at the office.

The above exceptions presuppose that there is no conflict of interest between the clients and also that the conveyancer does not participate in the negotiations leading up the conclusion of the deal. If the transaction develops into a contract race, then similarly the same firm may not act for both seller and buyer, unless there is no conflict of interest. Self-evidently, the same firm may not act for two or more competing purchasers.

161

A solicitor who sells property on behalf of a seller may also act for the seller in the conveyancing work. He may not, however, act for the buyer.

2 Acting for lender and buyer

It is common practice for the lender also to instruct the buyer's conveyancer to act for him. There are exceptions to this, particularly with regard to sole practitioner practices, and where a conveyancer is acting for himself in his own personal transaction.

So long as no conflict of interest arises, the conveyancer may—and generally will—represent both parties. In the very great majority of cases, this causes no problems. Sometimes compliance with the conditions of a mortgage offer do tend to prolong the conveyancing transaction and the requirements of certain lenders may be more stringent than those of an individual buyer. However, such instances do not generally precipitate a conflict of interest.

At the time of writing, there is much debate within The Law Society about separate representation of lenders and buyers, and views are divided. If there is to be separate representation of both parties, then inevitably costs will increase and additional delays may be involved. Such a system could also work against small firms of provincial solicitors, as the large firms are likely to be predominant on any select panels that the lenders may set up for the future. Membership of such panels could well demand compliance with strict management criteria controlling the quality of service offered and made available.

Costs

Strictly speaking, the solicitor incurs separate costs for acting on behalf of a lender and a scale of charges is suggested. In practice, most firms of solicitors do not now charge separately for dealing with the mortgage lender's formalities; it is included within the overall quotation provided. Of course, separate fees are applicable when acting only on a re-mortgage or a redemption.

Individual mortgage lenders

It is vital that the conveyancer should not act for both lender and borrower in a private mortgage situation. If you have two clients, for that matter, two members of the same family lending money to one another, then one of those individuals must take separate and independent legal advice from another firm. Although a loan between members of the same family may not be regarded as at 'arm's length' and therefore outside the scope of Rule 6, it is still better to err on the side of caution.

Fraud

Sadly, over recent years, there has been a significant increase in the incidence of fraud.

One of the most common instances in day-to-day private practice, where a solicitor can, possibly unwittingly, find himself involved in potential wrong-doing, is where a price for a property is renegotiated, and ends up being different to that notified to the mortgage lender. It is vital to make the mortgage lender aware of the correct purchase price, and that it is notified to the mortgage lender prior to completion of the mortgage.

In its warning to the profession about mortgage fraud, The Law Society have highlighted the following signs:

(1) A fictitious buyer—practitioners should beware of invented clients who you never meet in person, and to whom you cannot speak on the telephone.

(2) Unusual instructions or an unusual transaction: if things go wrong in a transaction, there may be an innocent explanation, but equally it may be that the behaviour of the clients, or those actually providing the instructions is irregular, because they have an unlawful design on the outcome.

(3) A deposit paid direct. If a deposit is paid direct from seller to buyer, you should ask why.

(4) Changes in the purchase price—this has been referred to above, and is probably the most common example of mortgage fraud. This happens particularly where a high percentage mortgage is required.

Certain steps can be taken to deal with the above situations:

(i) Insist on meeting the client.

(ii) Question unusual instructions. Do not be afraid to challenge your instructions if they worry you.

(iii) Discuss any odd cases or odd instructions with your partners or principal.

(iv) Do not witness pre-signed documentation. Only witness documents that are signed in your presence. If documents are returned signed but not witnessed, insist that they are re-signed in the presence of a witness.

(v) Check signatures—make sure that signatures on all documents are the same, to the extent that they purport to be by one and the same person.

There are a number of other examples of potential fraud which good and cautious conveyancing practice can eliminate. Full disclosure of a new mortgagee must be the order of the day.

Solicitors hardly need to be reminded that involvement—even passively or negligently—in a mortgage fraud is likely to constitute a criminal offence, and would of course lead to disciplinary proceedings.

3 Client care—Rule 15

Every principal in private practice must operate a complaints handling procedure which, *inter alia*, ensures that clients are informed who to approach in the event of any problem with the service provided.

In addition, every solicitor in private practice must, unless it is inappropriate in the circumstances:

(1) ensure that clients know the name and status of the person responsible for the day-to-day conduct of the matter and the principal responsible for its overall supervision;

(2) ensure that clients know who to approach in the event of any problem with the service provided; and

(3) ensure that clients are, at all relevant times, given any appropriate information as to the issues raised and the progress of the matter.

Many firms have devised a client care booklet, and this sets out the necessary information in a pleasing and well-presented way. Other firms send a standard form of letter which each conveyancing executive adapts according to his or her circumstances. In any event, the letter—with or without an accompanying brochure—must state who will be in charge of the day-to-day conduct of the matter; who will be the partner in charge of supervising the conduct of the matter; to whom complaints should be made if anything goes wrong; the extent of the work to be undertaken, and the fee structure applicable. Sometimes, clients are requested to confirm their agreement by countersigning a copy of the letter.

4 Dealing with non-solicitors

There are two classes of non-solicitor conveyancers; licenced conveyancers and unqualified conveyancers. The former should present few problems, the latter present many problems.

The significance of ascertaining the identity of the representative on the other side of a transaction is very important in conveyancing work, as so much of that work depends upon the exchange of undertakings, the operation of one of The Law Society formulae on exchange of contracts, the National Protocol and the code for completion by post. These are all matters of pure practice and not law. They are recognised as between solicitors, but are they recognised outside the profession?

(1) *Licensed conveyancers.* It is always wise to check that the representatives of the other party to a transaction are what they say they are. If you are dealing with licenced conveyancers, few problems arise. Licenced conveyancers are treated on an equal footing when it comes to conveyancing practice, and undertakings given by them should be recognised.

(2) *Unqualified conveyancers.* Under the Solicitors Act 1974, it is an offence for an unqualified person to prepare a contract for sale or a deed, unless it is done purely voluntarily without payment. Someone who attempts to do this, who is not a solicitor, barrister or licenced conveyancer commits a criminal offence. A conveyancer acting on the other side can be guilty of procuring the commission of such an offence.

Watch out for the notepaper you receive from representatives on the other side of a transaction. Sometimes, the notepaper will only provide details of academic qualifications.

5 Providing quotations

Rule 15 of the Solicitors Practice Rules 1990 effectively obliges a solicitor to provide a client with an estimate of the likely cost of a transaction — indeed this rule relates to work beyond conveyancing transactions. In practice, it has become a commercial necessity not only to provide an estimate, but to give a quotation. This is the invariable practice now in residential conveyancing, though not in commercial transactions, where a specific quotation may not be possible. A variety of different arrangements exist between solicitors and large business clients, but most business clients will be keen to obtain the most cost-effective provision of legal services to their own company.

Sometimes a bill is paid by another solicitor's client. If this is the case, then it is important that the solicitor of the paying client obtains an estimate of any such costs. It has been known for solicitors' charges raised against another solicitor's client to be higher than usual, and you should guard against this happening.

Provision of an estimate

It is important that one's anxiety to obtain the job does not lead one to mislead a client about the additional cost of disbursements or VAT. It is very important to make it clear to the client whether there will be disbursements, and if so, what they will amount to, and it is also important to make it clear as to whether the quotation of your firm's fees includes or excludes VAT. Some practitioners may not be VAT registrable, but most are. In former times, it was not unheard of to add postage and photocopying charges as disbursements, but this is no longer current practice.

Since quotations are now more common that estimates, a solicitor is not at liberty to charge more if the work turns out to be more complicated than originally anticipated. There is some advantage in providing a quotation, however. A quotation which has been accepted by the client is subject to s 57 of the Solicitors Act 1974. If the client has signed to accept it, and if it has been provided in writing, then the client cannot subsequently complain about it once the work is completed. Clients who refuse to pay a solicitor's bill because they consider it to be too high are entitled to apply to The Law Society for a remuneration certificate (see below). This is not available to a client where a s 57 agreement has been made.

Disputes concerning costs for all non-contentious business are governed by the Solicitors Remuneration Order 1972. This Order provides a procedure whereby The Law Society determines 'such sum as may be fair and reasonable, having regard to all the circumstances of the case' (Rule 2). The Law Society will take the following into account:
(1) The complexity or difficulty of the matter.
(2) The skill, or specialised knowledge required.
(3) The time spent.
(4) The number and the importance of the documents prepared and read.
(5) The amount or value of the transaction.
(6) The importance of the matter to the client.

The effect of Rule 15 of the Solicitors Practice Rules 1990 is expressly to state the elements in the contract between the solicitor and the client which might otherwise be deemed to be implied. Most firms' client care packages refer to the client's obligation to pay appropriate amounts for the services rendered.

It is important to send a bill of costs to the client fairly quickly after the end of the work undertaken. Disputes regularly arise in respect of those bills which follow six or 12 months after the work is finished. This is bad practice, and does not make for good client relations.

Dispute as to costs

If a client has not paid a solicitor's bill, then the solicitor is obliged to give one month's notice to the client, during which time the client can apply to The Law Society for a remuneration certificate. Appropriate standard wording to this effect is printed on the back of the bills of most large firms of solicitors. If the client fails to respond during this notice period, then the firm of solicitors in question may proceed directly to recover the amount of the bill through the usual county court procedures.

As an alternative to a remuneration certificate, the client may apply to have his bill taxed by the High Court. The costs of an application for taxation must be borne by the client. If the taxing officer allows less then one half of the sum charged to the client by the bill, he is under a duty to bring the facts of the case to the attention of the The Law Society. A third party who is responsible for paying the costs can apply for a third party taxation within three months of the delivery of the bill.

A lien exists by virtue of s 73 of the Solicitors Act 1974 in respect of the client's papers. Until the bill is paid, the solicitor is not under an obligation to release those papers, either personally to the client or to another firm of solicitors.

6 Issuing a contract to more than one purchaser

The conduct of a contract race is a matter of concern and interest to The Law Society. Contract races are an example of a situation where a solicitor may be unwillingly involved in a difficult transaction, and therefore strict rules provided by The Law Society must be followed. The procedure applies regardless of whether the original contract is sent out simultaneously to both buyers' conveyancers or at different times.

Many conveyancers and estate agents go out of their way to avoid a contract race from the beginning. It is, of course, always open to a seller to withdraw a contract from a buyer and send out the contract to an alternative buyer's solicitor. In this way, only one contract is out at any given point in time, and the rules for the engagement of a contract race do not therefore come into play.

The rules

The buyer's conveyancer must be notified at once when a contract race is to begin. Notification must be made in writing. It is vital that the precise terms of the race are set out. Each buyer must know what has to be done in order to win the race. For example, it may well be that the seller agrees to exchange contracts with the first buyer to deposit a signed contract and a deposit cheque at the seller's conveyancer's office.

The clear terms of the contract race must be discussed with, and explained to, the seller. The seller might also be told that because there is so much anxiety involved in contract races, he could lose the interest of both prospective buyers. Great caution must be exercised.

The existence of a contract race is not affected by the decision of the seller to allow each contract to contain a different price.

Conflict of interest

As explained above, conflict of interest rules must be carefully followed by conveyancers all the time. It is virtually impossible for the conveyancer to act for two prospective purchasers on a contract race, and instructions must be declined in such a situation.

7 Undertakings in the conveyancing transaction

The provision of undertakings most commonly occurs on completion, where tasks remain to be fulfilled. It is particularly common with regard to the discharge of the seller's subsisting mortgage. Generally, such discharge cannot take place until the proceeds of sale become available to pay off that mortgage. The receipted mortgage deed or the Form 53 will be sent to the buyer's conveyancer as soon as possible after the completion, and the appropriate form of undertaking, either in The Law Society's recommended form or as part of the replies to the completion information and requisitions on title form will be given.

Another common occasion for the provision of an undertaking is when your client is to be responsible for someone else's costs. This may commonly occur when acting for the acquirer of a lease or when a deed of easement is being granted. The extent of an undertaking as to costs in those cases should be limited by the provision of a maximum figure.

Undertakings must be given with caution, and on all occasions must be carefully worded. They are an obligatory commitment on the part of the solicitor and, for that matter, a licensed conveyancer. Breach of an undertaking can ultimately lead to disciplinary proceedings. It is professional misconduct.

Once an undertaking has been fulfilled, a formal discharge should be requested.

In order to remind oneself that undertakings have been given on a particular file, the file should be carefully marked. This makes it apparent to anyone else dealing with that particular file that undertakings remain to be fulfilled. It is important not to do anything on that file which makes it impossible to fulfil the undertakings (eg sending out the money to the client instead of using it to redeem a mortgage).

Part 4

Conveyancing and taxation

Chapter 20

Income tax

Taxation implications arising from land transactions are not necessarily foremost in the mind of the conveyancer and many conveyancers do not possess particular expertise in the law relating to taxation. The purpose of this chapter and Chapters 21–23 below is to alert the conveyancer to those occasions when a knowledge of taxation is important, if only to refer the client to more specialist advice.

1 Income tax relief (MIRAS)

Purchasers of a residential property which they intend to use as their main home are currently entitled to limited income tax relief on the instalments they pay to their mortgagee. At the time of writing, this has been reduced to 15% (tax year 1995/96). It is anticipated that the relief granted to mortgage payers will continue to be reduced and may within the lifetime of this book be completely removed as a concession to house purchasers.

The relief is limited to the first £30,000 of the loan, but most mortgages will be for more than this, and the bank or building society in question will usually make the appropriate adjustments to secure a net monthly payment on the first £30,000.

The relief is available only for mortgages used for purchase. It is not available for money raised for any other purpose, including home improvements.

It is important to ensure that your client is properly advised by the bank or building society with regard to their MIRAS entitlement. Clearly, the arrangements will not relate to a client of foreign domicile whose income comes from abroad. Not all building societies will offer a net payment at source. Sometimes, borrowers will have to make the claim at the end of the tax year by arranging to submit to the Revenue themselves the appropriate reclaim form or by arranging for their accountants to deal with this procedure on their behalf. This will particularly apply if the mortgage was on a property of mixed residential/commercial use.

2 Re-mortgages

It is particularly vital to check the position on a re-mortgage. Many conveyancers are currently involved in quite a lot of re-mortgaging instructions. Make absolutely certain that any new loan intended to replace an existing loan carries with it the same MIRAS entitlement. Sometimes, where the new re-mortgage is for more than the old mortgage, there will be two new loan accounts, thereby preserving the integrity of the first qualifying for tax purposes.

Chapter 21

Value added tax

1 In general

Generally, there is no value added tax in respect of residential dealings. VAT is, however, applicable to commercial property and extreme care needs to be taken when acting for a purchaser of freehold or of leasehold commercial premises.

If the vendor of a commercial property is registered for VAT, then in all likelihood you will have to add VAT to the purchase price. The implication for your client purchaser is not serious if your client is also registered for VAT, but if this is not the case, it can have a significant impact. The intention to charge VAT is often referred to in the special conditions on the contract.

The same applies to a quoted amount of rent under a lease. Some commercial landlords charge VAT and others do not. This question should always be asked of a prospective landlord's solicitors. Again, its significance is greatest when the proposed tenant is not registered or registrable for VAT purposes.

Where the price of the property includes VAT, stamp duty is payable on the total VAT inclusive sum. The same applies when calculating the amount of stamp duty payable on the rent under release. VAT will be added in order to calculate the total amount of stamp duty due.

2 Mixed property

In the case of a shop with a flat above, the purchase price of the entire building can be split—an amount can be attributed to the value of the shop and a further amount attributed to the value of the flat. Difficulties may arise, however, with regard to the foundations and the roof. The best advice is to check the position with the local office of HM Customs and Excise in order to be absolutely certain.

3 Charities

Many charities are in the business of acquiring shops up and down the country. If a charity uses a shop for the purpose of a business, then standard rate VAT is payable.

4 Building works

The cost of altering or enlarging an existing building attracts VAT. This applies, even if the building is for residential use. However, the reconstruction of a listed building may be zero rated. Again, it is important to check the position with the local office of HM Customs and Excise.

Chapter 22

Capital gains tax

The incidence of capital gains tax is a very important consideration when a client is proposing a deed of gift or when a client is purchasing a property in which he does not intend to live. A conveyancer may be able to give only generalised advice, and then refer the client to more specialist advice. It is, nevertheless, vital to discuss this issue with the client at the outset of a proposed acquisition or a proposed transaction which may give rise to CGT.

1 Private residence

The Inland Revenue has clarified its interpretation of a number of points concerning CGT relief for principal private residencies.

(1) *Sale of house and garden.* No relief is due on the sale of a garden when it is sold separately from the house and after the sale of the house. We have always known this but it is an important point to remember.

(2) *Delays in the occupation of a property.* Any delays in the occupation of a property as a residence at the start of ownership are regarded as periods of ownership for the purposes of relief. However, the delay must not exceed one year, or longer if there are good reasons for exceptional delay. The Inland Revenue's interpretation of this is that no extension is allowed where the period of delay is more than two years. If the delay is between one and two years, it is left to the discretion of local district inspectors to decide what constitutes a good reason for exceptional delay. The Inland Revenue expects the reasons to be factors outside the taxpayer's control.

(3) *Periods of absence.* Relief is due for periods of absence from the home only if the home was the taxpayer's residence at sometime both before and after the period of absence. The Inland Revenue takes the view that the question of whether, during the period

concerned, the property has been a residence is one of fact. A minimum period is not specified and the Inland Revenue does not want to impose one. It considers that it is the quality of occupation which determines whether a property is its owner's residence and not the length of occupation.

(4) *Elections by married couples.* When a couple marry and both spouses own a residence, a new two year period for making a principal private residence (PPR) election begins. Where one spouse owns more than one property and the other owns none and there is no change on marriage the Inland Revenue takes the view that a fresh election period does not begin since there has been no change in the combination of residences owned by either spouse and neither spouse needs to become party to any existing election to which they had not been a party. A notice has to be given by both spouses only where it affects them both.

Where the spouses jointly own more than one property but neither separately owns any other property a new period of election will still begin on marriage.

(5) *Anti-avoidance.* There is no PPR relief in cases where:
  (1) A property is acquired wholly or partly to realise a gain.
  (2) There is expenditure on a property wholly or partly to realise a gain.

Although the Inland Revenue acknowledges that most people who buy a home hope that in the fulness of time they will make a profit on its disposal, the legislation will be used where the primary purpose of the acquisition was an early disposal of the profit. The same approach is taken for (2) above. The second part is more often applied than the first and the common circumstances in which it may be applied are:
  (i) Acquisition by a leaseholder of a superior interest in the property eg the freehold.
  (ii) Conversion of an undivided property into flats.
  (iii) Barn conversions and other developments of outbuildings or of the land attached to the property.

In deciding whether a restriction to the PPR relief is appropriate under (ii) above the Inland Revenue will ignore cases in which the only relevant expenditure is incurred on obtaining planning permission or removing restrictive covenants.

(6) *Use of property for business.* PPR relief is restricted for parts of property used exclusively for business. It applies where the

part of the property concerned has been exclusively so used throughout the period of ownership. It does not refer to use only at the date of disposal. Where the restriction applies, no relief is due on the part of the property used for business even for the last three years of ownership. Since relief does not apply to the business part, no relief can be given for that part for any period.

(7) *Scope of 'dwellinghouse'*. An ancillary building cannot form part of a dwellinghouse for PPR relief purposes unless the building is within the 'curtilage' of the main house.

Where dispersed groups of buildings have a clear relationship with each other they will fall into a single curtilage if they constitute an integral whole. Whether one building is part and parcel of another will depend primarily on whether there is a close geographical relationship beween them. **Because the test is to identify an integral whole, a wall or fence separating two buildings will normally be sufficient to establish that they are not within the same curtilage**. Similarly, a public road or stretch of tidal water will set a limit to the curtilage of the building. Buildings which are within the curtilage of a main house will normally pass automatically on a conveyance of that house without having to be specifically mentioned.

(8) *Succession of spouse*. Where a spouse inherits a property from the other spouse, he or she also inherits any period of PPR ownership the other spouse might have obtained. The Inland Revenue has confirmed that this is not overriden by TCGA 1992, s 62 which provides that a legatee acquires an inherited asset for CGT purposes on the date of death.

(9) *Disposal by beneficiaries*. Where a beneficiary disposes of inherited property, the position is that the beneficiary's period of ownership begins at the date of death. Where the beneficiary does not become resident until a later date, the period prior to taking up occupation will not qualify for relief unless it falls within the final 36 months prior to disposal.

(10) *Deceased person's estates*. Relief is available to personal representatives when they dispose of a property which before and after the deceased's death has been used as the only or main residence by individuals who under the will or intestacy are entitled to the whole or substantially the whole of the proceeds of sale of the property. The Inland Revenue interprets 'substantially the whole' as 75% or more.

2 Holiday homes

If the owner has a second home for holidays or weekends, then that second home will not qualify for CGT relief. In fact, it is up to the owner to decide which of his two properties will qualify for CGT relief.

3 Payment of CGT

It is important not to forget that since separate taxation of married couples, each spouse has his or her annual allowance for CGT purposes (currently £5,800 per year). It is not impossible that any gain made on the sale of the property may be within these allowances. However, it is equally important to note that any other gains made in the tax year in question will also be taken into account at the same time, in order to provide an aggregate gain for the purposes of the client's CGT liability.

A conveyancer should check the position with regard to the likelihood of the payment of CGT upon receipt of instructions. Advice should be given at an early stage. It is easy to overlook the possibility of the payment of CGT when dealing with a deed of gift. If the recipient receives a property under a deed of gift, or indeed if the property forms part of an inheritance which is then not lived in and subsequently sold or subsequently redeveloped and sold in parts, then CGT will be payable upon realisation of all or part of the asset. The possibility that this may happen is something that should be mentioned to the recipient, and for that matter to any donor or testator, at an early stage.

CGT applies to businesses in the same way as it applies to individuals, but it does not apply to charities.

A 'disposal' of a property is made at the time of the contract, and not at the time of completion. It is the date of the contract that is used for the purposes of assessment to tax, although clearly, no tax becomes payable unless the contract is completed.

Chapter 23

Stamp duty

1 Stamp Office publications

The Inland Revenue Stamp Office issues a series of notes for guidance purposes only and these include the following publications which are obtainable from the Inland Revenue:
(1) Stamp Duty on buying a freehold house in England and Wales and in Northern Ireland—SO1.
(2) The Stamp Office Customer Promise—SO2.
(3) The Stamp Office Adjudication Customer Promise—SO3.
(4) How to Get The Most Out of Your Stamp Office—SO4.
(5) Common Stamp Duty Forms and How to Complete Them—SO5.
(6) Stamp Duty on Buying a Leasehold Domestic Property—SO7.
(7) Stamp Duty on Agreement Securing Short Tenancies—SO8.
(8) A Table of Ad Valorem Duties—SO9.
(9) Penalties: An Explanation of Penalties Payable When Having Documents Stamped Late—SO10.

2 Penalties for late stamping

It is obligatory to present your document to the Stamp Office within 30 days of its date. Delay authorises the Stamp Office to impose penalties pursuant to s 15 of the Stamp Act 1891. The full penalty is £10 plus interest at 5% per year on the outstanding duty where this is more than £10, plus a sum equal to the amount of duty outstanding. Section 15 also imposes a fine of £10, but in practice this is ignored.

3 Freehold property

The sale of freehold property where the price is £60,000 or more will attract duty at the flat rate of 1%. Where the price is less than £60,000 no stamp duty is payable; however, the transfer still needs to be submitted for a particulars delivered stamp to be impressed upon it. There is no need for the transfer to be sent separately to the Stamp Office for this purpose. As long as the appropriate particulars delivered form is complete, this can be dealt with by the Land Registry upon submission or first registration or registration of the dealing.

In order to avoid the payment of stamp duty on transactions of property costing less than £60,000, it is important to ensure that the following certificate of value is endorsed on all transfer deeds at the end thereof:

It is HEREBY CERTIFIED that the transaction hereby effected does not form part of a larger transaction or of a series of transactions in respect of which the amount or value or the aggregate amount or value of the consideration exceeds £60,000.

It will be noted that this certificate prevents splitting up a transaction into lots of small parts in order to avoid payment of duty on the whole. Any such procedure would be an illegal way of avoiding duty properly payable, and a solicitor who was party to such an action would find himself in trouble.

4 Leases

The sale of an existing lease is subject to stamp duty in the same way as freehold property. On the grant of a new lease, stamp duty is payable on the basis of the amount of rent and the length of the term. Most conveyancers will have stamp duty tables indicating the appropriate amount, and as mentioned above, you should not forget to add VAT when calculating stamp duty due on the rental quoted in the lease.

Leases are completed in duplicate—the original, plus a counterpart. £0.50 is the fixed duty applicable to a counterpart lease.

5 Exemptions

There are a number of documents set out in the Schedule to the Stamp Duty (Exempt Instruments) Regulations 1987 in respect of which no duty is payable. These are as follows:

A. The vesting of property subject to a trust in the trustees of the trust on the appointment of a new trustee or in the continuing trustees on the retirement of a trustee.

B. The conveyance or transfer of property the subject of a specific devise or legacy to the beneficiary named in the will (or his nominee).

C. The conveyance or transfer of property which forms part of an intestate's estate to the person entitled on intestacy (or his nominee).

D. The appropriation of property within s 84(4) of the Finance Act 1985 (death: appropriation in satisfaction of a general legacy of money) or s 84(5) or (7) of that Act (death: appropriation in satisfaction of any interest of surviving spouse and in Scotland also of any interest of issue).

E. The conveyance or transfer of property which forms part of the residuary estate of a testator to a beneficiary (or his nominee) entitled solely by virtue of his entitlement under the will.

F. The conveyance or transfer of property out of a settlement in or towards satisfaction of a beneficiary's interest not being an interest acquired for money or money's worth being a conveyance or transfer constituting a distribution of property in accordance with the provisions of the settlement.

G. The conveyance or transfer of property on and in consideration only of marriage to a party to the marriage (or his nominee) or to trustees to be held on the terms of a settlement made in consideration of the marriage.

H. The conveyance or transfer of property within s 83(1) of the Finance Act 1985 (transfers in connection with divorce etc).

I. The conveyance or transfer by the liquidator of property which formed part of the assets of the company in liquidation to a shareholder of that company (or his nominee) in or towards satisfaction of the shareholder's rights on a winding up.

J. The grant in fee simple of an easement in or over land for no consideration in money or money's worth.

K. The grant of a servitude for no consideration in money or money's worth.

L. The conveyance or transfer of property operating as a voluntary disposition *inter vivos* for no consideration in money or money's worth nor any consideration referred to in s 57 of the Stamp Act 1891 (conveyance in consideration of a debt etc).

M. The conveyance or transfer of property by an instrument within s 84(1) of the Finance Act 1985 (death: varying disposition).

Again, it is important that the above documents contain the appropriate certificate in order to avoid duty, and this certificate reads as follows:

It is HEREBY CERTIFIED that this instrument falls within Category [ ] in the Schedule to the Stamp Duty (Exempt Instruments) Regulations 1987.

In the above cases, the document does not need to be sent to the Stamp Office.

6 Exchanges of land

Stamp duty is now payable on the full value of each property being exchanged and is no longer confined to the value of any equality money paid. No duty is payable if both properties are valued at £60,000 or less, but where they are valued at more than this, then stamp duty is payable on either or both at the standard 1% rate.

7 Fixtures, fittings and contents

These are not subject to stamp duty, hence the fact that they are generally listed separately in a contract, and their value is not carried through to the transfer deed. It is very important that a valuation of these items is realistic and is not an over-valuation for the purpose of avoiding stamp duty.

It is important to note that where land is exempt from VAT, it is possible that the sale of the contents may attract VAT. The position needs to be carefully checked in each case, because there is no general rule. It will depend on the nature of the transaction and the identity of the parties to it.

Part 5

Conveyancing and agricultural land

Chapter 24

Searches and enquiries relating to agricultural land

1 Introduction

The procedure for buying and selling agricultural land is more or less identical to that involved in buying and selling residential properties.

There are certain ancient rights which may arise with agricultural land; but more commonly, the buying and selling of agricultural land will also involve the sale or purchase of a working farm. As with a transaction involving any other on-going business, there are questions that arise with regard to the apportionment of the price as between the land and the value of the fixtures and fittings or items sold with the farm and also the value of any growing crops or quotas that the land may have the benefit of.

On the sale of a farm, accountancy advice may also be important, in order to ensure that one is not unwittingly acquiring a tax liability. It is important to establish the VAT position.

2 Searches

As with residential conveyancing, the usual local and water authority searches must be carried out. However, with regard to the former, additional enquiries will be relevant. For example, it will be important to establish whether a footpath traverses the property. A commons registration search is particularly pertinent to agricultural land, and this will show whether you are acquiring any rights of common over adjacent land, or whether any part of the land that you are being offered for purchase is in fact registered land.

If the property is located in a mining area, then carry out the appropriate mining search to ascertain the position with regard to current workings.

3 Pre-contract enquiries

It is important to study the agents' particulars and to supplement that study with the knowledge you have gained from discussing the property with your client, in order to ascertain which additional enquiries you wish to raise with regard to the proposed acquisition of a farm. Such enquiries will vary in every case, and so long as the enquiries are specific to the property and not of a general nature, then you should not feel constrained in the questions you pose.

Some of the more usual extra enquiries might include the following:

(1) You will need to ascertain the position concerning growing crops. If these are not included in the sale, the vendor may wish to reserve for himself the 'right of holdover' beyond the completion date up to a likely latest date for harvesting. This applies to all the crops which are, by their very nature, harvested at different times of the year.

(2) It is important to ascertain whether the land carries with it the benefit of a milk quota, and if so you need to ascertain further details concerning that quota before you proceed (see below).

(3) The plan and the boundary lines are very important when dealing with rural property. In general, the rule of the country is that the boundary lies on the far side of the ditch from the hedge. This may or may not invariably apply, but it is certainly the way that most farmers regard the position.

(4) Land drainage is very important and easily overlooked by the conveyancer more accustomed to urban transactions. It is very important to establish the lie of the land and the ditches into which it drains, or otherwise to establish whether there are land drains under the land in question.

(5) You will often find water pipes have to travel some distance to get to the property from the nearest mains supply. It is important to establish the age of these pipes, because their repair or replacement could be the sole responsibility of your client acquiring the farm. Again, as in all cases, check the appropriate easement exists in case the pipes or any other services need to travel some distance over neighbouring land in the ownership of a third party.

(6) It is important to include questions relating to land which is 'set aside'. You need to find out the use of the land on 31 December 1991, even if the land was not part of the seller's holding at that time. At the very least, the contract must contain a warranty by the vendor as to that use. You will then need to go on to establish the cropping history of the land since 31 December 1991. Ask the seller to supply copies of the IACS forms.

Similarly, if the seller has already submitted a set aside claim, the buyer will be required to agree not to make competing claims and to comply with the set aside rules. In addition, the buyer will have to agree not to prevent entry by officials from the Ministry of Agriculture and Fisheries onto the land which is the subject of the contract.

It is possible for both the new and the old occupiers to apply for set aside. Accordingly, the solicitors should check who is to make the set aside claim.

(7) The local land charges search will indicate whether or not the property is listed as being of special architectural or historical interest. Although this is not peculiar to rural property, it is more likely to crop up with property in rural areas, and you should raise further additional enquiries of the vendor's solicitors concerning notice of this, and in particular watch for any alterations that may have been made to the property subsequently.

(8) Depending on the nature of the farm (eg pig farm) discharge licences granted by the National Rivers Authority or by HM Inspector of Pollution under the Water Act 1989, the Environmental Protection Act 1990 or the Water Resources Act 1991 may be required. It is important to ascertain the position and also to check that there have been no breaches of those licences or no unauthorised pollutants discharged into the water courses around the property that your client proposes to purchase. An Environment Bill is imminent and will set up a new Environmental Protection Agency to take over regulatory functions with effect from 1 April 1996.

(9) A plentiful supply of water is important in order to ensure the health of the crops on the farm. Many farms carry with them one or more water abstraction licences under the Water Resources Act 1991 and you should raise enquiries to confirm that these licences do exist and that the benefit of them may be assigned. Sometimes, you may find that a new licence or a new series of licences have to be drawn in favour of your client purchaser, and in this respect you should contact the appropriate Authority in order to ensure that your client has the benefit of the arrangements he will require in order to provide water for his farm.

Each licence carries with it a stipulation as to the amount of water that may be used. When the licence expires, there is no automatic right to the issue of a new one. An assignment from one person to another is possible only where the buyer buys precisely the same land as the seller owned.

It must not be overlooked that even for a domestic supply, many rural properties do not have mains water. Some have their own private water supply which may require pumping up from a well adjacent to the main farmhouse, for example. The position needs to be generally ascertained.

(10) The availability or otherwise of sporting rights is also a common question attaching to rural properties. Sometimes, sporting rights may be let to a third party, and you need to be particularly watchful of the existence of such a lease. Specific enquiries should be raised.

(11) If you are concerned with livestock (in particular pigs and cattle) you should ask questions about the history of notifiable diseases on the farm. You need to know whether the farm has had a recent history of disease.

4 Value added tax

As with the sale of any business as a going concern, the incidence of value added tax needs to be considered. Where both parties are registered for VAT, no tax is payable. However, if the buyer is not registered but the seller is, then VAT is payable in addition to the purchase price. VAT is chargeable on business property, and applies to 'chattels' and the land alike.

5 Planning

It is important to ensure that any agricultural buildings erected comparatively recently have the benefit of planning permission. Some agricultural buildings fall within the Agricultural General Development Order.

Something else to watch on the planning front with rural property is the not infrequent occurrence of a condition attaching to a planning permission for a property that may have been built some years ago, whereby it may be occupied only by someone who is employed for the purposes of agriculture. This practice is not current now, but at one time it used to be commonplace. Check the planning consents for properties built within the last 30 or 40 years in or around the farm in order to ensure that no such restriction subsists. Where one does exist, it halves the property value.

6 Pipes and pylons

In some parts of the country, rural property is often affected by the network of electricity cables above the land and a network of pipelines underneath the land. Sometimes a deed of easement will have been granted in favour of the appropriate electricity company or British Gas, but more commonly, there will be a wayleave consent. Wayleave agreements are commonplace and again, are more likely than not to apply to agricultural properties. Inspect any wayleave agreements carefully. If you are buying only part of the land covered by a wayleave agreement then the electricity company, or whoever may have the benefit of it, will need to issue a new wayleave agreement to you, dealing with that part of the land that your client is to acquire.

7 Highway agreement

Again, highway agreements are not peculiar to agricultural land, but quite often hidden amongst the title deeds there will be a dedication agreement whereby a corner or a boundary of a field has been dedicated to the appropriate highway authority for road straightening or road widening. It is important to raise the usual enquiries in order to establish the precise position.

8 Agricultural credits search

A fixed or floating charge made by a farmer in favour of a bank over agricultural land must be registered within seven days of its completion. If this is not done, it is unenforceable. In order to check the position, the purchaser of farming assets should make an agricultural credits search. Where the search reveals a subsisting charge, then the seller must discharge this on or before completion. If the search carries no priority period, a further search ought to be done before completion.

The search is made by sending form AC6 in duplicate to the Agricultural Credits Department, Burrington Way, Plymouth.

9 Completion arrangements

For most residential property completions, the balance of the purchase money is all that is required on completion. This is not likely to be the case in respect of the sale of a working farm, and the following might additionally need to be taken into account:

(1) VAT—as described previously.
(2) Apportionment of any agricultural rents, property rents or wayleave payments.
(3) Payments for items included in the sale such as agricultural machinery.
(4) Payment for stock at valuation.
(5) Any adjustments that may be agreed in respect of holdover arrangements.

Chapter 25

Agricultural quotas

Any sugar beet quota must be assigned to the buyer by express provision in the contract. The same applies to potato quotas. The position relating to milk quotas requires a little more analysis.

The Common Agricultural Policy of the European Union has regulated the amount of milk and milk products being produced in the EEC. A levy is payable if a producer exceeds his quota. The quota attaches to the land and therefore passes with the land.

1 Additional enquiries

It follows from the above that additional pre-contract enquiries should be asked in appropriate cases where a milk quota is likely to form part of the business of the farm. You will need to know the amount of the quota attaching to the land now being offered for sale. Sometimes, an apportionment of the quota will have been made if the land holding is to be split up.

Acting for a buyer of a farm which has the benefit of a milk quota, you should ask for evidence of the amount of milk produced to date and the allocation of quota and you will need to make sure that the quota is registered in the seller's name.

The buyer is well advised to secure details relating to livestock and cropping in 1983. 1983 was the year by reference to which levels of milk production were fixed at the time of the introduction of milk quotas.

2 The completion documents

It is important that reference to the transfer of the quota is included in the contract for sale, and transfer deed. In the former, the appropriate additional clause must refer to the transfer of the quota and commit the seller to the supply of the appropriate form duly signed for transfer of the milk quota. The transfer deed should contain a clause transferring the quota to the buyer.

On completion, the buyer must obtain a completed form T1/2 which is a consent to the transfer of the quota. Also, for collection on completion, you will need to obtain a licence to sell milk direct to the public.

Within two months of completion the buyer must give notice of change of occupation to the Milk Marque and send to them the quota transfer form (Form T 1/2).

3 Apportionment of quotas

If a buyer buys only part of a seller's land, he will acquire only part of the quota attaching to it. The parties therefore have to agree on the appropriate apportionment of the quota. If this is not possible within two months, then there is an arbitration procedure. The President of the Royal Institution of Chartered Surveyors will appoint an arbitrator to decide the matter on the payment of an appropriate fee. The arbitrator will consider in particular the milk production in the area of land being sold over the preceding five years.

Chapter 26

Agricultural tenancies

1 Tied accommodation

This relates to houses occupied by agricultural or forestry workers. The position depends upon occupation before 15 January or after 14 January 1989.

Occupation prior to 15 January 1989

Because low rents or agricultural holding exemptions usually exclude agricultural and forestry workers from the Rent Act 1977, they are protected by the Rent (Agriculture) Act 1976. To qualify, an agricultural worker must have worked full time in agriculture in at least 91 of the last 104 weeks. The worker must have exclusive occupation and the property in which he lives must be owned by his employer.

Such a worker will enjoy full security during his employment and after his retirement, redundancy or incapacity. The landlord can apply to the local authority to re-house the worker only if the property is required for another employee. The property can pass to the worker's spouse, or his immediate family may succeed to the tenancy on death under the Rent (Agriculture) Act 1976 or the Housing Act 1988 if after 14 January 1989. The rent is strictly controlled under the relevant Act.

Occupation after 14 January 1989

On expiry of the contractual arrangement, an assured agricultural occupancy will arise under the Housing Act 1988. The criteria for eligibility are similar to those under the Rent (Agriculture) Act 1976.

2 Grazing licences

Generally speaking, a grazing licence for a period of less than one year will not provide the licensee with any right to renewal or security of tenure. A grazing licence may well be appropriate when a landlord has a few acres to dispose of on a temporary basis, the land being surplus to his requirements. If security of tenure is to be avoided the licence document must be carefully drawn. An appropriate licence fee may freely be negotiated between the parties. A succession of licences should be avoided.

3 A *Gladstone v Bower* agreement

An agricultural tenancy will not have security of tenure under the existing agricultural holdings legislation where it is granted for a period of between 18 months and two years. Again the rent may be freely negotiated between the parties.

4 The Agricultural Tenancies Act 1995

This Act came into effect on 1 September 1995. It creates a new class of tenancy called 'the farm business tenancy' under which tenants will be able to diversify to non-agricultural enterprise, provided farming is the main business. A landlord and tenant will be free to agree a length of term, so long as at least one year's notice of termination is required. They will be able to agree on the appropriate level of rent and a landlord will have to pay compensation for any tenant's improvements. The Act is intended to free the parties, particularly landlords, from the restriction of the existing Agricultural Holdings legislation.

Part 6

Conveyancing and commercial leases

Chapter 27

Preliminary enquiries applicable to commercial premises

1 Introduction

The procedure and art of commercial conveyancing is very similar to that relating to residential conveyancing. The practical difference between the two is that most commercial acquisitions relate to leasehold property.

In being confronted with the acquisition of commercial property, the following questions should be posed:

(1) Is this to be the grant of a new lease by the freeholder of the property?

(2) Is this to be an assignment of an existing lease?

(3) Is this to be a sub-lease by a tenant of the property?

(4) Is this to a sub-lease or an assignment of part of a premises?

The procedure will vary slightly, depending upon which of the above paragraphs applies.

2 Enquiries of the seller/lessor/assignor

General points

In the most simple instance, the landlord will let the property to the tenant and the landlord will undertake responsibilities allotted to him in the lease and will have a direct relationship with the tenant. More professional landlords, such as those who manage a range of properties, will often appoint a firm of managing agents to deal with the administrative work on their behalf. Quite often, the fees of such agents can be recovered from the tenant on a proportionate basis as part of the service charge element catered for by the lease. Service charges are sometimes called 'additional rent'.

A management company assumes the responsibilities of a landlord most commonly in a block of flats. Generally each tenant will be required to acquire one share in the management company and therefore will be entitled to attend its general meetings. It is important to be advised of the name and address of your landlord or the secretary to the management company. It is important to ascertain the extent of the contributions towards the cost of maintaining the building.

It is important to raise practical questions abou the lease in case the practical reality has varied from the theory of the clauses in an existing leasehold document which it is sought to assign.

The significance of a rent receipt is that if one can be produced, it automatically implies compliance with the provisions of the lease by the existing tenant, who is now seeking to assign it. Ask to see a clear rent receipt.

Maintenance charges

These are more significant when dealing with the assignment of a lease relating to a unit within a large block. It is important to ascertain what the maintenance charges have been hitherto, as these can often be very expensive. It is important to ask whether any unusual expense is likely in the next year or two. This information is needed to enable the prospective tenant to make the necessary financial calculations in order to weigh up the cost of the premises.

Management company

As explained above the existence of a management company would be more likely where there is a block of residential flats than in dealing with a commercial lease. It is, however, worthy of mention at this point. Many landlords dispose of their day-to-day administrative responsibility for running the premises to a management company. The management company will have as its members each tenant. Upon acquiring the lease the tenant will have a share certificate to signify his membership.

In such a case, where a management company exists to administer the building on behalf of the landlord, you should ask for a copy of the Memorandum and Articles of Association of the company. You should ask to see the prospective assignor's share certificate. You should ask to see the management accounts for the last three years and also for contact names for the management company.

Sometimes, the freehold of the building will be disposed of by the landlord to the management company. It is important to ascertain the position in this respect, and equally to ascertain whether there is any imminent proposal to dispose of the freehold in this way.

Complaints

It is important to ascertain whether the assignee has received any complaints from the landlord, the management company or from any other tenant about the way that the property has been managed or conducted.

Insurance

It is common practice in commercial leaseholds for the landlord to insure the building and to recoup the cost on a proportionate basis from each tenant. Where the landlord maintains the insurance policy, you should ask to see a copy of it, so that you can satisfy yourself about the range of risks it covers. You will also need to know that the premiums have been paid up to date. You will need to know the extent of the current cover.

Maintenance responsibilities

If decoration inside or out, or both, is the responsibility of the tenant, you will need to know that the tenant has complied with his obligations in this respect prior to the assignment of the lease to your client. Check when the property was last redecorated in accordance with the convenants in the lease in order to be sure that there is no possibility of complaints being raised about the non-performance of such obligations prior to the assignment.

Alterations

Generally, a lease will prohibit alterations being made to the property of a structural kind, and other alterations are likely to be allowed only with the landlord's consent. You should ask whether any alterations have been made, with or without the consent of the landlord.

Planning permission

Detailed enquiries about the precise nature of the subsisting planning permission are extremely important when dealing with commercial property. Becuase of the range of use classes applying to different forms of commercial activity, you must obtain a copy of the current planning permission, and if a slight variation is likely as a result of your client's proposed business use, then you should write to the planning officer of the relevant district council. You will be concerned to establish the position under the Town and Country Planning (Use Classes) Order 1987 (SI No 764).

Access

Probably the most basic point of all—but rather crucial—is the right of access to the property if this runs through other parts of the building that are let to other tenants. It is important to establish rights of access and also rights for services to pass and repass through other property to your client's property. Your client may also need rights to dispose of his/her rubbish, to park motor vehicles and rights to use his/her property at the times of day that he/she requires it. All of this should be considered carefully by reading the draft lease in great detail when it arrives from the landlord's or assignor's solicitors.

Chapter 28

Searches applicable to commercial premises

1 Local authority search

A local land charges search and local authority search are as applicable to commercial premises as they would be to residential premises. Always carry out a local authority search whether upon the granting of a new lease, the assignment of an existing lease or the granting of an underlease of whole or part.

The local authority search will reveal:

(1) Details of the planning position in respect of the property, together with reference numbers of any planning papers which should be made available to you.

(2) Details of any proposed rearrangements concerning the highway, parking schemes etc. The position concerning the highways adjacent to the property may be of commercial significance to your client.

Environmental questions may be of particular significance to a commercial tenant, and you should note the replies to the questions in this respect particularly carefully eg whether the property is in an area zoned for smoke control.

2 Water authority search

Again, this is just as important as for a freehold property.

3 Land Registry searches

It is not normal to investigate the freehold title of the property unless you are acting for a client who is taking a long lease. Accordingly, one would not normally search either in the Public Index Map or undertake a Form 94(A) or 94(B) search. The superior title is relevant, however, to the extent that if there is a mortgage you will want to see a consent to dealing by the mortgagee prior to completion.

If you are taking the assignment of a lease which is registered (ie one over 21 years) then a Form 94(A) or 94(B) search will be necessary against that leasehold title.

4 Land charge searches and company searches

Since it is now common practice to have commercial leases running for short periods of time (eg five, or no more than ten years), most commercial leases are not registered at the Land Registry. It is therefore important to carry out a land charge search against the landlord in order to check for the usual information against him as referred to earlier in this book (see head 2 of Chapter 4).

Where a prospective landlord is a limited company, a company search should be carried out in order to check that there are no liquidation proceedings and whether there are any subsisting mortgages or debentures which would be relevant to the proposed lease in favour of your client.

5 Other searches

Other searches might apply in the same way as they would to conveyancing in respect of residential land and as is described earlier in the book (see Chapter 4).

Chapter 29

Business leases

1 The assignment of an existing lease

When dealing with the assignment of an existing lease, the assignor's solicitors will send you a copy of their client's lease. Whether or not they also send you an agreement to take the assignment varies. Sometimes, an agreement will be utilised, and on other occasions there will be no agreement on the understanding that the matter remains subject to contract until completion.

Scrutinise very carefully the lease that your client is to take. You will need to satisfy yourself from the content of this document whether or not you can advise your client to sign up to it. If it is an existing lease, there will be little you can do to alter its terms.

In most business leases, it is likely that the landlord's consent to the assignment will be needed. Generally, there will be a provision which prevents the landlord from unreasonably refusing to give that consent. The landlord may, however, with justification, ask to see references from the prospective assignee's bank and two trade references or a personal reference. Therefore, the first task when acting for a prospective assignee is to obtain the relevant references and to pass them to the assignor's solicitor. In turn, the assignor's solicitor will pass those back to the existing landlord's solicitor. If they are satisfied with the references, their permission will be granted and a licence to assign will be prepared. The form of the licence to assign will vary slightly. Apart from reciting the landlords' permission to the existing tenant to assign the lease to a new tenant, it will also commit the new tenant directly to the landlord to observe the terms and provisions of the existing lease. This direct covenant is of importance and of value to the existing landlord.

It is also common practice for the existing tenant to pay the costs of the landlord for granting a licence to assign and, generally speaking, the landlord's solicitors will not begin work until they have received an undertaking from the tenant's solicitors that their costs will be paid, regardless of whether or not the matter proceeds to completion.

Once the licence to assign is dealt with, the prospective tenant's solicitor will examine the lease, carry out the necessary searches, raise pre-contract enquiries and then report to his client on the lease.

A deed of assignment is necessary in order to transfer an existing lease to a new tenant, and, once this is drawn and executed by both parties, completion can take place. Again, this particular part of the process is generally paid for by the incoming tenant, and his solicitors will have given an undertaking for costs at the beginning of the transaction.

2 Granting a new lease

The procedure when dealing with a brand new lease is slightly different. If coming directly from a new landlord, there is no need to be concerned about a licence to assign. However, the landlord may still want to see references in respect of the proposed tenant.

There is also much greater flexibility in negotiating and agreeing the terms of the new lease as between landlord and tenant. Typical provisions found in a lease are covered in the next chapter. Clearly, the landlord's solicitors will dispatch a draft lease which will be very favourable to the landlord in the first instance. It is the duty of the tenant's solicitors to balance the lease so that a number of the provisions are of help, support and assistance to the proposed new tenant.

On the granting of a new lease, it is very important to carry out the searches described above, and very important to ensure that no planning application is needed in order to change the authorised use of the premises. When taking an assignment of an existing lease from a business whose trading activity is roughly the same as your own client, one can anticipate, although not take for granted, that the planning use is already authorised. This is less likely to be so on the granting of a brand new lease. An existing lease will generally have a use clause which will fix the use of the premises, often regardless of whether planning permission exists or not. If taking a new lease, it is important to have this clause as wide and flexible as possible because, if you wish to assign that lease in a year or two's time, then those to whom it can be assigned will be that much greater in number.

If you allow yourself to be confined to a restrictive and unhelpful lease from the tenant's point of view, then difficulties might arise if that tenant wishes to assign. The only way that an existing lease can be varied is by a deed of variation, and subsequent negotiations for a deed of variation can be difficult and costly. It is better to have a lease which is right first time.

3 Granting a sub-lease

Most hand-leases prohibit an assignment or a sub-lease of part only of the premises, and permit an assignment of whole only with the landlord's consent—such consent not to be unreasonably withheld. Subletting, even of the whole, is very often prohibited.

The recession has meant that many more tenants have had to revert to their landlords in order to ask for the terms of their leases to be varied in order to secure their own financial survival. In difficult economic times, many landlords have seen fit to oblige, and have permitted underletting as well as assigning and of part as well as of whole.

An underlease is a new document, and the difference between granting an underlease and an assignment is that with the latter, the existing tenant remains in place and becomes known as the 'immediate landlord'. The rent in the sub-lease may or may not be controlled by that in the head-lease. The sub-lease is a new and continuing contract between the immediate landlord and the undertenant. It is important to ensure that the underlease does not contain provisions which are inconsistent with those in the head-lease. Although there is a measure of freedom in negotiating the terms of an underlease, it is very much constrained by the provisions in the head-lease which are, of course, not available for renegotiation.

4 Licence to occupy

Licences to occupy as a means of avoiding security of tenure are not to be recommended for premises fully and entirely occupied by the same licensee. However, licences to occupy do have their uses. They are appropriate for a franchisee, eg someone within a large department store who takes a certain amount of floor space. That franchisee may be moved around the store at the whim of the franchisor and, in such a case, a licence which does not confer security of tenure is the proper document.

There is, however, one particular situation where licences are not uncommon. If it is mutually agreed between the parties that there is to be no security of tenure, then it is common practice for an application to be made under the Landlord and Tenant Act 1954, s 38 that the provisions of ss 24–28 of the 1954 Act be excluded. A new tenancy ought not to begin, and occupation ought not to be taken, until the order of the court has been made. A tenant who is impatient to go in, may go in under licence prior to the granting of the order. An appropriately worded form of licence—which may be in the form of a letter from the prospective tenant to the prospective landlord—would suffice. This obliges the parties to enter into a lease as soon as the court order is made.

5 The Landlord and Tenant Act 1954

Definitions

This deals with business tenancies and Part II of the 1954 Act defines a business tenant as 'a tenant who occupies premises for the purposes of his business'.

(1) Premises include *land*.

(2) Business includes *trade, profession and employment*.

Excluded are *agricultural holdings, mining leases, public houses, lettings for six months or less* and certain other tenancies.

Determination

The landlord can terminate it ONLY by *forfeiture* or *by notice in statutory form*. OTHERWISE a tenancy within Part II of the 1954 Act is *automatically continued by the Act on the same terms*.

Landlord's statutory notice

(1) This must be in the statutory form.

(2) It must specify *a date six to 12 months ahead on which the tenancy is to end*.

(3) A fixed term tenancy may not be determined before the end of the term provided.

(4) It must also state whether the landlord would oppose an application to the court for a new tenancy, and if so on what ground.

If the notice *is not in the statutory form*, it will determine the *contractual tenancy*, but the tenant can continue in possession under the 1954 Act until a proper notice is served.

If the tenant wants a new tenancy he must inform the landlord within two months that he is not willing to give up possession, and he must apply to the court for a new tenancy not less than two months nor more than four months after the landlord's notice.

New tenancy

The tenant can request a new tenancy provided:

(1) The tenancy was for a term certain exceeding one year.

(2) The new tenancy will begin six to 12 months ahead.

(3) The request is in statutory form and contains proposals as to the terms of the new tenancy.

Application to the court

Failing agreement, application for a new tenancy is to:

(1) the *county court*—if the rateable value is less than £5,000.

(2) the *High Court*—in other cases.

The application must be made between two and four months after the landlord's notice or tenant's request.

The court *must order* a new tenancy not exceeding *14 years* at such rent and on such terms as, in the absence of agreement, it thinks fit, UNLESS the landlord can establish *one* of the following grounds set out in *Section 30*:

(a) Tenant's failure to repair.

(b) Persistent delay in paying rent.

(c) Other substantial breaches of covenant.

(d) Offer of reasonable alternative accommodation.

(e) Applicant the sub-tenant only of part and it would be more profitable to dispose of the property as a whole.

(f) The landlord has a *firm and settled intention before the end of the hearing* to demolish and reconstruct the premises.

(g) The landlord wants possession for his own business or as a residence. (Ground (g) does not apply if the landlord purchased within five years before the end of the tenancy).

The court's powers

(1) The new lease may include no greater part of the property than that originally let.

(2) In default of agreement the court must fix the 'open market rent' *without regard to the effect of the tenant's occupation*.

(3) The court may fix an interim rent to apply between the expiry of the old tenancy and commencement of the new one.

Compensation

Compensation is available to the tenant, where a new tenancy is refused on a ground relating to the landlord's convenience. The amount of the compensation equals the rateable value of the premises or if the business is at least 14 years old, twice the rateable value.

Compensation may also be available for *improvements* under the Landlord and Tenant Act 1927. The improvements must:

(1) add to the letting value; and

(2) have been carried out with the consent of the landlord.

Generally, compensation must be claimed within three months after the end of the tenancy, unless the tenancy comes to an end by effluxion of time when a claim must be made between three and six months before the end of the term.

Chapter 30

Hints for the commercial conveyancer

There follow some hints for the commercial conveyancer with regard to provisions to be found in a typical commercial lease.

(1) *Sureties.* If the proposed new lease or assignment of an existing lease is to be vested in a limited company then it is not unusual, particularly in the case of a small company, to ask for sureties or guarantors as to the performance of the covenants in the lease and in particular, the covenant to pay the necessary rent. Generally, the directors of the company will have to guarantee the company's obligations. This will provide the landlord with additional protection.

In such a case, it is very important to advise the sureties of the liability that they are accepting. It may be appropriate for them to be independently advised for fear of a conflict of interest arising between the proposed tenant company and those individuals who are required to guarantee the performance of its obligations.

(2) *Length of term.* It is currently common practice to have shorter term business leases. If the landlord insists on a longer lease, then it is not uncommon for a tenant to insist on a break clause to allow the tenant to give up the premises should his business fail. This is most important for new businesses where it is difficult to determine their future profitability. Be certain to provide this advice to a tenant starting up in business for the first time.

If properties are difficult to let in the particular locality, the landlord is not likely voluntarily to agree a surrender of the lease if the tenant subsequently gets into trading difficulties. Extracting oneself from a business lease can therefore be very costly and in the worst case, a tenant can be saddled with rental obligations lasting until the end of the contractual term unless, of course, it is possible to assign the lease or grant an underlease. Watch the provisions in any given lease for such disposal possibilities.

(3) *Stamp duty*. Clearly, the longer the term the more stamp duty is payable. We have already observed that the Inland Revenue will add VAT to the rent in order to assess the stamp duty payable (see head 4 of Chapter 23).

(4) *Registration*. A lease for 21 years or less is not capable of being registered but where a tenant is in occupation of the property the lease takes effect as an overriding interest under the Land Registration Act 1925, s 70(1)(g).

(5) *Mortgages*. If the landlord's title is subject to a mortgage, it is important to obtain the consent of that morgagee prior to the grant of the lease. Such consent is given in letter form and a commitment on the part of the landlord to hand it over prior to completion must be sought.

(6) *Landlord's covenants*. Commonly, these normally amount to two. First, there will be a covenant for quiet enjoyment and secondly, the landlord will check responsibility for insurance.

(7) *The mechanics of preparing the lease*. The lease is prepared by the landlord's solicitor in draft form. It is submitted in duplicate to the prospective tenant's solicitor for analysis. One copy may then become known as the 'travelling draft'. This will be the document on which the amendments are made in different colours by each party on each occasion that it goes to and fro.

The terms of the lease will be negotiated in accordance with the comments above. Remember that a lease for three years or less need only be in the form of a tenancy agreement. Remember also, The Law Society's Standard Business Lease, which is helpful particularly for smaller firms without a range of precedents on disk.

It is more common than not to dispense with the need for a contract. However, in so doing it is important to remember that the Inland Revenue now require the following paragraph to be added to your Lease:

We certify that there is no agreement or 'tack' to which this Lease (or tack) gives effect.

(8) *Completion*. Once the preliminary formalities have been dealt with, the lease will be ready for engrossment and this is done in two parts. The counterpart will be signed by the tenant and kept by the landlord and the original will be signed by the landlord and kept by the tenant. The original attracts ad valorem stamp duty and the counterpart attracts 50p standard duty only. Completion takes place when the two parts of the lease are formally dated and

exchanged. Rent will run from that date or from any other date from which it is agreed the lease term begins.

Rightly or wrongly, it is not unusual for tenants to take occupation prior to the completion of the leashold formalities. A cautious landlord will require some form of licence but others allow the practical arrangements to overtake the legal formalities. In such circumstances, it may therefore be agreed that the rental liability be back-dated, for example to the preceding quarter day.

In business leases, it is usual for the rent to be paid quarterly in advance by standing order. Completion may take place mid-way through a quarter and therefore, the first rental payment will relate to only a portion of that period.

(9) *Liability between the landlord and the original tenant.* It is important to advise a prospective tenant about the rules relating to 'privity of contract'. Basically, this means that the landlord and the original tenant remain liable to one another on all the covenants in the lease at any time during its contractual term. This liability on the part of the tenant continues even if the landlord changes.

The effect of this is that if an assignee of the lease cannot meet his obligations to the landlord, then the original tenant may have to resume responsibility for such matters. Most significantly, the original tenant remains liable for the rent. There has been much comment about these rules, and legislative proposals to change them.

(10) *Liability between the landlord and tenant for the time being.* The relationship between successors in title, both to the freehold and to the leasehold, is based on the doctrine of 'privity of estate'. This means that the parties are liable to one another during the currency of their tenure. They are liable for covenants 'which touch and concern the land'.

(11) *Liability between a head landlord and a sub-tenant.* A contractual relationship will be established between these two if the subtenant has entered into direct covenants with the landlord. Such a requirement is common and the appropriate provisions will be incorporated into the licence to sub-let.

The sub-tenant ought to ask to see the head lease on the grant of the sub-lease. Indeed, he will be deemed to have knowledge of the contents of the head lease even if he does not exercise his right under the Law of Property Act 1925, s 44 to inspect it.

(12) *Undertakings for landlord's costs.* In most cases dealing with the assignment of a commercial lease, the landlord is entitled to ask

the tenant to pay his reasonable charges in connection with the preparation of the necessary documents. Most landlord's solicitors will not take any steps until they have received such an undertaking from the proposed tenant's solicitor. These undertakings are given whether or not the matter proceeds to a satisfactory conclusion.

It is important not to give an open-ended undertaking. When acting for a prospective tenant you should ask for an estimate of the landlord's solicitors' costs, or otherwise you should limit the undertaking to a contribution of a certain amount.

Do not provide an undertaking as to costs unless you have your client's express instructions. Explain to your client what an undertaking means. It may be wise to obtain a sufficient sum from your client in advance. This is particularly important if the transaction fails to materialise.

The prospective tenant's solicitor can assist in keeping down costs. If he is ready with the appropriate references and prepared to let matters proceed in a relatively uncomplicated way, then this reduces the time and expense of conducting the transaction.

Chapter 31

Typical pitfalls in commercial conveyancing

1 Introduction

The purpose of this chapter is to alert you to common errors and omissions. These are all too easy to make when impatience on the part of others involved in the transaction requires you to proceed more expeditiously than you might otherwise consider prudent. This chapter therefore serves as a checklist of minimum requirements which you ought to observe prior to being persuaded to exchange contracts on the grant or the assignment of a lease, or to complete the lease itself:

(1) If it is decided to do without an agreement and proceed directly to the lease, emphasise from the beginning that all communications prior to completion are to be construed strictly subject to contract and are not in themselves capable of comprising a formal agreement to take a lease.

(2) Carry out a local authority search, and pay close attention to the authorised planning use of the premises. Insist on seeing copies of the planning permissions.

(3) Raise standard enquiries before contract and pay particular attention as to whether the rent will attract VAT or not. The landlord may elect to charge VAT and this decision will depend upon the identity and intention of the landlord. The decision is of significance to those tenants who are not themselves registered or registrable for VAT purposes. See Chapter 21.

(4) Always read the lease very carefully, even if it is extremely lengthy. When reporting to your client on its terms, send a copy of the lease as well. If the client is pressing you to go ahead speedily, you may not have the time you would otherwise wish to have to try to negotiate alterations. You should point out any clauses in the lease about which you—as the conveyancer—are unhappy and the client is then left with the decision as to whether to proceed according to his preferred timetable or whether to take a

little longer and allow you to negotiate adjustments in any aspect of the documentation about which you are unhappy.

(5) If the prospective landlord is a company, undertake a company search to check that the company is not the subject of any liquidation or receivership. If borrowing is secured on the property, ensure that appropriate consents from the mortgage lender are handed over to you on completion.

(6) Check the arrangements for access. This is particularly important if the commercial premises involved carries with it car parking in the vicinity. You will need to know that there are rights of access between the main business premises and the car parking spaces.

(7) Make certain that your client understands what the financial cost of the building will be over and above the rent. Watch carefully the service charge clauses in the lease and alert your client to the additional liability for the business rates and other outgoings. As previously mentioned in this text, make sure that there are no large expenditures in the offing which could give rise to a disproportinately large service charge in the future accounting period.

(8) If the landlord is under an obligation to insure, check the wording in the lease carefully to make sure that you know which risks will be covered. Ideally, obtain a copy of the policy from the landlord's solicitors—not just the policy schedule—the tenant may have to supplement the cover.

(9) Make sure that the current condition of the property is clearly recorded at the commencement of the lease. This is particularly important with older premises, where the lease is a full repairing lease. The aim is to ensure your client is not acquiring an obligation to put the property in a better condition than it was at the commencement of the term. It may be wise to arrange for a surveyor to prepare a schedule of condition which should then be incorporated as part of the lease. Sometimes, a schedule of condition incorporates photographs in order to avoid the possibility of misunderstanding. The reason for all of this is that there will be a standard clause in the lease requiring the tenant to leave the premises in the same condition in which it was at the commencement of the term.

(10) Make sure that your client understands the difference between the demised premises which will be available for his exclusive occupation and those other parts of the building which he will have to share in common with others. In this latter category will be likely to fall entrance halls, landings and stairs, toilet facilities, car parking spaces and driveways.

(11) Most leases will require the prospective tenant to comply with all Acts of Parliament, whatever these may be at present and in the future. Acts of Parliament will include local bylaws and detailed regulations following from delegated legislation. It is vital that you ensure the building complies with these requirements at the outset. Again, draw your client's attention to these provisions. You might even try to persuade the landlord's solicitors not to have to comply with future legislative programmes in view of the impossibility of knowing what these might comprise, however, such an attempt to revise this fairly standard requirement in a lease is likely to fail.

2 Conclusion

If you are persuaded to proceed expeditiously with the granting of a commercial lease, the client must be warned in writing of any loose ends about which you remain concerned, so that he fully appreciates any risk that may remain.

As a commercial conveyancer, you have to strike the proper balance between care and diligence on the one hand and meeting the legitimate commercial aspirations of your client on the other hand. Generally, the two are happily reconciled, but the above pointers will hopefully serve as a reminder of the key issues that must be dealt with regardless of the pressures under which you may be placed.

Part 7

Conveyancing and
residential leases

Chapter 32

Short-term leases—assured shorthold tenancies

Aspects of short-term leases, which because of their complexity and importance are not dealt with in this book, are rent control and security of tenure under the Rent Acts. They demand a book to themselves of which there are a number, to which readers are referred.

1 Assured shorthold tenancies

The provisions of the Housing Act 1988 were intended to reverse the decline of rented housing and to improve its quality.

Most practitioners will appreciate that the first part of the above objective has undoubtedly been achieved. Rarely a day goes by in the experience of many conveyancing practitioners without their being asked to organise an assured shorthold tenancy for a landlord, or peruse the content of a draft agreement for a prospective tenant. In fact the time has come when it is rare to be asked to organise a residential tenancy in any other form.

The concepts of the 'assured' tenancy and 'shorthold' letting were first introduced by the Housing Act 1980.

Some progress has been made in securing a greater element of contractual agreement between landlord and tenant.

An assured tenancy differs from a regulated tenancy in so far as the rent will be the market level rent agreed on a contractual basis between the landlord and the tenant as at the commencement of the tenancy. There is, in general, no subsequent recourse to a rent assessment committee on such an agreement.

Assured shorthold tenancies are for an agreed fixed term of not less than six months. The landlord has the right to vacant possession of the property at the end of the agreed term on service of notice. There are no rights of succession under the assured shorthold tenancy, should the tenant die before it concludes.

If a tenant does not move out upon the date specified in the notice to quit, a landlord may regain possession of the property by the issue of the appropriate summons in the local county court without having to provide suitable alternative accommodation.

An assured shorthold tenancy can be for as long a period as the parties may agree between them. If it is mutually desired between both landlord and tenant that the period run on beyond the contractual date, the landlord will not lose the entitlement to regain possession on the above terms, but may do so only on the conclusion of the next anniversary date. For example, an assured shorthold tenancy for 12 months may run on for a further 12 months without the need for the preparation of any additional documentation, but the landlord may bring the arrangement to an end only by the service of the appropriate notice two months before the conclusion of the second period of 12 months. Although the tenancy will effectively be converted to a periodic tenancy, the landlord does not acquire a secure tenant by allowing the term to run on.

The provisions of the Housing Act 1988 have not totally repealed the Rent Act 1977 but have amended and repealed certain of its provisions.

The provisions relating to assured shorthold tenancies came into force on 15 January 1989.

The 1988 Act is a weighty tome and the reader is referred to Gerald Bowden's annotation published by Shaw & Sons in February 1989.

In practice, the preparation of a shorthold tenancy agreement is very simple. Basically, most conveyancers, and indeed many firms of estate agents, keep their own standard precedent, which is then used with the necessary amendments as to parties, rent and the terms etc. It is usual to take a deposit against breakages or damage in the sum of one month's rent. This is repayable at the end of the term, as long as the property is returned in good condition.

The agreement must refer to s 20 of the Housing Act 1988 in order to enable possession to be recovered upon the expiry of the fixed term of the agreement. A minimum of not less than two months' notice is required in order to bring the tenancy to an end in accordance with s 21 of the 1988 Act. A similar notice is required in order to terminate any subsequent periodic tenancy arising.

The most important piece of advice I can give you is that before tenants take possession they must have received a standard form of notice informing them that the agreement is to be an assured shorthold tenancy. If this notice is not served on the tenants before the commencement of the term, the protection of an assured shorthold tenancy will not be available to the landlord. The notice is therefore a most vital document and is normally produced in duplicate with one copy being countersigned by the tenants in order to acknowledge safe receipt of the top copy. Both copies will clearly have to be signed by or on behalf of the landlord.

If there is a subsisting mortgage the mortgage lender will require a similar notice to be signed by the new tenant agreeing to vacate if possessive proceedings are instituted. This notice is pursuant to Schedule 2 ground 2 of the Housing Act 1988.

Once the notice has been dealt with, and once the agreements have been signed (usually in duplicate), then the tenants can go into possession, and the shorthold tenancy begins.

As indicated above, many letting agents are now bypassing conveyancers altogether and issuing their own standard forms. I have seen many such forms that are badly drawn and that omit any sensible provisions on the part of the landlord, which might protect the tenants. It is curious how tenants' enthusiasm to be in the new property as fast as possible makes them so rash as to fail to take professional advice.

2 The role of letting agents

As market conditions have shifted from the sale and purchase of freehold residential property to the increasing popularity of rented residential property, many estate agents have set up departments to manage residential property. Such departments provide a comprehensive service to include finding tenants, vetting the tenants, making arrangements for inventories to be drawn and for the tenants to enter once the appropriate shorthold tenancy documentation has been dealt with.

Once the tenants are satisfactorily installed for their minimum period of six months, the letting agents will charge a weekly management fee and will collect the rent and deal with any other practical query that may arise from the tenant about the condition, the services, or the nature of the property.

Disputes do arise with the letting agents. Sometimes they fail to deal promptly with the tenants' requests. Sometimes they misjudge a tenant and the rent falls into arrears. Sometimes they fail to pass on the rent sufficiently speedily to the landlord's account. Occasionally, errors are made in the preparation of the documentation at the outset. Solicitors are often requested to pick up the pieces if the relationship between the landlord and the letting agent comes to grief in one of the above ways.

Solicitors are usually always involved for the purpose of serving a formal Notice to Quit upon a tenant who either fails to pay his rent or whose term is coming to an end. If a tenant does not respond to such a notice, then county court possession proceedings may be necessary. A solicitor may also be requested to examine the conduct of the letting agents to ascertain whether there may have been any negligence in the conduct of his responsibilities.

3 Short-term leases

The first point to consider is whether a full lease is necessary, or whether a tenancy agreement will be sufficient. In the case of a letting of three years or less, an agreement under hand only is permissible, and usually adequate. In general, use the simpler form of agreement under hand where this is applicable. If the lease or tenancy to be granted is an *underlease*, ensure that its terms comply with those of the head lease, and in that case it may well be convenient to provide for the periodic payment of rent in advance a few weeks earlier than rent is payable under the superior lease so that your client, the landlord, may receive that rent in time to pay out of it the rent reserved by the head lease.

Costs

Take instructions as to who is to pay the costs. From time immemorial, the lessee used to pay the lessor's costs of a lease, in the absence of specific agreement to the contrary; in the case of tenancy agreements, in the absence of such agreement, the custom was for each party to pay their own costs, although this was often varied by agreement. Under the Costs of Leases Act 1958, each party to a lease or tenancy agreement bears their own costs, and their own costs only, in the absence of agreement in writing to the contrary.

When demand for rented property exceeds supply, many landlords will seek to pass on their costs to tenants; but the Act is directed at what had come to be recognised as an anomaly, and departure from the Act can be resisted by a tenant. Nor is it a part of your professional duties (having advised your client of the legal position) to persuade a landlord-client to seek to reverse the progress of the law by written agreement to the contrary. But most landlords—especially the property-owning companies—are well aware of the position and their power, and the purpose of the Act is more often honoured in the breach than the observance.

Because the work involved in a short-term tenancy is usually less than that for a lease, the costs charged in the case of a mere tenancy agreement are commonly less than they would be for a full-fledged lease. Perhaps another reason for this lies in the fact that, whilst only a conveyancer may properly charge for preparing a lease, an estate agent—anyone, indeed—may by law prepare and charge for preparing a tenancy agreement of three years or less.

As well as taking particulars of the bare bones of the transaction—the parties, the property, the term, the rent etc—one or two matters always call for rather special consideration.

Parcels (ie description of the property)

If the letting is of the whole of the property owned by the lessor it will in general be sufficient to state the address.

It often happens, however, that the owner is letting a part only of his property—a flat in a building, a cottage in the grounds of the lessor's house etc. Then you need to be particularly clear and specific, often by reference to a plan. Note particularly the warning given by the case of *Scarfe v Adams* [1981] 1 All ER 843. Every such case demands careful consideration to ensure: (i) that the tenant is *granted* all the rights that will be needed for the full enjoyment of the property let; and (ii) that the lessor *reserves* all the rights that will be needed for the full enjoyment of the remaining property. Consider these requirements always under three headings, namely:

(1) rights of way giving access to and from the dominant or servient tenement;

(2) rights of water, gas, electricity, drainage, and any other services; and

(3) provision for the use, maintenance and repair of common structures, etc, such as a party wall, a shared bathroom and lavatory, the roof and main walls, a combined drain serving two or more tenements, the cleaning of a common hall and stairway etc.

In many cases—particularly in lettings of flats and parts of a building—it is desirable that leases of all the flats shall be in identical terms, otherwise it may be found, when seeking to enforce a right granted to one tenant, that in some respect it is unenforceable against another.

You will often best learn of these, and the provisions that need to be made, by talking discursively to your client of the nature of the premises and the letting. Consideration of a plan of the property may suggest provisions that have not occurred to either party, as may its inspection.

Fixtures and furniture

In the case of furnished lettings all the contents will be specified in the agreement, usually by reference to an inventory annexed to it, or signed by the parties. It is important, from the viewpoint equally of lessor and lessee, that the *condition* of any article less than perfect should be stated in the inventory: otherwise there will be dispute and possible loss for one party or the other if neither admits that they disembowelled the grand piano, leaving only the eviscerated container. In many unfurnished lettings, too, it is important to list fixtures and fittings included with the property. If not supplied by the lessor, then acting for the lessee in a proper case ask for such a list, and if it's not forthcoming specify in a letter what your client declares them to be. Checking and agreeing the contents of the inventory at the commencement and end of the term is important. As above, it is also wise to take a deposit from the new tenant to be held against breakages and damage.

Rent reviews

It is established practice, in lettings for terms of more than five years, to provide for periodic rent reviews under which the rent payable for successive periods shall be either that paid during the previous period, or the market rent that the premises could command at the date of the review, whichever is the higher. Acting for landlords, advise them of the dangers of freezing a rent for too long a period.

Insurance

Make it perfectly clear in the lease who is to insure, and against what risks. If the tenant insures, provide that the insurance shall be in the full value of the property from time to time with a society to be approved by the landlord, and in the joint names of tenant and landlord. If the landlord is to insure, it is not uncommon to provide that the insurance for which the tenant pays shall include one or two years' loss of rent and architect's and surveyor's fees on any necessary repair or rebuilding. Comprehensive cover against fire and other risks, and 'index linked' cover are common and desirable.

In connection with insurance it is also common and reasonable to provide that rent shall cease from the time the premises may be destroyed by fire.

Outgoings

You will of course take specific instructions from your client as to who pays the outgoings. Be specific as to who bears the burdens.

Repairs and decorations

The provisions in a lease or tenancy agreement on this subject are the most frequent cause of dispute between the parties, and the draftsman should therefore be most precise and specific on the subject. Whatever may be excluded from the tenant's covenant should be included in a corresponding covenant by the landlord.

As to what is a reasonable division of liability for repairs, if you are asked to advise on the point, the general rule is that the shorter the term, the less the liability commonly fastened on the tenant. So in a monthly letting an agreement by the tenant 'to keep the premises in as good a state of internal decorative repair as the same are now in', perhaps excluding fair wear and tear, would be reasonable; in a letting of seven years or more, a full repairing lease might be appropriate. But when a part only of a larger building is let (as in the case of a flat or maisonette) it is reasonable for the landlord always to remain liable for the 'foundations, roofs, main walls and timbers' and the common parts of the entire building, and also for the decoration of the outside and common parts and to give a covenant to that effect.

The full form of lease includes both a covenant by the tenants to carry out whatever may be their agreed share of the repairs, *and* a covenant to permit the landlord to inspect periodically, and then to carry out any repairs of which the landlord gives notice to the tenants, and which the tenants then fail to execute. See that such a covenant provides that the tenants are only to do repairs 'for which they may be liable under their hereinbefore contained covenants', or some such words, otherwise this second covenant may unintentionally impose a liability wider than this. Ensure, too, when acting for tenants, that the period provided for doing the repairs is adequate—sometimes this is not the case. A reasonable form will provide that the repairs shall be *commenced* within a specified period, and thereafter proceeded with diligently.

Remember, and in a proper case advise your client of the implications of the Landlord and Tenant Act 1985, ss 11–16 (formerly the Housing Act 1961, ss 32 and 33), whereby in lettings of dwellings since 24 November 1961, for terms of less than seven years, the landlord is responsible for the structure; for the outside; and for water, gas, electric, sanitary and heating installations. It's an obligation that, in general, the parties can't contract out of except so far as the lessees would be liable under their duty to use the premises in a tenant-like manner.

In the case of short tenancies, most law stationers sell a satisfactory printed form of tenancy agreement. Since the costs that can properly be charged in many such cases are not high, feel no embarrassment in using such a form in a suitable case; as well as saving costs to the client, you will also save valuable typist's time. For many of us these are now superseded by our own firm's precedent stored on disk.

Always enquire (and this is of special importance when acting for tenants) as to the *present* state of the property, as to whether this is to be put into a good and tenantable state of repair, and if so, whose responsibility that is to be. If (as not uncommonly occurs) the point has not been considered or discussed between the parties, point out to prospective tenants that a covenant to *keep* in good repair 'and so to deliver up the premises at the end of the term' may involve their *putting* them into better condition than they are now in. The importance of this cannot be over emphasised, as horrible consequences can follow.

Assignment and subletting

All tenancies and leases should contain some limitation on or prohibition of assignment or subletting. In the case of a short (monthly, quarterly, or even sometimes longer) tenancy an absolute prohibition is not unreasonable or unusual; under a lease the most common provision is that a tenant may not assign without the landlord's licence, but provision is usually made that this shall not be unreasonably refused in the case of a respectable and responsible person. However, it isn't unusual for there to be an absolute prohibition against dealings with a part of the property (as distinct from the whole).

Always take specific instructions on the question of right to assign from whichever party you act for. Remember that under the Landlord and Tenant Act 1927, s 19, when a lease contains a covenant not to assign etc, without licence, there is always implied, if it is not already in the clause, a proviso that such licence shall not be unreasonably withheld; but the section does *not* apply when there is an *absolute* covenant against assignment, without any reference at all to a licence. In general, in all but the shortest terms, tenants can fairly expect some right to assign, however qualified, even though, when you ask them, they say they have no intention of ever assigning, for neither they nor you can foresee what the future holds. So in general, when you act for a lessee, seek reasonable provision in this respect.

When the landlord is particularly concerned not to let to anyone not personally approved (as may be the case, for example, when the tenant of a part of the landlord's home will become a neighbour), provide that before subletting or assigning a landlord is to have the option of accepting a surrender of the term. This will sometimes be a useful compromise. Such a term has become so common that it is 'built in' to some of the printed forms of tenancy agreement sold by law stationers, but it should be used only in a proper case, not as 'common form'.

Landlord's covenants

Having reached the landlord's covenants in the standard form of lease, insert (on the principle of being explicit) appropriate covenants as to the repairs, insurance and outgoings, if any, for which the landlord is to be responsible, as well as the invariable covenant for quiet enjoyment and the proviso for cesser of rent in the event of fire. If the landlord is to insure, provide that he or she shall furnish the tenant with a copy or sufficient extract from the policy and that the tenant will also be notified of any subsequent modification of or addition to the policy.

The covenant that should always be in long leases (see head 1 of Chapter 33), that if required the landlord will enforce covenants (such as not to disturb neighbours) in leases of other parts of a building, is equally appropriate in short-term leases. So is a covenant by the landlord that all leases in the building shall be in similar terms.

Ensure that the tenant's and the landlord's covenants, taken together, cover the repair and maintenance of the whole of the premises let, including in the case of a flat the structure, roofs, foundations and common parts such as entrances, halls and stairs of the building, and any garden included in the letting or of which the tenant has the use.

A landlord's covenant to repair does not include an obligation to 'rebuild', so if a wall, for example, collapses and complete rebuilding is required this would not come within the scope of a covenant merely to keep in repair—so when acting for a tenant (or a landlord, for that matter) see that the missing word is included in the landlord's covenant. (See [1984] *Gazette* 5 September, 2369.)

Option to purchase reversion or to renew lease

A lease sometimes contains an option for lessees, on giving notice within a prescribed period, to purchase their landlord's reversion to the lease, whether freehold or leasehold. It's easy in such a case to overlook the fact that in the case of unregistered land the option must be registered by the lessees in the Land Charges Register as an *estate contract*, and this should invariably be done. Otherwise, if the lessor sells the property subject to the lease, the option will be unenforceable against the new reversioner, and the lessees' solicitors will be liable for their professional negligence in failing to register.

Similarly, if the landlord's title is registered, the lessees' interest should be protected by registration on the charges register of a *notice* that an option to purchase is contained in the lease.

An option to renew a lease must be registered in similar manner if it is to bind a buyer of the reversion. An option to renew is regarded by the courts as a privilege. Accordingly, if to be exercisable the option is expressed to depend on observance of the tenant's covenants, the tenant must have complied strictly with all the terms of the lease, and particularly with the covenants to pay rent and to decorate and repair.

It's easy to overlook the need to register an option in a lease: the item to this effect on your post-completion agenda should serve as a reminder.

For a learned article on the problems of options void for uncertainty, and conditional options to renew by D W Williams see [1985] *Gazette*, 11 December, 3801.

Notice to quit

Before serving a notice to quit for a landlord, ensure not only that it complies with the terms of the lease but also that notice of any change of landlord has been given to the tenant. Once notice has been served, there's always a danger that by subsequently accepting payment of rent, a landlord will have waived his or her notice, and will have to start all over again should he or she wish to proceed. The danger is greatest when management is in the hands of agents, who may inadvertently accept rent. The danger may be avoided by adding to the notice to quit (the printed form of notice available at law stationers is to be recommended) the following notice:

> Take notice that without prejudice to this notice the landlord will accept payments of rent from you only until this notice expires. After that date all payments will be accepted only as mesne profits for your use and occupation of the said premises and by accepting such payments the landlord must not be considered to have waived this Notice to Quit or the landlord's right to recover possession of the said premises.

The duty of a lessee's conveyancer

It is of course the prime duty of the conveyancer acting for lessees to explain to them all the terms, and in particular any unusual ones, contained in the document. The operative word is *explain*. It isn't enough to gabble verbatim through the document to a stunned client. This duty was demonstrated by the case of *Sykes v Midland Bank Executor & Trustee Co Ltd* [1970] 2 All ER 471. In that case a solicitor for the plaintiff underlessees, a firm of architects and surveyors, had failed to draw his clients' attention to the effect of a clause prohibiting any user other than that of the plaintiffs' business unless 'the permission in writing of the lessor *and the superior lessors* has first been obtained, such permission *by the lessor* not to be unreasonably withheld'. The plaintiffs entered into the underlease on the mistaken belief that the *superior* lessor's consent could not be arbitrarily withheld, as in fact it was. The Court of Appeal held that the clause was unusual, that it might and did affect the plaintiffs' interest, who should therefore have been warned of the possible arbitrary refusal of the superior lessor to a change of use; and that the solicitor (or rather his estate, the defendants being his executors) was liable to the plaintiffs in negligence. In that particular case the damages awarded were merely nominal (£2) because the court found that even if the clause had been fully explained, the plaintiffs would nevertheless have proceeded; but the warning light as to a convey-ancer's duty is no less clear for that.

The case decided one other matter *in favour of* solicitors: the lower court had found that in the case of a partnership, a solicitor should explain the effect of a lease to *all* the partners. The Court of Appeal reversed this, holding that it is sufficient for the solicitor to tender advice only to the partner dealing with the matter.

In your own protection it is desirable to have proof that you have explained the terms of a lease to lessees; therefore always mention in a letter that you want to see them for that purpose or confirming such an appointment. And when there are unusual or unduly onerous terms which your lessee-clients nevertheless accept, record this, and the advice you have given them as to the possible effect of such terms, in a letter to them.

Chapter 33

Long leases—enfranchisement

1 The terms of a long lease

Turning now to long leases at a ground rent, commonly created for the consideration of a cash payment. See for general considerations affecting either a lessee or his mortgagee head 4 below. The most common term (because a longer term attracts higher stamp duty) has until recently been 99 years although 999 years is not uncommon. Recently, following the practice in right to buy procedure (Chapter 9) a term of 125 years is becoming more and more common.

Many buyers prefer freehold to leasehold property, on the general principle that, an Englishman's home being his castle, it is undesirable that any outsider should be entitled to enter and inspect it, dictate as to when it should be repainted etc. Today, however, the long leasehold interest has a special application of great importance in connection with the 'sale' of flats and maisonettes, being specially appropriate to the disposal of part of a building, where sometimes complicated rights of mutual support, way, and other easements have to be granted and reserved, and countless positive covenants will run with leasehold land and the reversion to it, which will not run with a freehold, as our law stands at present. For this reason the client contemplating the purchase of a flying freehold should be firmly advised against it for the foregoing reasons and also because building societies refuse to lend on the security of a flying freehold.

The duty of a lessee's conveyancers to explain all, and particularly any unusual term of a proposed lease to their client is of course identical to their duty in the case of a short lease. Similarly, a lessor's conveyancers are under an obligation to explain to their client all the terms of their draft, and any proposed amendments to it.

In taking instructions for both a long and a short lease, careful attention to the parcels and the ancillary rights and liabilities is called for. If you are instructed by the lessor in such a case, find out what common services (water, electricity, drainage, etc) are to be shared or are to pass

228

through one flat on the way to another; which parts of the building are to be party walls and structures, and what is to be the nature of the rights and liabilities in respect thereof—for example, who is to be responsible and in what measure or proportion, for the horizontal division of the ceilings and floors between one tenement and another? What common entrances, halls and stairways are to be used by which tenants, and who is to be responsible for the lighting and maintenance thereof? What provision is to be made for the storage of fuel, dustbins etc? What provision is to be made for the maintenance of the grounds? Has the lessor a scheme of rules or regulations for the good domestic government of the building, which might usefully be incorporated in a schedule? In what proportions are the costs of maintenance and insurance of the building to be borne by the lessees? Remember to ensure the numbering of the pages of all lengthy documents such as leases to facilitate reference.

Long leases of separate buildings are invariably full repairing leases; in the case of leases of flats or maisonettes, however, the lessor will usually be responsible for the common parts of the building such as entrance hall and stairs, roofs, foundations, main walls and timbers. It is essential that there should be a covenant by the lessor, or sometimes by a management company, in a lease of part of a building, for such maintenance and for the lessee to be able to enforce this obligation. The absence of such provision is bad conveyancing, and adverse to the lessee's interest, and a prospective lessee or mortgagee should be warned of its effect. Most building societies and other mortgagees will not accept as their security for a loan a lease which lacks such a covenant, enforceable by the lessee, for maintenance of the structure and common parts of the building.

Lessors' covenants

Covenants by lessors to repair, maintain gardens, etc, will usually include provision for the lessee to pay a fair proportion of the cost. Acting for lessors, beware of providing unfairly that they shall, in effect, be judge and jury in their own cause by including the provision that the construction of the covenant as to what is or is not included therein shall be determined by the lessors' surveyor, whose decision shall be *final and unchallengeable*. Such provision, the court has decided, is contrary to public policy and void as totally ousting the jurisdiction of the courts on a question of law (*Re Davstone Estates Ltd's Leases; Manprop Ltd v O'Dell* [1969] 2 Ch 378). Safer, therefore, to exclude from the clause the provision making the surveyor's decision *absolute*.

Remember that at common law there is no implied covenant by a lessor to repair. So in a lease of premises for 21 flats imposing full repairing covenants on the lessees, the lessees had an implied right to use a drain running under a mews over which they had rights of way. But the lessor was under no obligation to contribute to the repair of the drain. And under the law of easements a servient owner is under no obligation to keep the servient property in repair (*Duke of Westminster v Guild* [1984] 3 All ER 144). So when a tenant is to be granted easements over property retained by the landlord, care should be taken to ensure that the landlord's covenant to repair extends to that property.

In a letting of a separate building, again, there will usually be a covenant by the lessee to insure, but in a lease of a *part* of a building the lessor will probably and preferably covenant to insure the whole, recovering under the covenants (and perhaps as rent) from each lessee a fair proportion of the total premium.

A lease of more than one flat in a building, whether purpose-built as a block of flats or a converted dwelling-house, should contain provision that the leases of all the flats shall be in the same terms other than variations relevant to a particular flat such as rent, etc. This provision is normally made, not as a covenant by the lessor but by a recital of the lessor's intention. It is essential, however, that the lessor should *covenant* with each lessee that, if reasonably required, he or she will enforce the covenants entered into by other lessees on the complaining lessee indemnifying the lessor against the cost of such enforcement. Without that covenant, a lessee has little or no remedy against nuisance or annoyance by neighbours, such as loud music late at night. In the absence of such a covenant, building societies refuse to make mortgage advances.

There's one exception to this when leases are drawn so that each lessee *covenants with the other lessees* as well as with the lessor; thus each can enforce directly covenants by another lessee.

Landlords sometimes seek to evade their responsibility for the maintenance of a building by requiring all the lessees to do this together; and landlords will sometimes seek covenants from each lessee to insure their flats, and for individual lessees to redecorate the outside of their flats in conjunction with the other lessee or lessees redecorating the outside of their flats in similar manner.

This is bad conveyancing, is likely to lead to dispute and quarrels between neighbours and to an omission fully to insure the whole building. It can lead to the outside of a building being decorated like a layer cake. If a lessor is so against accepting any responsibility as a landlord, then the leases should be drafted in reasonable terms and the landlord should offer to sell his or her reversion to one or more or all of the lessees, or to a company formed for that purpose in which each lessee will hold a share. Lessees, if they are wise, will jump at the opportunity of becoming their own freeholders and will pay somewhat in excess of the investment value of the reversion for that privilege; both parties are then better off for the deal (see below).

So the usual covenants by a lessor should include the following:

(1) for quiet enjoyment;
(2) to maintain, repair and replace the roofs, main walls and timbers (or load-bearing walls and timbers) and the foundations;
(3) to maintain the grounds or garden, if any, and the paths and steps leading to the building;
(4) to maintain, decorate, clean and light the common entrance hall, passages and stairs;
(5) to insure the building;
(6) to paint and decorate the outside of the building;
(7) to enforce the covenants of other lessees;
(8) and to prepare annual accounts of the cost of the foregoing.

And there will, of course, be a covenant by every lessee to pay a share of the lessor's expenses of complying with the covenants.

Management companies

A development in the case of newly built or converted flats, beneficial alike to lessor and lessee, is the provision whereby each lessee takes up shares in a company which, after all the flats have been sold, takes over the freehold reversion. The lessor is thus relieved of such burdens as cleaning and lighting common halls and stairways, and the lessees themselves assume the management of such matters, and become in effect, through their holdings in the company, the freeholders of their flats. The landlord, who will be foregoing the right to receive the ground rents of the flats, sells the freehold to the company for an agreed price as soon as the development of the property is completed.

Another not uncommon arrangement (but less beneficial to the lessees, since they do not thereby become the freeholders and their own landlords) is for the control and maintenance of the building to be the responsibility of a *management company* in which each lessee holds a share, the rents continuing to be paid to the landlord. This still has the advantage for the lessees that the decoration, maintenance and servicing of the building are in their hands and not those of a rapacious or indifferent absentee landlord, interested only in the collection of rents. The former arrangement with the higher price for the reversion, is preferable for lessor and lessees alike.

Maintenance

A matter that sometimes troubles lessors is the liability for repair and maintenance of the grounds, roofs and common parts of buildings. The lessor of a block of flats will probably have in mind the ultimate sale of the freehold ground rents (ie the freehold property subject to the leases and with the benefit of the rents) in the investment market. If the lessor does not sell to a management company, as mentioned above, after all the individual flats have been disposed of, and if the freehold is incumbered with duties to clean and light the entrance halls and stairways, to maintain the gardens etc, investors will be shy of purchasing, or will expect a substantial abatement of the price they will pay.

The problem can be overcome either by a management company as mentioned above, or by providing in the *lessees'* covenants that they will pay a specified proportion (eg a twentieth, if there are 20 flats) of all money spent by the lessor in carrying out the obligations of his or her specified covenants: and in the *lessor's* covenants that the lessor will maintain the foundations, roofs, structure and common parts of the building; pay rates thereon; plant and maintain the common garden etc; and *a specific proviso that the lessor can delegate all this work* to any other person or company, and charge a percentage of the total cost by way of a management charge. The lessor is thus put in the position of doing no more than collect rents, whilst there is no financial disincentive for the property being well maintained. The provisions call for fairly careful draftsmanship. From the lessee's viewpoint this method is less satisfactory than the suggested alternatives, and probably less so for the lessor, having regard to the price the lessee will probably be prepared to pay.

Lessees should be guarded against increase in their proportion of maintenance charges by a lessor's covenant that in the event of any flat being vacant the landlord will observe and perform the covenants and make payments in respect of such other flats as the occupiers thereof would be liable to observe, perform and make as if the flats were let under leases in the same terms as this lease other than parties, rent and term.

Proviso for forfeiture

The universal proviso for forfeiture on breach of covenant should never in a long lease (otherwise in a short one) provide for forfeiture on *bankruptcy* of an individual, or liquidation of a corporate lessee. Mortgagees will refuse to advance if the lease contains such a provision, and a lessee should refuse to accept it.

Registration of assignments etc

Lastly, it is undesirable to provide for the *production* of an assignment etc, to the lessor's solicitor. Draw such a clause to provide for giving *notice* of assignment only, not forgetting payment of the solicitor's fee, which, with continuing decline in purchasing power, continues to rise in modest harmony.

Remember, acting for a lessor when in due course an assignment or mortgage is registered with you, to notify your client of the change of ownership and to whom future demands for rent should be sent. It's a convenient practice to attach to the counterpart lease all notices of assignment etc, received on behalf of a lessor. If the counterpart has been sent to the lessor, write with any such notices, advising the lessor to attach them to the document.

2 Illegal premiums and long residential leases

Although as mentioned above in the context of short leases, this book does not deal with rent control, there is one aspect of that subject that directly affects the conveyancer in the long leasehold field: the possibility of an illegal premium being asked for and paid on the grant or disposition of a lease.

If the grant of a long lease falls within the Rent Act 1977, the payment of a purchase price might be illegal. Section 127 of the 1977 Act has been amended by s 115 of the 1988 Housing Act.

A lease falls within the scope of the Act if the rent, as defined by the Act, exceeds two-thirds of the rateable value of the dwelling on the 'appropriate day' as defined by the Act—commonly 23 March 1965. 'Rent' is defined by the Act, as amended by s 79 of the Housing Act 1980, as including any payments to the landlord, but certain 'disregarded items' include payment for water rates, maintenance and insurance.

A problem arises when there are periodic increases in ground rent, which may take the rent (as defined by the Act) 'over the top'.

3 Leasehold Reform Housing and Urban Development Act 1993

This Act came into force on 1 November 1993. It deals with collective enfranchisement for tenants of flats. The 1993 Act gives most long leaseholders of flats a collective right to buy the freehold of their building at the market value. A 'qualifying tenant' is one who holds a lease of more than 21 years or is one who has a perpetually renewable lease or, is one whose lease was granted under the right to buy in the Housing Act 1985 or, is one who holds a 'shared ownership lease', where the tenant's share is 100%.

If a tenant qualifies on one of the above criteria, then it is important to establish that the tenant pays a low rent. In very broad terms, the rent for the first year must not exceed two-thirds of the open market rent for the flat at the date of the commencement of the lease. At least two-thirds of the flats in the building must be let to 'qualifying tenants' and at least two-thirds of them must give notice of their desire to purchase the freehold. Tenants who qualify and choose enfranchisement are then 'participating tenants'. At least one-half of the participating tenants must also pass a 'residents' test.

There are a complicated series of criteria which need to be examined in order to establish whether the building is enfranchisable or not. Whilst a block of flats is likely to qualify, a building involving fewer than four units, or where the owner or a member of his family has occupied part of it for at least 12 months, or where the landlord resides in the property will not qualify as enfranchisable. It is also important to establish that a premises is used for residential purposes. Non residential lettings do not qualify for enfranchisement.

Participating tenants must hold at least one-half of the flats in the block. The collective right of enfranchisement is exercised through a 'nominee purchaser'. Generally, this will be a company formed for the purpose which ultimately takes the transfer of the freehold. There is a counternotice procedure and a timetable for exercising the right to enfranchise.

An unwilling freeholder will be forced to sell unless he can show that he intends to redevelop the block and also that two-thirds of the long leases in the block are due to end within the next five years. An unwilling freeholder will be compensated for the fact that he was not a willing seller. Readers are referred to a very helpful article in the *Estates Gazette*, 28 May 1994 by Tony Elliot and Judy Gough. The article contains three flow charts which establish whether enfranchisement is possible or not.

Notwithstanding the complexity and restrictions inherent within the terms of the 1993 Act, it is having some impact on the housing market in London and on the South coast.

4 Sale of lease

When you act on the sale of an existing lease, there is of course no opportunity to vary its terms; the buyer must take it or leave it, unless there is provision in the contract for sale that, for example, the seller is to obtain the lessor's licence to variation of the use of the premises. When acting for buyers, it's just as essential that they really *understand* the terms of the lease they propose to buy as it is on the initial granting of a lease (head 3 of Chapter 32). Read and *explain* it to your buyer-clients. Any failure by them to grasp the nature of their rights and obligations will be a measure of your failure as their conveyancer, for it is largely in that explanatory capacity that they have engaged your services. Liability for negligence in failing to explain the terms of the lease to the client will be no less than on the grant of a new lease. Particular care should be taken to explain and advise the client on any unusual or unduly onerous terms, and on the absence of any that should be included (head 3 of Chapter 32 above). It is wise, in any such case, to record your advice by letter to the client. See head 3 of Chapter 34 as to the defective lease.

When you act for the buyer of a leasehold interest, you'll find it a great saving of time in a simple case to keep in your office (stored in your word processor or computer), a draft assignment that you can complete and adapt to any particular case.

Prepare your own standard draft from the forms favoured in your office, remembering to include in it provisions appropriate to recital of devolution; to joint ownership; an indemnity of the assignor against continuing liability under the lease; a certificate of value; and any other provisions that may sometimes be useful in your particular practice. Using such a rough draft it is only a matter of seconds to delete inappropriate clauses, but they are invaluable reminders to include or adapt them in a particular case.

Broadly speaking, most of the points made already in this book about sales and purchases of freehold properties can relate to sales and purchases of leaseholds.

When acting for an original lessee who is selling his or her lease, be careful to include in the contract and to ensure that there is included in the assignment or transfer (which will be drafted by the buyer's conveyancer) the following:

(1) An indemnity by the buyer against subsequent breach of the lessee's covenants for which, as the original lessee, your client will have a continuing liability. Acting for the buyer, seek to limit liability during period of the buyer's ownership only.

(2) An indemnity by the buyer against any previous breach of repairing and decorating covenants (you will remember that in transferring as beneficial owner with full title guarantee the implied covenants by the seller, include one that the lessee's covenants in the lease, which include those to repair and decorate, have been observed and performed).

See special conditions of sale D, E and K in head 6 of Chapter 3.

Chapter 34

Conveyancing hints on dealing with residential leaseholds

1 Checklist for lessors

The lessor's conveyancer has the duty of preparing the draft lease, and there's little to be said in favour of drawing it in terms unduly favouring the client: this will only lead to disputation with the lessee's lawyer, delay and possibly to bad feeling between the parties. We are not (or ought not to be) engaged to seek an unfair bargain. So the checklist for lessees (head 2 below) should also be the lessor's.

(1) *The parties.* Be meticulous about names and addresses, and persuade your secretary to be, too. If a woman's name is 'Ann' don't call her 'Anne'. Check the lessor's name against his or her title to the property.

(2) *The parcels.* Be meticulous about these, too; check them against the title, and if necessary, inspect the property, particularly if your client is disposing of a part only. If a plan is required (always necessary on a lease of a flat or part of the lessor's property), ensure that it is adequate—see head 2 of Chapter 3. Remember that it's for your client to provide this: don't volunteer to do work for which you aren't professionally qualified or you may be held professionally liable if you make a mistake. Consider carefully what easements are necessary—rights of access, dustbin area, use of garden or whether this is to be included in the letting etc.

(3) *Rent.* This is now very commonly paid in advance, even ground rent, which once was invariably paid in arrears. Market rents are often high. A useful provision, particularly common in rent review clauses, but no reason why it should not apply to all rent payments, is for interest to be chargeable for any period of delay in payment. See an up-to-date book of precedents—and it's useful, too, to base your own draft lease on such modern precedents.

(4) *Reservations.* Consider carefully what rights need to be reserved

to enable the lessor and other tenants to have the full enjoyment of the remainder of the building in the case of a letting of part. If there are mutual rights (eg to services running through the property, to support etc) see that both grant and reservation are as far as possible in identical terms.

(5) *Tenant's covenants*. Provide for the tenant paying a fair proportion of maintaining *party* walls, sewers etc, as well as a covenant in a suitable case to pay a proportion of the maintenance, repair and decoration of the building, which the landlord covenants to do. If the reversion is leasehold or if, being freehold, it is subject to any restrictions, ensure that the tenant is liable to perform these, either by reference to the document containing them or by reproducing the relevant provisions in your draft lease.

(6) *The user clause*. This needs to be carefully drafted. Consider, in the case of a private dwelling, whether provision that the property is to be occupied by one family only will preserve the character of the premises.

In a business letting containing a rent review clause remember that the more restricted the permitted user, the lower may be the rent obtainable in the open market (normally the basis of the renewed rent), which will blow back on your client to his or her detriment. So instead of providing that 'the premises shall be used as an architect's office only', it may be preferable to say 'as an architect's offices or as the offices of any other profession or business', perhaps excluding any particular businesses that would compete with those carried on by other tenants of the landlord.

(7) *Landlord's covenants*. It is essential, and not only from the tenant's viewpoint (head 3 of Chapter 32), that a lease should make someone enforceably liable for the repair of the whole building. In a full repairing lease of a house this is simple: the tenant does everything. In a lease of a flat or part of a building, liability is commonly divided between the tenants, who are liable for the interior of their flats, and the landlord, who is commonly responsible for the roof and structure and for the decoration of the outside and the common parts (entrance steps and hall etc) of the building, recovering the cost by contributions from all the lessees. Whatever the provisions in a particular case, ensure that they cover the *whole* building, including the grounds and right to use these: failure to do so might constitute professional negligence.

(8) *Law of Property Act 1925, s146*. Take care that the invariable provision for recovering the costs of a notice under ss 146 and 147

of the Law of Property Act 1925, notwithstanding that forfeiture is avoided otherwise than by relief granted by the court, is wide enough to cover both costs of preparation and service of the notice, and costs subsequent and incidental to the notice and the enforcement thereof.

(9) *The rent review clause*. Although the courts tend to find that under the various forms of this clause, time is not of the essence of the contract (House of Lords authority for this in two cases heard together: *United Scientific Holdings Ltd v Burnley Borough Council* and *Cheapside Land Development Co Ltd v Messels Service Co* [1977] 2 All ER 62), it is wise to state this specifically. Draw the clause so that each party has a reasonable time to act, that the old rent shall continue to be paid pending the determination of the new, and that the new rent shall date back to the commencement of the latest review period. And don't forget to provide for interest on an increase of rent from the rent day to actual payment to cover a possibly long delay in agreeing or arbitrating the amount of increase. For dangers — and to emphasise a solicitor's duty to explain to clients the terms of a lease — see an article by the Law Society's Legal Practice Directorate 'Solicitors beware rent-review cases', inspired by the scandal of the *Blue Dolphin Fish Restaurants Ltd* case [1988] *Gazette* 21 September, 10.

Rent review clauses are clearly of great importance to landlords and tenants alike, and have long exercised the minds of draftsmen. In 1985, the Incorporated Society of Valuers and Auctioneers, in conjunction with The Law Society, published a suggested form of rent review clause [1985] *Gazette* 18 December, 3664. For a learned and detailed consideration and criticism of the form by Steven Fogel and Philip Freedman see [1986] *Gazette* 12 February, 430.

(10) *Re-read the checklist for lessees*. This ensures that all reasonable terms are included by you in the lease, so that they are in your favoured wording, not that of the lessee's conveyancer.

(11) *Lessor's covenants*. As well as the invariable covenant for quiet enjoyment, commonly provided for:
  (i) Landlord's covenant to repair etc — a common source of litigation. The landlord wants to be clear and specific, the tenant to be comprehensive. Combine both these purposes in the clause — such wording as 'maintain, repair, cleanse, repaint, redecorate and renew'. Include gutters and down rainwater pipes. See an article, 'Damages for breach of

repairing obligations' by Nic Madge, pointing to increasing measure of damages [1988] *Gazette* 20 July, 17, and an article by Joseph C Harper, 'An update on repairs' [1988] *Gazette* 5 October, 37. It's a tricky subject because the courts seem to be formulating new principles and definitions of 'repair'. One might formulate a conundrum: 'When is repair not a repair?' Answer: 'When it is not an item of disrepair.' So cast the net wide (especially when you act for the tenant), and as the hymn says, 'watch and pray'.

(ii) To insure. Again, be specific, be comprehensive. Such words as 'for the joint benefit of all persons having an interest in the insured premises' are useful. Vital to both lessor and lessee that there is no shortfall in cover: such wording as 'full reinstatement value including all professional fees, site clearance and two years' loss of rent inflation-linked such that the amount payable shall be the reinstatement value at the date reinstatement is effected'.

Include covenant 'to lay out policy money in reinstatement'. Cover fire and 'risks covered by a comprehensive householder's policy'.

(iii) To enforce lessees' covenants in leases of other flats if reasonable request and an indemnity against costs.

(iv) To clean, maintain, decorate and light the common parts — hall, stairs, passages, garden etc.

(v) To keep and supply proper accounts of past and proposed expenditure.

2 Checklist for lessees

(1) *The parties*. As for a lessor, be meticulous about names and addresses when you take instructions, and see that these are correctly reproduced in the draft lease. Go through the lease clause by clause with your client. Remember that it is negligence not to explain unusual or obscure clauses.

(2) *The parcels*. In the case of a lease of a flat or part of a building, particularly a converted one, confer *with your client* as to whether any stairs (eg the stairway leading to a top flat, which none but your client will use), loft or roof-space etc, should be included. Check the plan with your client (head 2 of Chapter 3).

(3) *Rights of way etc*. Check that there is adequate access to the flat, to the garden if its use is included, to a dustbin area (and that the lessee has the use of it) etc. Check that easements of support,

supply of services etc, are adequate, and in the case of a flat that the grant and reservation of easements and of covenanted rights (such as right of entry to the rest of the building by the lessee to repair the flat, and right of entry to the flat by the lessor to repair other parts of the building) are in complementary terms.

(4) *Term and rent*. Check that your client gets what was originally offered. It sometimes happens in the case of a lease at a market rent that the lessee was never told by the selling agent of a rent review clause; or in the case of a long lease, that there would be periodic increases in ground rent. Ensure that the terms of the clause are fair. Check that there's no chance of an illegal premium. Look out for unduly high maintenance charges (the object of your request in your preliminary enquiries for recent accounts), which may be high, sometimes to the point of highway robbery, and advise your client. Remember (but who wants to litigate?) the wider remedies for a lessee contained in the Landlord and Tenant Acts 1985 and 1987.

(5) *Tenant's covenants*. Check that these are all fair and reasonable and be especially careful to explain them to your client.

(6) *Stamp duty*. This is simply calculated by comparing the annual rent with the period of years over which the lease provides for it to be payable. For a lease of less than seven years, stamp duty starts at £550 annual rental.

(7) *The ground rent trap*. In a long lease with periodic rent increases, it's the *average* rent that determines whether a premium may or may not attract the full rate of duty. Although on rents charged in the past the average annual rent has rarely exceeded £250, with inflation and the corresponding increase in rents it's becoming more and more of a risk. Remember that the initial, lowest rent is payable only *from the date of the lease*, not from the commencement of the term (which for good reason may be some years earlier), and this can sometimes operate to increase the *average* rent throughout the lease above the critical figure.

Again, long leases are subject to the Rent Acts in the same way as other leases if the letting is not at a 'low rent'; ie a rent not exceeding two-thirds of the rateable value. The effect of inflation created a danger that with higher ground rents and increasingly common long-term rent increases in long leases the rent payable would bring some leasehold flats and houses within the scope of the Rent Acts, with disastrous consequences for a seller who was then debarred from taking a premium on a sale. That problem was first solved by the Housing Act 1969, s 81 (replaced by the Rent

Act 1977, s 127) but compliance with its safeguarding provisions was sometimes overlooked. Now the Housing Act 1980, s 78, provides that in the case of leases granted *before* 16 July 1980 a premium can be charged on the assignment of a lease provided that:

(i)   a premium was lawfully charged when the lease was granted;
(ii) at that time the rent was a low rent within the meaning of the Rent Act 1977, s 5; and
(iii) the terms of the lease allow assignment or subletting of the whole of the premises.

The restrictions relating to premiums were further relaxed by s 115 of the Housing Act 1988, as noted above. In the case of a lease granted *after* 16 July 1980, it is exempt from the possibility of being converted to a regulated tenancy if it complies with one or other of two alternatives: *either* it complies with the conditions applying to leases granted before 16 July 1980, *or*: (*a*) the lease was at a low rent when it was granted; (*b*) *the terms of the lease ensure* that the rent, disregarding sums paid for rates, services, repairs or maintenance, does not exceed two-thirds of the *current* rateable value *at the date of any variation*; and (*c*) any variation of the rent occurs not less than six years after the grant and thereafter not more often than once in every seven years.

Note that under the second alternative, *the lease itself* must ensure that, in the terms of the statute, 'any variation of the sums payable by the tenant otherwise than in respect of rates, services, repairs or maintenance, cannot lead to those sums exceeding an annual rate of two-thirds of the rateable value of the dwelling-house at the date when the variation is made'.

(8) *Long leases*. In the case of a long lease, check that there's no sort of limitation of the free right to assign or sublet—see below. And there should never be a rent *review* clause (as distinguished from the now common rent *increase* clause, every 25 or 33 years) in a long lease.

(9) *Lessor's covenants*.It's essential that, in the case of a letting of part, the repair and maintenance of the *whole* building and the redecoration of the outside and common parts should be provided for—apart from your client's interest, any mortgagee may refuse to advance unless such is the case. See all that's said above, under 'Lessor's covenants'.

Go through all the covenants carefully, checking that there's nothing unusual or unreasonable. In the case of a flat or maison-ette see that there is a covenant by the lessor to enforce all the lessee's covenants, if required to do so, against all the lessees of other flats, and a further covenant that all the leases of the remaining flats in the building will be in terms similar to yours. Also a covenant that lessors will themselves observe the covenants of empty flats whilst they remain vacant.

(10) *Subleases*. When the lease offered is a sublease, demand a copy of the head lease to satisfy yourself that the sublease is not in breach of its terms, or if it is, that an adequate licence has been obtained. Get a covenant by the lessor to observe its terms.

(11) *Insurance*. See all that is said above under this heading for lessors. Be precise. Not merely 'such sum as the lessor may determine' but 'against all damage or destruction by fire and all other risks normally covered by a householder's comprehensive policy in the full reinstatement value of the property from time to time'. In the case of a flat or part of a building, the lessor usually insures (unless there is a management company to do so). Tenants should have the right to inspect or have a copy of the policy—and they should always give the insurers notice of their and their mortgagees' interest in it (head 8 of Chapter 13), so that they and their mortgagees will be notified of any lapse of the policy. Moreover, failure to notify might render tenants responsible for the results of their own negligence, enforceable by the insurer on the principle of novation.

The covenant should include an obligation to repair or rebuild with all speed. Remember to include 'rebuild' (head 3 of Chapter 32).

(12) *Enforcement of covenants in other leases*. Unless a lease is so drawn that lessees can enforce the covenants of the lessees of other flats in the building, they are without defence against unreasonable noise or behaviour *unless* the lessor will enforce covenants against other lessees, which he or she may have no personal incentive to do. The only exception to this is if the nuisance is so great that it constitutes a breach of the lessor's covenant for quiet enjoyment. So always seek such a clause. Without it building societies will refuse to advance on the security of a lease.

(13) *Regulations*. Sometimes restrictions on the use of a flat are incorporated in a schedule to the lease. Check when going through the lease with your client that these are not unduly onerous, and won't prohibit any particular purpose, such as keeping a pet; or provide for occupation by one family only if two unrelated persons wish to occupy the premises.

(14) *Rent review clauses*. These vary considerably in their terms and

are of special relevance in business and commercial leases (in all but the shortest, almost invariable). They have no place in long leases.

(15) *Registration of option to renew or to purchase the reversion*. If a lease contains an option to renew it *must* be registered by notice against the landlord's registered title or as an entry on the Charges Register that the lease contains an option to renew, or, in the case of an unregistered title, as an estate contract if it's to be enforceable against an assignee of the reversion (*Kitney v MEPC Ltd* [1978] 1 All ER 595). An option to purchase the reversion should be protected in the same manner.

(16) *Investigation of title*. If a premium is being paid for the grant of a lease, investigate the lessor's title to the reversion. If the title to the lease is to be registered try to ensure that an *absolute* title will be granted. There's no problem about this if title to the reversion is itself registered as absolute. (In your requisitions, require the lessor's land or charge certificate to be lodged in the Land Registry on completion to await registration of the lease.) If it is unregistered, you'll deduce the lessor's title as in any other application for first registration. In the now rare cases where a leasehold reversion is registered with only good leasehold title, you must bow to the inevitable and seek no more for your under-lease unless, because of the period the good leasehold title has persisted, your lessor is now entitled to have his or her good leasehold title converted to absolute and agrees to make that application.

(17) Landlord's liability for vacant flats. In the case of a development comprising flats or maisonettes, where all the units have not been sold, there should be a covenant by the lessor that he or she will accept the liability of a lessee of any flats unsold or unlet until such time as they shall have been disposed of. See also head (l) above.

(18) *After completion*. Register any mortgage (and assignment, in a purchase of an existing lease) with the lessor or the lessor's solicitors in accordance with the terms of the lease. Register with the insurers (if the landlord insures) notice of the interest of the tenants and their mortgagees. When a mortgage is supported by a life policy as collateral security, notify the insurers. In the case of a registered title to the lease, or the grant of a lease in an area of compulsory registration, register in the District Land Registry.

Notify the insurers, when insured by the lessor, of the interest of your client and your client's mortgagees (head 8 of Chapter

13). But this may now be unnecessary if, as some policies provide, the benefit of the insurance is for all lessees, mortgagees and others having an interest in the property. See head (k) above.

(19) *Leases under the Housing Acts*. The Acts establish a wholly new scheme of conveyancing in the case of purchases of freehold or leasehold houses or flats from local authority and some other bodies. See Chapter 9 on 'right to buy' conveyancing.

(20) *Mortgage of leasehold property*. If your client needs mortgage finance, ensure that your client's mortgagees accept the terms of the lease or draft lease offered as security before you exchange contracts; otherwise your client might be faced with a purchase that cannot be completed and you with a claim for negligence.

(21) *The maintenance trap*. As with right to buy purchases, the unwary buyer of leasehold property can walk into a concealed trap if major works of maintenance or repair are contemplated by the freeholder but have not yet been carried out. In almost all leases there will be provision for such costs being shared between all the lessees, and in such a case a buyer or an original lessee can be faced with a heavy and unexpected bill fairly soon after completion.

Always raise the question in your practical enquiries by enquiring of the lessor's or seller's solicitors, or in a suitable case of both, as to such a possibility:

Have any substantial works of maintenance or repair, such as to render a purchaser liable to be called on for a contribution to the cost thereof, been carried out recently but not yet charged for, or are any such contemplated in the near future?

Make this one of your standard practical enquiries; the reply to the standard printed enquiry will give you particulars of the lessor, to whom the enquiry can be repeated by letter in a purchase of an existing lease.

(22) *Clog on assignment*. A long lease, unlike a short-term lease for a market rent, ought not to contain any restriction on the lessee's right to assign, mortgage, sublet, *except* a prohibition against disposing of a part as distinct from the whole—a provision considered reasonable to preserve the character of a building or an estate. Resist any attempt to clog the right to assign etc—some lessors do seek to restrict unfairly the rights of their lessees. *Never* agree any such provision without first warning the lessee and the lessee's mortgagee that the provision is unusual, and if they still wish to proceed, confirm this in writing.

A restriction on the right to assign etc, commonly takes the form of a tenant's covenant not to assign without the landlord's written consent, such consent not to be unreasonably withheld in the case of a respectable and responsible assignee. Although a buyer of a prospective lease, perhaps for a substantial sum and a low ground rent, may have little or no difficulty in supplying references to secure the licence, the operation may result in considerable expense, delay and frustration. Some lessors 'make a meal' of it, referring the grant to their managing agents as well as to their solicitors and surveyor whose costs will have to be paid. Acting for a lessor of a long lease, advise your client against such a provision if it is suggested as being likely to delay and perhaps frustrate a sale. Acting for a lessee, delete the provision, advise your client firmly against accepting it.

There are one or two institutions, of which the Church Commissioners are the largest, who insist on such a clause in all their leases. Here it's a case of take it or leave it—idle to waste time arguing the virtues of the matter, and those who wish to live in the sanctified atmosphere of their estates must bow to the landlord's will. But advise your client fully and carefully.

3 Principal defects

It's the duty of the conveyancer for the buyer and the buyer's mortgagee to point out any major defects in a lease offered for sale or as security, and to advise them. Leases come in all shapes and sizes (one wonders sometimes where draftsmen found their precedents) and every one must be carefully scrutinised. In the case of a new lease, of course, where you act for the proposed lessee, the draft is open to amendments; not so once a lease has been completed unless all concerned will agree to a deed of variation.

Principal defects, most of which have been considered above, are as follows:

(1) A clause in a long lease for forfeiture on bankruptcy of the lessee. Advise buyer and building society or other mortgagee not to proceed unless the seller can procure a deed of variation deleting the offending provision. Such a clause is appropriate only in a short-term lease at a market rent.

(2) Provision in a long lease against assignment of the whole (as distinct from a part) without the lessor's licence, albeit not to be unreasonably withheld. Advise buyer and mortgagee to reconsider proceeding unless modified—see above.

(3) Absence of adequate provision for the maintenance and repair of the structure, roofs and common parts (head 3 of Chapter 32). Advise client and mortgagee not to proceed unless satisfactory amendment obtained.

(4) Inadequate provision for decoration of the outside. Sometimes a lessor, in an effort to evade all responsibilities, will provide for each lessee to decorate their own section of the outside. Awkward, but not insuperable (see (5) below). A possible source of dispute, and ultimately litigation with an awkward neighbour. On the original grant of a lease, press strongly for more satisfactory provision. On an assignment, of course, it's too late for that.

Advise buyer and mortgagee to think carefully before proceeding. If they decide to, there must be some enforceable provision for decorating the whole of the outside.

(5) Absence of a covenant by the lessor to enforce covenants by other lessees if required to do so, coupled with a declaration or covenant in the lease that leases of other flats will be in similar terms (head 3 of Chapter 32). If this provision is absent, advise buyer and mortgagee to withdraw. But point out that in many older leases the covenant is missing, as it is in 'right to buy' leases. Indeed, until perhaps 15 or 20 years ago, it was seldom included in leases, so buyers and mortgagees may bow to the inevitable and accept the lease. Or the lessor may be persuaded (on payment of the lessor's costs) to enter into a deed of variation incorporating the clause in the lease. Remember that it's often one of the terms of offer of an advance by banks and building societies that the lease shall contain such provision. So always advise against proceeding without revision.

(6) Absence of a covenant by the lessor to insure the whole building, the lease providing, instead, a covenant by each lessee to insure their flats against fire etc. This again results from a lessor's evasion of his or her proper responsibilities, and it can backfire. For, if the other flats are under-insured, there's little hope of the building being rebuilt. Even if your client's flat is fully insured, the mere receipt of its rebuilding cost (not its value in the open market, which will have to be paid if one home is to be replaced with another) is quite inadequate compensation for a home lovingly created over the years. A lessee of a flat in an otherwise inadequately insured building may never see it rebuilt. So advise your clients to have none of it unless the position is somehow amended.

They could, of course, insure the whole building themselves, but that would be unacceptably expensive. Or a mutual deed of variation and covenant by the lessor and all the lessees providing for the lessor insuring on the usual terms of the lessees paying the premiums would serve. Or a deed of covenant between all the lessees that one of them insure and each contributes to the premium might be a possibility.

(7) A lease being negotiated should provide for the landlord observing the lessees' covenants in respect of vacant flats (head 17 above). If the lessor rejects such a provision, advise, explain and take the client's instructions.

(8) Avoid the flying freehold (head 1 of Chapter 33) at all costs. Advise the client firmly not to proceed.

(9) In the case of new or recently constructed purpose-built blocks of flats, ensure that they are built with NHBC protection (see Chapter 9)—absence thereof may not only prejudice the lessee but also a mortgage or subsequent sale. Advise against proceeding if built since NHBC protection was extended to flats if without that protection.

(10) Beware the illegal premium trap (head 2 of Chapter 33). If a danger, advise client and take instructions.

(11) It's impossible to predict all the possible unfair, fatal or absent provisions of the leases that will come your way. Go through each with a pin. A beady eye and a suspicious mind are your client's best protection—and yours. Vigilance must be your guide.

4 Advice on procedure

So, acting for the proposed original lessee under a long lease now to be granted, what's your plan of action?

(1) First, secure for yourself adequate time to give the matter the full undisturbed attention that it demands. You'll have your client's instructions in your head and on your instructions sheet before you, and perhaps on the selling agents' particulars; satisfy yourself that these are embodied in the contract and draft lease. Get off your local search (or make a personal search, if urgent) unless, on enquiry, the lessor's solicitor has a current search certificate.

(2) Go through the drafts with a pin, checking all the provisions of the lease as you reach them in your perusal. The drafts may have been submitted with the time-honoured, time-saving ploy that leases of all the flats in a building must be in similar terms, and that no amendments can therefore be accepted. Disregard it: other drafts can be varied to agree with yours, and good sense should

still prevail. If, however, the terms of other leases have in fact been finally agreed, you are in real difficulty if a material amendment is desirable: then you must seek your client's instructions, and if some really important term is lacking—such as provision for enforcing the covenants in other leases—advise your client— *including your client's mortgagees* if you act also for them, to consider seriously whether or not to proceed.

(3) There is one provision you should always seek, namely, that your clients will not be liable under their covenants after they've parted with all interest in the premises. The law, you'll remember, makes original lessees liable under their covenants throughout the term and any number of assignments, and there have been disastrous, even tragic cases of original lessees being called on to remedy the default of assignees of whom they had never heard. There has been a recent Consultative Paper published by the Law Commission on the subject, for consideration and comment by interested bodies and individuals, which hopefully may lead to a Report being laid before Parliament, and then, with yet more optimism, to legislation. But until that happy event you are your client's sole shield. A lessor's plea that other leases are silent on the point is irrelevant here because other lessees are not affected by the presence or absence of such a clause in your lease. In the face of stubborn refusal to accept it by the lessor, take instructions. As with other unreasonable sticking points, it's sometimes effective to explain it to the selling agent (who wants a commission and might as well do something for the money) who may be able to soften the lessor's heart to agree the saving provision. Similarly on the purchase of an existing lease beware of your client being put in the position of the original lessee.

(4) Continuing your journey through the lease, check every provision as you read it; be satisfied that the description of the property is adequate, and in the case of a top-floor flat consider whether the stairs leading to it from the floor below should be included in the demise and whether the roof should be excluded. Check that provision for repair of floors, joists and ceilings is fair and comprehensive (a not uncommon source of confusion). See that all necessary easements in favour of your client are included—rights of access, of drainage and services, of support, of use of garden or grounds, of dustbin area, etc, and be alert for both typing errors and for irrelevant provisions being carried over from leases of other properties—more common nowadays with dilution of skilled staff and the use of one standard draft lease stored in word

processor or computer. Check everything with the suspicious mind and eye of the professional lawyer.

(5) Acting for the *lessor*, bear in mind, when drafting the lease, all that's been said above about the lessee's task: we aren't paid to be oppressive, and a lease that is reasonable to both lessor and lessee saves time, argument and delay, to the benefit of your client.

(6) There is really no professional duty to modify the general conditions commonly incorporated in the agreement to grant a lease: they have been settled by leading conveyancing counsel, and if anything favour the seller or lessor. No harm in some modifications favoured by many solicitors in rather parrot-like fashion, but observe what's been said about the penal clause on delay in completion: there is no need, without specific instructions, to modify it in deference to imagined client cupidity.

(7) But there is one useful financial provision that has crept into many modern leases, particularly commercial ones, to the effect that interest shall be paid for any delay in payment of rent at, say, 4% above bank base lending rate (a rate lower than the interest paid by a tenant to his bank might not be an effective disincentive to delay). Not in the case of long leases, of course, where ground rents are trivial. A punctual payer has nothing to lose by the clause: it is fair that a tardy one should be kept to the bargain.

(8) Lastly, when you act for the buyer of an *existing* lease it is of course impossible to vary its terms, but go through it with the same meticulous care, noting any defects of omission or commission; explaining them, and all the provisions of the lease, to your client as you would in the case of an original grant—remember that it is not the least of your duties to explain to your client just what are the rights and obligations of the tenant under the lease contemplated, giving clear and firm advice.

(9) Remember, the Protocol procedure will relate to residential leasehold conveyancing.

Appendix I

Table of stages in a simple conveyancing matter: sale and purchase of freehold or leasehold and grant of long lease

(NOTE—*Steps that can normally be taken at the same time are all listed under the same number. Page numbers in brackets indicate where the step is considered in the text. (L) followed by a page number indicates that a specimen letter is given in Appendix II.*)

Part I: Acting for a seller/lessor

1 Take client's instructions; complete instructions sheet (p 11).

2 (*a*) Write client, acknowledging instructions (L, p 256). Include client care details.
   (*b*) Write buyer's/lessee's conveyancer (L, p 258); or
   (*c*) Write buyer/lessee (if no estate agent) for particulars of his conveyancer.
   (*d*) Write estate agent concerned (p 36).
   (*e*) Write the client who introduced the seller/lessee (L, p 257).
   (*f*) Write client's mortgagees for title deeds (L, pp 257–58).
   (*g*) Write Land Registry on Form 109 for office copy entries on the Register and filed plan.

3 Upon receiving title documents:
   (*a*) Peruse title; make notes on title (p 81).
   (*b*) Prepare draft contract and additional copy (p 26) and if acting for lessor, draft lease and copy.
   (*c*) Make copies of lease, restrictions or other matters to be disclosed to buyer (unless copy entries on Register to be sent) (pp 26–33).
   (*d*) Write buyer's/lessee's conveyancer with 'package' letter—(p 11) (L, p 257).

(*e*) Write client, acknowledging receipt of the title deeds and reporting position (L, p 259). Enclose Protocol forms for completion.

(*f*) If unregistered, copy abstract of title or prepare epitome of title, to enclose with 'package' letter.

(*g*) Write buyer with 'package' letter (L, p 257).

NOTE If the seller leaves the title deeds on originally giving instructions, stages 2 and 3 can be combined.

4 On hearing from the buyer's/lessee's conveyancer with draft contract [and draft lease] approved and any additional enquiries or requirements

(*a*) Peruse draft contract [and lease] and agree amendments.

(*b*) Deal with further queries (L, p 259).

(*c*) Telephone buyer's/lessee's conveyancer and agree any outstanding points on the contract [and lease]. Also if linked with a purchase, arrange exchange by telephone (p 43).

(*d*) Write buyer's conveyancer confirming the same and with replies to any additional enquiries.

(*e*) Engross contract.

(*f*) Write client to call and sign (or send) contract, and report position (L, p 260).

5 Upon receiving the contract signed by the buyer and any deposit payable:

(*a*) Exchange contracts by telephone or otherwise.

(*b*) Write client, reporting.

(*c*) If property is in mortgage, get precise redemption figure having previously received a rough estimate of the redemption figure (L, p 259).

(*d*) On an exchange by telephone, write recording this.

6 On hearing from the buyer's conveyancer with requisitions on title and draft transfer:

(*a*) Prepare replies to requisitions on title.

(*b*) Peruse and approve draft transfer.

(*c*) On grant of lease, engross lease and counterpart, with copies.

(*d*) Write buyer's conveyancer with replies to requisitions and draft transfer approved.

(*e*) Prepare your 'before completion', 'completion' and 'after completion' agendas (p 278).

(*f*) Attend to such matters on 'before completion' agenda as can be dealt with at this stage (p 278).

(*g*) Write lessee's conveyancer with counterpart lease and copy.

(*h*) Write client with copy replies to requisitions and reporting, and on grant of a lease, to call and execute the same (L, p 259).

7 Upon hearing from the buyer's conveyancer with engrossment of transfer:

(*a*) Check same against approved draft.

(*b*) Write seller to call and sign document and as to any completion requirements, which can now be dealt with (L, pp 259–60). Alternatively this could be sent by post.

8 On client calling:
   (*a*) Obtain seller's signature of transfer, and any undertakings or documents requiring seller's signature.
   (*b*) Take client's instructions on giving possession of the property; keys; disposition of sale proceeds etc.
   (*c*) Telephone buyer's/lessee's conveyancer to arrange method of completing—by CHAPS, etc.
   (*d*) Prepare letter of undertaking to discharge mortgage (L, p 261).
   (*e*) Attend to any other matters still outstanding on your 'before completion' agenda.

9 Immediately prior to completion:
   (*a*) Go through and dispose of any items on 'pre-completion' agenda not yet ticked.
   (*b*) Go through 'completion' agenda with whoever will attend completion.

10 Completion. On completion go through methodically and deal with all items on your 'completion' agenda, ticking each one as it is disposed of:
   (*a*) Completion by post/credit transfer/CHAPS, etc (pp 132–33) (L, p 261).
   (*b*) Undertaking as to outgoings (L, p 261); to discharge mortgage (L, p 261).

11 Immediately after completion:
   (*a*) Write client reporting, with completion figures and cheque etc. (L, p 262).
   (*b*) Go through and deal with all other items on 'after completion' agenda, which can be dealt with, making diary notes of any items that cannot be finally disposed of now (p 136).
   (*c*) Redeem mortgage.
   (*d*) Pay estate agents.
   (*e*) Write seller's/lessor's insurers (L, p 263).
   (*f*) Write seller's/lessor's bank (L, p 263).

12 Later, after completion:
   (*a*) On receipt of LR form 53 (registered land) *or* discharged mortgage (unregistered land) *or* consent to dealings write buyer's/lessee's conveyancer therewith.
   (*b*) On receipt of discharged mortgage of life policy, write insurers with notice of discharge (L, p 264).
   (*c*) On return of discharge of mortgage, write client therewith, and with policy (L, p 264).
   (*d*) Go through papers and after completion agenda, put in order, file away.

Part II: Acting for a buyer/lessee

1 Take client's instructions; complete instructions sheet (p 15).

2 (*a*) Write client, acknowledging instructions (L, p 264), and include client care details.

  (*b*) Write seller's/lessor's conveyancer; or

  (*c*) Write seller/lessor (if no estate agent) for particulars of conveyancer or write seller's conveyancer 'package' letter (p 266).

  (*d*) Write estate agent concerned.

  (*e*) Write the client who introduced the buyer/lessee (L, p 265).

  (*f*) Dispatch local search and enquiries.

  (*g*) In 'right to buy' purchase write landlord (L, p 265).

3 On receiving draft contract/draft lease and the search results and Protocol forms and title:

  (*a*) Write or telephone client upon any points arising thereon.

  (*b*) See client, go through lease, if leasehold purchase or grant of new lease; and for client to sign contract if terms agreed.

  (*c*) Draw amendments to draft contract, and on the grant of a *new* lease, to the draft lease, copy these into additional print or copy contract.

  (*d*) Prepare additional enquiries arising on draft contract, and additional copy.

  (*e*) Write seller's/lessor's conveyancer with this and subject thereto with draft contract approved by 'package' letter (L, p 266).

  (*f*) Arrange exchange by telephone or otherwise in linked sale and purchase.

4 With regard to local search:

  (*a*) Peruse and mark replies.

  (*b*) Write seller's/lessor's conveyancer on any point arising.

  (*c*) Write buyer/lessee likewise (L, pp 266–67).

5 With regard to property information form and fixtures, fittings and contents form:

  (*a*) Peruse and mark replies (p 119).

  (*b*) Write seller's/lessor's conveyancer on any point arising.

  (*c*) Write buyer/lessee likewise.

6 On hearing from seller's/lessor's conveyancer approving your amendments to the draft contract, or making further amendments:

  (*a*) Telephone conveyancer and agree any further amendments necessary.

  (*b*) Write buyer to call and sign, or send contract if not already signed.

  (*c*) Write seller's/lessor's conveyancer acknowledging letter etc.

7 On client signing contract:

  (*a*) Exchange contracts (by post or telephone) (p 43) (L, pp 267–68).

  (*b*) Write client, reporting exchange (L, p 268).

8 With regard to the abstract or epitome of title:

  (*a*) Peruse title, prepare notes on title when unregistered title (p 81).

    (*b*) Prepare requisitions on title and additional copy (p 85).
    (*c*) Prepare draft transfer and copy (p 85).
    (*d*) Write seller's conveyancers with requisitions and draft transfer etc.
    (*e*) Write mortgagee's conveyancers with title.
        (*alternatively omit this for letter 9 (f)*)

9 On hearing from seller's/lessor's conveyancer with answers to requisitions and with draft transfer approved:
    (*a*) Engross transfer (with additional copies, if necessary, for mortgagee's solicitor and Land Registry, if unregistered title is to be registered).
    (*b*) Prepare 'before completion', 'completion' and 'after completion' agendas (p 278).
    (*c*) Attend to such matters on 'before completion' agenda as can be dealt with at this stage (pp 278–80).
    (*d*) Write client, reporting as to completion and any matters now arising, and (if required) to call and execute transfer, lease mortgage, etc (L, p 268–69).
    (*e*) Write seller's conveyancer with any observations arising on replies; with engrossment of transfer if this need not await buyer's signature; with completion requirements (L, p 269).
    (*f*) If a mortgage is being obtained, submit title, searches, requisitions and replies, draft transfer etc, to mortgagee's solicitor (L, p 269), or;
    (*g*) If you act for a building society or other mortgagee, write with report on title and request for cheque (L, p 270).

10 On client calling:
    (*a*) Obtain client's execution of transfer or counterpart lease if required, and of any mortgage, undertakings or other documents requiring client's signature. Sometimes this may be done by post.
    (*b*) Take final instructions on completion, taking possession of the property, finding the balance of completion money etc.
    (*c*) Write seller's/lessor's conveyancer as to completion, on any other matters arising (L, p 270).

11 As completion approaches:
    (*a*) Check sum due from client.
    (*b*) Write client for balance of purchase money, with bill of costs and on any matters arising (L, p 270).
    (*c*) Dispatch final searches (Land Registry or land charges) and if necessary make personal company search (p 124 and Chapter 4).
    (*d*) Attend to any remaining items on 'before completion' agenda still outstanding.
    (*e*) Telephone seller's/lessor's conveyancer, arrange CHAPS payment and discuss any points outstanding.
    (*f*) Write seller's/lessor's conveyancer confirming completion etc (L, p 271).

(*g*) Similarly, if a mortgage is being obtained, make final arrangements for transmission of the advance with mortgagee.

12 Immediately prior to completion:
   (*a*) If you do not have your own CHAPS terminal, telephone bank to arrange sending of CHAPS payment and follow this up with written instruction.
   (*b*) Go through and dispose of any items on 'before completion' agenda not yet ticked.

13 Completion. On completion, go through and deal with all items on your 'completion' agenda, ticking each as it is dealt with:
   (*a*) Completion by post (L, p 271).
   (*b*) Completion by CHAPS (L, p 271).

14 Immediately after completion:
   (*a*) Write client reporting (L, p 272).
   (*b*) Go through and deal with all other items on 'after completion' agenda, which can now be dealt with, give instructions for stamping and registration of conveyance etc, and diary all items that cannot be finally disposed of now (pp 136–41).
   (*c*) Write building society if you act for it reporting completion (L, p 273) (not always required).
   (*d*) Register transfer, assignment, mortgage, with lessor's solicitors in case of leaseholds (L, p 273).
   (*e*) Write insurers in case of leaseholds (L, p 274).
   (*f*) Write mortgagee if you act for him or her (L, p 274).
   (*g*) Write seller's/lessor's conveyancer for NHBC notice of insurance cover and particulars of completion form.

15 Later, after completion:
   (*a*) Send transfer/lease after stamping, or land or charge certificate after registration, to client or mortgagee (L, pp 273–74).
   (*b*) Alternatively retain same or send to client's bank (L, p 276).
   (*c*) Write client, reporting (L, p 276).
   (*d*) Go through papers and 'after completion' agenda, put in order, file.

Appendix II

Specimen letters

(NOTE *For economy of space the letter-headings, which should invariably be given, are omitted from most of these specimen letters.*)

Part I: Acting for a seller/lessor

LETTER TO CLIENT

Dear

re

Thank you for your instructions to act for you on the sale of your freehold property to Mr Cutbush for the price of £95,000, which I shall be very happy indeed to do.

To enable me to prepare the contract of sale of your property, we shall need to see your title deeds. Could you please let me know the whereabouts of these deeds, so that I may acquire them with the minimum of delay.

I propose to operate The Law Society's National Protocol in the conduct of this transaction. In order to assist in this, would you please complete the fixtures, fittings and contents questionnaire, which is enclosed, and would you also read and then complete the property information form [additional property information form]. In each case it is a simple question of ticking the relevant box. If you require assistance with the completion of these forms, would you please let me know.

It would also be helpful if you could forward any copy planning papers or builders' guarantee certificates etc that you may have in your possession.

We operate a Client Care Scheme, and the enclosed booklet explains precisely how we provide our service to you, and the terms upon which it is provided. Please note that I will be your point of contact throughout this transaction.

I am also pleased to be able to confirm my quotation to you, whereby we agreed to carry out this work on your behalf in the sum of £   plus VAT at the current rate. This sum, together with the expenses that we will incur for the searches will amount to approximately £   .

Kind regards.

Yours sincerely,

STAGE 2(*b*)—'PACKAGE' LETTER TO BUYER'S OR LESSEE'S CONVEYANCERS

Dear Sirs,

We now enclose the following documents and look forward to hearing from you approving the draft contract:
- (*a*) draft contract in duplicate;
- (*b*) office copy entries on the Register and filed plan;
  or epitome of title and accompanying documents;
- (*c*) property information and fixtures, fittings and contents form;
- (*d*) replies to requisitions on title;
- (*e*) copy lease;
- (*f*) copy of last available maintenance accounts;
- (*g*) copy/particulars of insurance policy;
- (*h*) copy certificate and guarantee re timber infestation;

Yours faithfully,

LETTER TO CLIENT WHO INTRODUCED SELLER

Dear Mr Robinson,

Thank you so much for your introduction to Mr   , who called on us yesterday and for whom we shall be very happy indeed to act.

Yours sincerely,

LETTER TO CLIENT'S MORTGAGEES (BUILDING SOCIETY)

Dear Sirs,

re
Borrower:
Mortgage No:

We have been instructed by your borrower, Mr   , in connection with his proposed sale of the above property. If you would be good enough to send the title deeds to us you may accept this letter as our undertaking to hold them on behalf of the society, to return them to you direct, as you may demand and to part with them to a third party only on repayment of all money due to the society [or so much thereof as you may indicate to us].

Yours faithfully,

LETTER TO CLIENT'S MORTGAGEES (PRIVATE MORTGAGE)

Dear Sir,

re
Mortgagor:

We act for the owner of the above property, Mr   , who is proposing to sell it and redeem the outstanding mortgage.

To enable us to prepare the contract for sale of the property we shall need to inspect the title documents which you hold as your security; we should be very grateful if you would transmit these to your solicitors as soon as possible and let us know their name and address, when we will communicate with them and will also make arrangements with them as to the repayment of your loan.

We enclose a stamped, addressed envelope for the courtesy of your reply.

Yours faithfully,

STAGE 3(d)—LETTER TO BUYER'S OR LESSEE'S CONVEYANCERS (ESTATE DEVELOPMENT)

Dear Sirs,

re Flat No   and Garage No
Podlingford.

We have been instructed by the proposed lessors of the above leasehold property for a premium of £   and an annual ground rent of £   rising to £   and we understand that you act for the proposed lessee. We therefore enclose the following documents:

(1) draft contract with additional copy for your use, and engrossment print;
(2) replies to standard preliminary enquiries;
(3) draft lease of flat in duplicate and plans;
(4) draft lease of garage in duplicate and plans;
(5) office copy entries on the register of the lessors' title;
(6) copy superior lease;
(7) copy restrictions contained in conveyance of;
(8) copy indemnity policy;
(9) copy planning and byelaw permits.

You will observe that our clients' development of the property constitutes a breach of the old restrictive covenant to use it only for the erection of detached and semi-detached dwelling-houses, and an insurance indemnity policy has been issued against the unlikely contingency of any objection being taken to this development. (The lessors have no knowledge of any such objection or anticipated objection.) You will observe from the terms of the enclosed copy policy that the benefit of this enures for individual lessees, and no notice to the society or endorsement of the policy will therefore be necessary for that purpose.

An estate development plan has been lodged with the Podlingford District Council and it will not, therefore, be necessary for you to send a plan with your search; it will be sufficient to refer to the deposited plan reference   .
Similarly, an estate plan has been lodged at HM Land Registry, and when in due course you make your search against part (Form 94B) reference to the plot alone will be sufficient without sending a plan.

Lastly, you will appreciate that in the development of an estate such as this it is essential that the wording of all the leases should be consistent, and accordingly no substantial variation of the drafts enclosed herewith can be accepted.

Yours faithfully,

LETTER TO CLIENT

Dear Mr

Thank you for your letter of   enclosing your deeds and documents of title. Thank you also for the Protocol forms.

I have sent the draft contract documentation to the buyer's conveyancer.

I will let you know if any further queries arise, but otherwise will inform you when the contract is ready for signature.

Yours sincerely,

STAGE 5(d)—LETTER TO MORTGAGEES (BUILDING SOCIETY)

Dear Sirs,

We act for the owner of the above property who is proposing to sell it. Contracts for sale have now been exchanged and the date fixed for completion is 29 October next. Will you kindly let us have a redemption figure for this date; and please indicate the daily rate.

Yours faithfully,

STAGE 6(h)—LETTER TO CLIENT

Dear Mr

We have received from your [buyer's] [lessee's] solicitors the customary 'requisitions on title', which we have answered to the best of our ability. We enclose a copy of those requisitions and our replies; will you kindly consider the latter carefully and let us hear from you, in the stamped, addressed envelope enclosed for the purpose, confirming, correcting or adding to our replies.

In particular please clarify the arrangements for handing over the keys on completion and confirm you have or will pay the outgoings up to the completion day.

Yours sincerely,

LETTER TO CLIENT

Dear Mr

The [transfer] [lease] of the above property is now ready for your execution [if you will telephone to arrange a mutually convenient appointment to call here for that purpose.] [and we enclose the document for your signing in the presence of a witness. You should sign where your initials appear in pencil, and the witness also signs, adding his or her address and occupation, where indicated in pencil. If you will then return it in the stamped, addressed envelope for that purpose we will hold it pending completion of the matter.]

[Will you kindly let us have] [You will remember that we are still waiting for] the last receipts for [ground rent and] outgoings to enable us to prepare the completion statement, and perhaps you will bring these with you when you call, if you have not let us have them before then. At the same time we can finalise the arrangements for collection of the keys of the property on or before completion.

[*In the case of a builder, add:*

We shall require, to hand over on completion, the notice of insurance cover issued by the National House-Building Council together with [the common parts notice of insurance cover when this is issued and] the declaration of purchase price, [both of] which should have been sent to you by the NHBC on completion of the building. If you have not yet received them please let us know when they may be expected.]

Lastly, we enclose a copy of the estate agent's commission account. Please let us know whether you agreed the amount of this with him when you put the property on the market, in which case we will pay him out of the proceeds of sale coming into our hands.

Yours sincerely,

LETTER TO BUYER'S OR LESSEE'S CONVEYANCERS

Dear Sirs,

We now enclose completion statement for Friday of next week, 29 October, together with additional copy thereof for your client's use [and the last demands or receipts for outgoings to enable you to check the figures].

[Kindly credit our client's account as arranged with the completion money as early as possible on the day. If you could do so on the previous day it would be a great help, since we also have a purchase to complete for our client on the day of completion.]

[On completion please let us have your undertaking to have the conveyance

executed by the buyer immediately after completion and to supply us with a
copy of his execution, since this document, you will remember, contains a
covenant by him.]

Yours faithfully,

UNDERTAKING TO DISCHARGE MORTGAGE

Dear Sirs,

In consideration of this matter being completed today we hereby undertake
forthwith to pay over to the   Building Society from the proceeds of sale
of the property the money required to redeem the mortgage/legal charge
dated   and to forward the receipted mortgage/legal charge [*or* to forward
a signed Form 53] to you as soon as it is received by us from the society.

Yours faithfully,

LETTER TO BUYER'S CONVEYANCERS (COMPLETION BY
POST/CREDIT TRANSFER/CHAPS)

Dear Sirs,

[Thank you for your letter of yesterday enclosing bankers' draft for the completion money of £   and release of the deposit in the selling agents'
hands.] [We confirm that our clients' banking account was duly credited by
your bank yesterday with the completion money of £   and we thereupon
telephoned the estate agents to release the keys to your client.]
To complete the matter we enclose the [transfer] [lease] to your client
together with the [title deeds set out on the accompanying schedule in duplicate, one copy of which kindly receipt and return] [land/charge certificate]
[Form 53/undertaking as to discharge of registered charge] [lease dated
and subsequent title deeds] [undertaking as to outgoings].

Yours faithfully,

UNDERTAKING AS TO OUTGOINGS TO BUYER'S
CONVEYANCERS

Dear Sirs,

In consideration of the above matter being completed today we hereby
undertake on behalf of the seller to pay all rent/maintenance (if any) charged
on the above premises up to this date.

Yours faithfully,

LETTER TO CLIENT

(NOTE—*To his NEW address, if the house sold was his home.*)

Dear Mr

We completed your sale of the above property yesterday, when we received from your buyer the sum of £40,500 made up as shown on the enclosed copy completion statement.

Out of this money we repaid your outstanding mortgage of the property to the Freehold Building Society amounting to the sum of £13,600, and we take this opportunity of enclosing a note of our own charges and disbursements, for which many thanks. We therefore [enclose herewith cheque for] [have credited your banking account with] [have in hand towards your purchase—see letter to you in that matter] the sum of £25,573 made up as follows:

Money received on completion		£40,500
Paid your mortgagee	£13,600	
agent's selling commission	900	
Our bill of costs	427	
		14,927
[Cheque herewith] [Paid to your bank account]		£25,573
[applied to your purchase]		

We have written to the estate agents for the deposit less their selling commission, and we will deal with this in the same manner as soon as the money comes to hand. We have also written to the insurance society surrendering your insurance policy, and we will let you have any available unexpired premium which they may refund to us.

We return herewith the last receipts for outgoings and other papers which you left with us.

[Lastly, we enclose our client services directory to enable you to avail yourself of our wide range of services should we be able to assist you in the future.]

Yours sincerely,

LETTER TO BUILDING SOCIETY

Dear Sirs,

We completed the sale of the above property and the discharge of the society's mortgage today, and we enclose our cheque for the sum of £13,600 redemption money. We also enclose [the original mortgage for the completion and sealing of the vacating receipt endorsed thereon] [LR form 53 for sealing by the society] and return to us, when we will transmit the document to the buyer's conveyancers.

Yours faithfully,

LETTER TO ESTATE AGENTS

Dear Sirs,

We completed the sale of the above property today, and we enclose herewith cheque for £900 as shown on your attached account which kindly receipt and return.

Yours faithfully,

LETTER TO SELLER'S INSURANCE SOCIETY

Dear Sirs,

re
Policy No

We act for your assured, Mr   , who has now sold the above property; we therefore enclose the above policy by way of surrender, his interest and that of his mortgagees (for whom we also act) in the policy having now determined. We shall be grateful if you will let us have a cheque in favour of our client for any unexpired premium which may be available for him.

Yours faithfully,

LETTER TO SELLER'S OR LESSOR'S BANK

Dear Sir,

re
Account: Mr

We completed the sale of the above property last Friday, and in accordance with [our previous undertaking] [the instructions of our mutual client] we enclose herewith cheque in his favour for the sum of £25,573, representing the net proceeds of sale in our hands, to be credited to his account. Kindly acknowledge safe receipt.

Yours faithfully,

LETTER TO SELLER'S LIFE INSURANCE SOCIETY

Dear Sirs,

re
Policy No
Your assured: Mr

We act for your assured who previously charged the above policy to secure a loan from the   Building Society [for whom we also act]. That loan has now been repaid and we enclose for your inspection and return the discharge of the mortgage. Kindly cancel the note of the mortgage on your records.

Yours faithfully,

LETTER TO CLIENT

Dear Mr

re
Mortgage of Life Policy

You will remember that when you bought the above property with the help of a loan from your building society you mortgaged, as well as the property itself, a policy on your life as collateral security for that loan. Now that the society has been repaid, the mortgage of the policy has also been discharged, and we enclose the policy together with the discharge thereof, which should of course be kept together in a safe place.

Yours sincerely,

Part II: Acting for a buyer/lessee

STAGE 2 (a)—LETTER TO CLIENT

Dear Mr

Many thanks for your instructions to act for you on your purchase of the above freehold (leasehold) property in the sum of £99,000.

We write to confirm our quotation of £   for dealing with this transaction on your behalf. As explained to you on the telephone there will additionally be VAT at the current rate, together with disbursements for searches, stamp duty and the land registration fee.

We enclose our Client Care booklet, which sets out the basis on which our service is provided to you. If you have any queries about this do not hesitate to let me know. I will be your principal point of contact and if you have any queries you should contact me.

I have written to the seller's conveyancers for the draft contract documentation and I will advise you as soon as I hear from them.

Kind regards.

Yours sincerely,

LETTER TO CLIENT WHO INTRODUCED BUYER

Dear Mr Jones,

Many thanks for your introduction to Mr   , who called on us yesterday and for whom we shall be very happy to act.

Yours sincerely,

LETTER TO CLIENT'S MORTGAGEES (BUILDING SOCIETY OR LOCAL AUTHORITY)

Dear Sirs,

[Thank you for your instructions to act for your society in connection with the proposed advance of £20,000 to the above, for whom we also act, and for all the accompanying papers. We have not yet exchanged contracts for sale and purchase, but as soon as we have done so we will report to you on the title.]

[We act for Mr   , the buyer of the above [freehold] [leasehold] property, and a copy of your council's offer of an advance to him is before us. We have not yet exchanged contracts for sale and purchase, but as soon as we have done so we will let you know and will then report to you on title.]

Yours faithfully,

'RIGHT TO BUY' LETTER TO SELLER

Dear Sir,

We act for the proposed buyer of the above property from your council, and we are concerned lest, in the event of his completing his purchase, he should find himself liable for a proportion of the cost of repairs not amounting to the making good of structural defects, recently or to be expended by the council on this Estate.

Would you be good enough, therefore, either to confirm that no such works have been recently carried out or are contemplated or anticipated in the near future such as to render a buyer liable for a contribution; or, if there be any such, kindly to let us have an estimate of the actual or probable cost thereof, although it may not be possible for you to give an exact estimate.

Yours faithfully,

LETTER TO SELLER'S OR LESSOR'S SOLICITORS ('PACKAGE LETTER')

Dear Sirs,

Thank you for your letter of the   with all the enclosures you mention. We now enclose the following:

(a) draft transfer in duplicate—if you approve its terms please retain the top copy for use as the engrossment;

or (if joint buyers, or fresh covenants imposed) kindly return the top copy for execution by the buyers;

or you will observe that it has already been executed by the buyers;

(b) requisitions on title in duplicate;

Please let us have replies to the following additional enquiries: . . .

We confirm the provisional date of   for completion, subject to our clients (*or* our respective clients) exchanging contracts for the synchronised completion date for their sale or purchase.

Yours faithfully,

STAGE 4(c)—LETTER TO CLIENT

Dear Mr

We have now received replies to the search and enquiries from the local authority, from which we learn that the road on which the above property abuts has not been made up and taken over by the appropriate authority. This means that at some future date it may be so taken over when you, as frontager, would have to pay road charges, and in the meantime there would seem to be no authority who can be charged with the responsibility of maintaining the road.

We should like your instructions on this point, and if you would care to discuss it by all means telephone.

Other information which we learn from our local search is that [the drainage is combined with that of adjoining properties, as indeed we were already aware from the terms of the draft contract.] [there is no main drainage; drainage is to a cesspool which is cleared by the council.] [the property is in an area which is zoned in the local town and country planning scheme as an area of special historical or landscape beauty.] [in 1980 an application to build two bungalows on the property was refused by the planning authority.]

Yours sincerely,

LETTER TO CLIENT

Dear Mr

We have now heard from your seller's conveyancers on various enquiries we made of them, and they tell us that their client believes that the drainage ditch on the northern boundary of the property is the responsibility of the neighbouring farmer.

We are waiting for information on one or two other points but subject thereto we have agreed the terms of the contract for your purchase and [the engrossment is ready for your signature if you will telephone to arrange an appointment for that purpose.] [we enclose the engrossment thereof for your signature where your pencilled initials occur on the last page. If you will then return it in the stamped, addressed envelope enclosed for that purpose we will proceed to exchange.]

Yours sincerely,

LETTER TO SELLER'S OR LESSOR'S CONVEYANCERS — EXCHANGE BY POST

Dear Sirs,

We now enclose our client's part of the contract, together with a cheque for the agreed deposit money.

Please proceed to exchange contracts with completion fixed as at the   day of   as agreed between us.

If you are not able to exchange contracts on this basis please advise us immediately and, in the meantime, hold the enclosures to our order.

Yours faithfully,

LETTER TO SELLER'S OR LESSOR'S CONVEYANCERS — EXCHANGE BY TELEPHONE—FORMULA A

Dear Sirs,

We now submit our client's part of the contract, together with a cheque for the deposit as agreed between us.

Would you please telephone us in order to proceed to exchange contracts pursuant to Law Society Formula A.

When we exchange contracts we shall wish to agree the completion date and we will also wish you to confirm that both parts of the contract are identical in all respects.

Yours faithfully,

LETTER TO SELLER'S OR LESSOR'S CONVEYANCERS—EXCHANGE BY TELEPHONE—FORMULA B

Dear Sirs,

Pursuant to exchange of contracts this afternoon at 3.50 pm in accordance with Law Society Formula B we now enclose our client's part of the contract, signed and dated as agreed between us, together with the deposit cheque.

We look forward to hearing from you with your client's part similarly signed and dated.

Yours faithfully,

STAGE 7(*b*)—LETTER TO INSURERS

Dear Sirs,

re
Assured: Mr

We act for Mr   , of   , the buyer of the above property, and we should be grateful if you would hold him insured under a householders' comprehensive policy in the sum of £50,000. The property is semi-detached, brick-built and tile-roofed.

If you will let us have a proposal form, we will have this completed and signed by our client for return to you but please hold him covered forthwith.

Yours faithfully,

LETTER TO CLIENT

Dear Mr

We have now exchanged contracts for the purchase of the above property in accordance with your instructions. Completion is fixed for the   day of   next, and should completion be delayed beyond that date (except by your seller's default) interest on unpaid purchase money will be payable by you for the period of delay. [We simultaneously exchanged contracts for the sale of your present home, to be completed at the same time.]

We are proceeding with our investigation of the title to the property, and we will report all developments to you.

Yours sincerely,

STAGE 9(*d*)—LETTER TO CLIENT

Dear Mr [and Mrs]

We have now prepared the transfer deed of the above property, and since this document requires your signature [(because it contains a covenant by you to fence and to observe certain restrictions)] [(because, the purchase being in your joint names, the document contains provisions as to the terms on which you will together own the property which must be assented to by both of you)] we should be grateful if you would telephone to arrange [for both of you] to call here for that purpose before we send the document to the seller's conveyancers for his signature.

At the same time we shall have the mortgage of the property and one or two other documents ready for your signature and we can discuss the final arrangements as to finance etc, at our meeting.

Yours sincerely,

LETTER TO SELLER'S CONVEYANCERS

Dear Sirs,

Thank you for your letter of yesterday enclosing draft transfer approved, and we enclose the engrossment thereof for signing by the seller. [You will observe that it has already been signed by the buyer.] [You will observe that the document has not yet been signed by the buyer but you may accept this letter as our undertaking to use our best endeavours to obtain his signature within seven days after completion, and to supply you with a copy of his signature.]

[On completion kindly let us have, in addition to the transfer and title documents, authorities to the tenants to pay future rents to the buyer, undertaking on behalf of the seller to pay outgoings up to completion, and the keys of the property or an authority to hand these over addressed to whoever may hold them.] [Please see that the seller [directors] sign[s] [and seal] the plan as well as sign[s] the document.]

Yours faithfully,

LETTER TO MORTGAGEE'S SOLICITORS

(if title not previously sent at Stage 8(f))

Dear Sirs,

We have now completed the exchange of contracts and our investigation of title, and we are therefore in a position to send you all the documents specified in your letter to us of the   , as follows:

(*a*) search and additional enquiries of the local authority;

(*b*) property information form;

(*c*) contract for sale;

(*d*) abstract of title [*or* office copy entries on the Register and filed plan with authority to inspect in your favour];

(*e*) our requisitions on title and replies thereto;

(*f*) approved draft [conveyance] [transfer] [assignment] [lease];

[(*g*) copy planning and byelaw permits.]

We shall be glad to receive your own requisitions on title, if any, together with draft mortgage for approval [*or, in the case of a building society*, with the society's form of mortgage for execution by our client].

Yours faithfully,

STAGE 9(G)—LETTER TO MORTGAGEES (BUILDING SOCIETY)

(*not usually required*)

Dear Sirs,

We have now completed our investigation of title and enclose herewith our report thereon and cheque request.

We hope to complete this matter on 29 October and accordingly we should be grateful if you would let us have the society's cheque for the advance in good time for completion.

Yours faithfully,

STAGE 10(C)—LETTER TO SELLER'S CONVEYANCERS

Dear Sirs,

[We enclose engrossment of the [transfer] [lease], which you will observe has already been signed by the buyer.]

We are now ready to complete this matter.

[As arranged, we will credit your clients' account with the completion money early on completion day, or if possible the day before.]

[*Other completion requirements if not already included in letter* p 269]

Yours faithfully,

LETTER TO CLIENT

Dear Mr

We hope to complete your purchase of the above property on Friday of next week, when we shall be paying your seller the sum of £40,500, made up as shown on the enclosed copy completion statement.

Towards this money we shall be receiving your building society advance of £20,000, less the society's legal expenses, and we take this opportunity of enclosing a note of our own costs and disbursements in the matter. We shall be grateful, therefore, if you would let us have your cheque for the sum of £22,099, made up as follows:

	£	£
Money payable on completion		40,500
Our bill of costs and disbursements herewith		491
		40,991
Building society advance	20,000	
Less their costs and disbursements (including stamp duty and land registry fees)	1,108	18,892
Monies payable by you		£22,099

Immediately before completion you should satisfy yourself that the property is vacant, or will be so by completion. Please telephone if in doubt.

Yours sincerely,

(NOTE—*It is more modern practice to type the statement separately from the letter.*)

STAGE 13(*b*)—LETTER TO SELLER'S CONVEYANCERS (COMPLETION BY POST)

Dear Sirs,

As arranged over the telephone, we enclose banker's draft for the completion money of £   as shown on the completion statement, together with release of deposit in the agents' hands. We should be grateful if on receipt of this letter you would telephone the estate agents for release to our client of the keys of the property now in their hands and thereafter complete the matter through the post.

Yours faithfully,

STAGE 13(*c*)—LETTER TO BUYER'S CONVEYANCERS' BANK (COMPLETION BY CHAPS)

Dear Sir,

We should be grateful if you would forthwith credit the client's bank account of Messrs Robinsons by CHAPS with the sum of £   and debit our client's

account therewith. Messrs Robinsons' bank is   Bank plc of   ,
telephone number   , sorting code number   and the number of
their client's account is

Please debit our office account with your charge for this service.

Yours faithfully,

(NOTE—*If completion is effected by CHAPS (head 8 of Chapter 12) no letter is required if instructions are given on the form supplied by the bank*.)

LETTER TO SELLER'S CONVEYANCERS
(COMPLETION BY CHAPS)

Dear Sirs,

As we advised you over the telephone, we confirm that we have today credited your clients' banking account with   Bank plc with the sum of £   ; thank you for releasing the keys of the above property to our client.

We look forward to hearing from you with all necessary documents to complete the matter through the post.

Yours faithfully,

LETTER TO CLIENT

(NOTE—*To his NEW address if he is taking immediate possession*.)

Dear Mr

We duly completed the purchase of the above property today, when we paid to your seller the sum of £40,500, being the completion money you had previously paid to us, together with the mortgage advance as set out in our letter to you of the   . We also acknowledge with thanks the receipt of our own costs and disbursements mentioned in that letter.

You will no doubt be hearing shortly from your building society as to the first payment under your mortgage, and meantime we enclose a completed copy of that document together with a copy of the rules of the society for future reference.

[*Or if there is no mortgagee concerned*:—We are proceeding with the stamping of the transfer and other completion formalities, whereafter we will transmit all the title documents to your bank to hold in safe custody for you, in accordance with your previous instructions. As we explained to you, as the first buyer for value since registration became compulsory, the burden of first registration lies upon you. We will make the necessary application on your behalf but it will probably be six months before the new land certificate is issued by the Land Registry.]

As you know, the property has been insured under a householder's comprehensive policy in the sum of £50,000 with the   Insurance Society plc [by the building society].

[Lastly, perhaps you should consider whether this change in your property investment makes any amendment of your will desirable. If so we would be happy to assist you.]

Yours sincerely,

LETTER TO BUILDING SOCIETY

(NOTE—*The contents of this letter, and the documents, if any, to be enclosed with it, will be determined by the instructions you have received from the particular society. Check these again at this stage. They may have sent a 'completion particulars' form which will replace this letter.*)

Dear Sirs,

We duly completed this matter today, and we enclose herewith your form of notice of completion.

[We are proceeding with the stamping of the [transfer] [lease] and other completion formalities, whereafter we will [transmit the title documents to you] [make application for first registration of the title. Current delay in the Registry is about six months.]]

[We are proceeding with the stamping of the transfer of the property and other completion formalities and will then register the same and the society's mortgage in HM Land Registry. Current delay in the Registry is about six months.]

Yours faithfully,

LETTER TO LESSOR'S SOLICITORS

Dear Sirs,

We act for Mr   , who has just completed his purchase of the above leasehold premises. We understand you act for the reversioners, Messrs   , and in accordance with the covenant in that behalf contained in the lease we enclose herewith cheque in your favour for the prescribed fee of £   and notice of assignment/transfer/mortgage in duplicate, one copy of which kindly receipt and return to us [together with the original assignment/transfer/mortgage also enclosed for registration with you.]

[We also enclose a certified copy of the assignment/transfer/mortgage which we trust you will accept in place of the original required by the terms of the lease.]

Yours faithfully,

LETTER TO INSURERS

Dear Sirs,

We act for the buyer of the above leasehold property, Mr   , who desires to take over the benefit of the above policy, which we enclose herewith for the endorsement thereon of a note of his interest. You will observe that the solicitors for your previous assured, Mr   , have endorsed a note that he is no longer interested in the policy.

[Would you also please note the interest of our client's mortgagee,   , and endorse the policy accordingly.]

Yours faithfully,

LETTER TO PRIVATE MORTGAGEE

Dear Mr

We duly completed the mortgage of the above property to yourself yesterday, when we paid to your borrower the sum of £9,000 which you had previously sent to us.

You will remember that interest is payable under the mortgage at the rate of 10% per annum or 2% above your bank's Base Rate from time to time (whichever shall be the greater) on the usual quarter days so that the first payment of interest for the period from yesterday until Christmas falls due on 25 December next.

We enclose a completed copy of the mortgage which you may care to keep by you for future reference [and we are effecting registration at HM Land Registry of the document].

Kindly let us know whether you would like us to send to you or to your bank, or to retain on your behalf, the original documents after we have completed all formalities [when we receive the charge certificate, which will constitute your security. As we have explained to you, the title to this property must now be registered, and this will take about six months].

Yours sincerely,

(NOTE—*In such cases a borrower must be separately advised.*)

LETTER TO SELLER'S CONVEYANCERS (FOR NHBC FORMS)

Dear Sirs,

You will remember that we still await the NHBC notice of insurance cover and declaration of purchase price, and we shall be glad to receive these as soon as possible to complete the matter.

Yours faithfully,

LETTER TO CLIENT

Dear Mr

We have now attended to stamping and other formalities of your purchase and enclose herewith [the lease of the above property safe receipt of which kindly acknowledge in the stamped, addressed envelope enclosed for the purpose. Your next payment of £   ground rent to your lessor will fall due on the next quarter day, the   .] [the land certificate which [with the enclosed lease] constitute your title, and safe receipt of which kindly acknowledge in the stamped, addressed envelope enclosed for that purpose.]

Yours sincerely,

LETTER TO CLIENT

Dear Mr

We have now completed the stamping of the [transfer, etc] and other completion formalities and have sent [the new charge certificate which [together with the lease of your property] constitute your title] to your building society, from whom you will no doubt be hearing, if you have not already done so, as to the first payment to be made under the mortgage.

Yours sincerely,

LETTER TO BUILDING SOCIETY

Dear Sirs,

We now enclose the [charge certificate [and lease] and other documents] set out on your accompanying schedule in duplicate, one copy of which kindly receipt and return to us.

Yours faithfully,

LETTER TO CLIENT

Dear Mr

We have now completed the stamping of the lease/transfer and all other completion formalities [including registration in HM Land Registry], and in accordance with your instructions [have sent your title documents to your bank, of   to hold in safe custody for you] [we are holding your title documents in safe custody for you.]

Yours sincerely,

LETTER TO CLIENT'S BANK

Dear Sir,

We enclose herewith the charge certificate and other documents relating to the above property set out on the accompanying Schedule in duplicate in accordance with the instructions of our mutual client, Mr   for you to hold in safe custody for him.

Kindly acknowledge safe receipt on one copy of the Schedule.

Yours faithfully,

Appendix III

Useful precedents

1 Instructions to act on sale/purchase of freehold/leasehold property

Property
1 Date received:
2 Client: Seller/Buyer/Mortgagor/Mortgagee

Name:

Address:

Occupation:

Phone   *Office*:   *Home*:

3 Old client/Introduced by:
4 Seller/Buyer:
5 Seller's/Buyer's conveyancers:
6 Estate agent:
7 Price:
8 Fittings etc, included:
9 Preliminary deposit: £   paid to:
10 Deposit arrangements:

Seller
11 Title documents:
12 Local search, notices:
13 Deposit:
14 Linked sale and purchase:
15 Receipts:
16 Planning consents:
17 Plans:
18 Insurance:
19 On sale of a flat
   (i)   get lease;
   (ii) outgoings;

   (iii) maintenance accounts;
   (iv) insurance;
   (v)   management co, shares;
   (vi) lessor's licence;
   (vii) grant of a new lease.

20 Replies to Protocol forms:
21 Possession:
22 Mortgage to repay?

Buyer

23 Deposit:
24 Instructions for search:
25 Linked sale and purchase:
26 Joint purchase:
27 Insurance:
28 Mortgage arrangements:
29 Survey arrangements:
30 Life Insurance:
31 *If available*, go through special conditions of sale, lease, replies to Protocol forms.

Both parties

32 Other terms:
33 Cost estimate:
34 Instructions for will?

2 Conveyancing agendas—before completion

SELLER/MORTGAGOR

1 Deposit pd us/agents
2 Get last rects/title deeds
3 Arrange discharge of mtge
4 Arrange exchange of contracts by telephone
5 Send client prelims/requons to check
6 Take up refs
7 Get licence to assign
8 *Prepare*: (*a*) sched of docs; (*b*) list re outgoings; to discharge mtge; to obtain NHBC cert (*c*) authy to tenant(s); (*d*) LR Form 53/staty rect/withd N/dep; (*e*) Co Form 395; (*f*) Co resns; (*g*) LR cover; (*h*) notice to lessor of mtge; (*i*) share transfer; (*j*) B/C
9 Write with requirets
10 Get exd by client: mtge/transfer/lease/Form 53/staty rect/withd N dep/authy to tenants/Co Form 395/rect for chattel money/unds to pay outgoings; share transfer/ctpt licence to assign/notice to lessor of mtge
11 Keys arrange release to byr
12 Confirm all mtgee's requirements satisfied
13 Arrange completion by post or credit transfer (telephone or CHAPS)

BUYER/MORTGAGEE

1 Deposit pd seller's solrs/agents
2 Confirm replies satisfactory to searches etc
3 Arrange exchange of contracts by telephone
4 Take up refs
5 Check replies to Protocol forms
6 Exchange contracts
7 Examine deeds
8 Requisitions on title
9 Draft transfer/mtge
10 Insurance
11 *Prepare*: (*a*) rel of dep; (*b*) Form L (A); (*c*) und re outgoings; repairs; (*d*) rect for chattel money; (*e*) Co Form 395; (*f*) Co resns; (*g*) LR cover; (*h*) R/T; (*i*) ctpt licence to assign; (*j*) notices to lessor of asst/mtge; (*k*) share transfer; (*l*) notice to insce soc; (*m*) B/C; (*n*) assignment of life policy
12 Write with complon requirements
13 Get complon money, costs, from client
14 Get mtge advance
15 Get exd by client: transfer/ctpt lease/mtge/unds
16 Obtain banker's drafts or arrange TT
17 Make final searches
18 Confirm all BS/LA/bank/mtgee's requirements satisfied
19 Arrange completion by credit transfer (telephone or CHAPS)

3 Conveyancing agendas—completion

1 Inspect/produce deeds/land or charge certe/last rects
2 Get/hand over transfer/lease/licence to assign/title docs/ land or charge certe (requon no   )
3 Get/hand over und to dischge mtge/LR Form 53/staty rect/withd N dep/consent to dealing.
4 Get/hand over mtge/LC sch agnst borrowr/LR sch/LR cover/L(A) Form
5 Get/hand over rel of dep/ctpt lease/sched of docs/share certe and transfer/NHBC certe, agreement or und re do
6 Get/hand over und as to outgoings, repairs/ctpt licence to assign
7 Get/hand over authy to tenant(s)/keys/licence to assign/fire pol (endd)/rect for chattel money/Co Form 395/Co resns
8 Endorse memo of sale on
9 Get/give deposit no of land certe
10 Get/hand over
11 Complete drafts and mtge blanks
12 Get banker's drafts or by TT for £   and £
13 Pay seller/mtgor/mtgee (redem)
    (*a*) draft or by TT £
    (*b*) draft or by TT £
14 *Or* transfer direct to Seller's clients' account £   by phone or TT

4 Conveyancing agendas—after completion

1 Write seller/buyer reporting complon; re dep; re insce (and recover all premiums); with B/C; with cheque/copy mtge/last rects, etc; re keys; re deeds; re will
2 Write mtgee/bank reporting complon; with cheque; with Form 53 or staty rect; with fire pol, etc
3 L(A) and stamp convce/transfer/asst/lease/share transfer
4 Register with Regr of Cos Co Form 395
5 Register asst/mtge/with lessor's solr and pay fee
6 Register share transfer
7 Register in LR transfer/lease/withd of N of dep/Form 53/mtge/N deposit/notice of option in lease
8 Write estate agent re deposit
9 Lodge sllr's land certe in LR; give/get dep no
10 Write insce soc of bldg soc's interest in life endowment policy
11 Write insce soc re byr's/mtgee's interest in fire policy/surrender policy
12 Notice to local authority and water authority
13 Send NHBC form
14 Credit seller's banking account with £
15 Get costs; pay or transfer to office bank account
16 Send ctpt licence to assign to lessor's solr
17 Diarise land registration due date

Index

281